THE Baseball Research JOURNAL

Volume 38
Number 1
Summer 2009

I0894195

Published by
the Society for American Baseball Research

THE BASEBALL RESEARCH JOURNAL, Volume 38, Number 1

Editor: Nicholas Frankovich
Production and Design Coordinator: Lisa Hochstein
Cover Designer: Clay Eals
Fact Checker: Scott Flatow
Copyeditor: Aldene Fredenburg
Proofreaders: Norman Macht, Ted Wagstaff
Photo Consultant: Mark Fimoff

Cover: Kenesaw Mountain Landis, National Baseball Hall of Fame Library, Cooperstown, N.Y.

Published by:
The Society for American Baseball Research, Inc.
812 Huron Road, Suite 719
Cleveland, Ohio 44115-1165

Phone: (216) 575-0500
Fax: (216) 575-0502
Email: info@sabr.org
Web: www.sabr.org

ISBN 978-1-933599-13-7

Postage paid at Hanover, Pennsylvania.

Contents

Note from the Editor

"There are no facts, only interpretations," wrote Nietzsche. The Society for American Baseball Research is founded on the principle that he's wrong about that. And that's a fact. We start from the premise that point of view doesn't matter. If the first-base umpire calls it fair, so it is. And that's what we want to know—what it is, not what it is as you saw it. For decades, armies of volunteer researchers have been laboring quietly, without fanfare, gathering and verifying and then organizing all manner of data and information from official scorebooks, newspaper box scores, court records, you name it. See the photo of Sandy Piez on page 70. It comes from the Bain Collection at the Library of Congress. How does the Library of Congress know that's Piez, a fairly obscure figure, who played for the New York Giants in 1914? A note in the record for the digital image credits "research by the Pictorial History Committee, Society for American Baseball Research, 2006."

Whether it's the Baseball Index, the Minor Leagues Database, the Baseball Biography Project, or any of the other various research products (did I mention the Batterymates Project?) that SABR makes available to its membership and, in many cases, the rest of the world, the value of the work done by SABR researchers is—well, I would say "incalculable," but is there anything baseball-related that the Statistical Analysis Committee won't eventually quantify? Let's just say that the present state of our collective baseball knowledge owes a lot to SABR and its passionate commitment to historical accuracy and analytical precision.

In our love of logic and empirical evidence, SABR acts as light that enables us to examine prejudice in the literal sense of that word. Most of us have baseball beliefs that are born of the inevitable and entirely human, and probably necessary, impulse to prejudge. Maybe we think Greg Maddux is the best-fielding pitcher of the past quarter century. We look at all those Gold Gloves. We've heard his defensive skills praised often over the years. And maybe we can recall seeing him in action, reaching to snare a line drive or lunging to snag a sharply hit ground ball and then throwing a strike to first to nail the runner by half a step. Now John Knox comes along (see page 49) to tell us, in effect, that Maddux was outstanding at all that but, no, not the best. Kirk Rueter was better. Kirk Rueter? This news conflicts with our prejudice. Is Knox right? Read and judge for yourself.

It's in this spirit of casting light on prejudice that Norman Macht, whose article is the centerpiece of the exchange that is the cover story of this issue, looks at Kenesaw Mountain Landis and his reputation for supporting segregation in Major League Baseball. We've heard it said often over the years. Macht asks for evidence—evidence not that it's been said often but that what has been said often is true. He notes that Landis in 1942 declared his readiness to accept the signing of African American players to major-league clubs. Lee Lowenfish in his response to Macht adds that Landis made the statement in the wake of a substantial grassroots movement that had resulted in a mountain of letters and telegrams calling for baseball's integra tion—a fact suggesting that Landis's intention was merely to fend off criticism, not to lead the way. To which the skeptic might reply: What difference does his intention make? The issue is not Landis's character but something narrower, more focused—what was his position on the integration of baseball?

A strong response to Macht's argument comes from Larry Lester in his article "Can You Read, Judge Landis?" which appeared in the journal *Black Ball: A Journal of the Negro Leagues* (fall 2008). Lester quotes Landis's successor Happy Chandler: "For twenty-four years Judge Landis wouldn't let a black man play. I had his records, and I read them, and for twenty-four years Landis consistently blocked any attempts to put blacks and whites together on a big league field. He even refused to let them play exhibition games." That Chandler said this is a fact, or at any rate that he was said to have said it is a fact: Lester cites his source. Is what Chandler said (or is said to have said) factual? Is it true?

What marks SABR's work of building baseball knowledge is that we proceed on the assumption that the answers to questions like this do exist, even if the answers end up forever defying all our strenuous efforts to arrive at them. Baseball knowledge is a destination, not a journey. It involves a journey, which we enjoy, but only because we have hope that we'll continue to advance from base to base on our way to the truth, which we're hardwired to home in on.

Nick Frankovich

Correspondence

Hitting Streaks and Psychology

I am writing this in response to Trent McCotter's piece on hitting streaks ("Hitting Streaks Don't Obey Your Rules: Evidence That Hitting Streaks Aren't Just By-Products of Random Variation," *BRJ* 2008). I want to begin by commending Trent on this fine piece of work. In short, a series of Monte Carlo tests revealed that the number of actual hitting streaks of lengths beginning with 5 games and ending with 35 games or more between 1957 and 2006 was, in each case, noticeably greater than what would have been expected by chance. It is always good to see evidence inconsistent with our "received wisdom." What I have to say here in no way attempts to contradict his research findings. My problem is with his attempt to explain them.

Trent first proposed three "commonsense" explanations for what he found. The first was that a batter might face relatively poor pitching for a significant stretch of time, increasing the odds of a long streak. But, in his words, "the problem with this explanation is that it's too short-[sighted]; you can't face bad pitching for too long without it noticeably increasing your numbers, plus you can't play twenty games in a row against bad pitching staffs, which is what would be required to put together a long streak." He then goes on: "The same reasoning is why playing at a hitter-friendly stadium doesn't seem to work either, since these effects don't continue for the necessary several weeks in a row." His third commonsense explanation is that, as hitting overall is thought to be better during the warm months, hitting streaks may be more common than expected during June through August. This is because, and this is critical, "hitting streaks are exponential. . . . a player who hits .300 for two months will be less likely to have a hitting streak than a player who hits .200 one month and .400 the next . . . [because] . . . hitting streaks tend to highly favor batters who are hitting very well, even if it's just for a short period." This is absolutely correct. Unlike the first two proposed explanations, in this case Trent looked for relevant evidence, claiming that he looked for more streaks in June, July, and August and found no more than in May. Trent, how about April and September?

Anyway, rejecting all three of these, Trent then proposed two possible psychological explanations. The first is that hitters aware of a streak intentionally change their approach to go for more singles, particularly when the streak gets long; and he has evidence that longer streaks occur less randomly than shorter ones, which would occur under this assumption (players would more likely think about keeping their streak going when it was long ongoing). The second is that hot hands really exist, and his claimed evidence is that taking games out of his random sample in which the player does not start increases the number of predicted hitting streaks, bringing it more in line with the number that actually occurred. Makes sense; a hitting streak is easier to maintain the more at-bats one has in a game. He proposes that this could reflect real life because managers would start a player proportionally more often when he was hitting well. True, but we should keep in mind that the same statistical effect for starting games would occur whether there is a hot hand or not. In other words, I don't think his evidence is very telling.

I want to be very clear here about my position on this issue. I have absolutely no problem with the suggestion that players' performance is impacted by psychological factors; I don't see how they aren't. My problem is with the way in which those suggestions are treated. If we are serious about sabermetrics as a science, then we have to meet the standards of scientific explanation. As esteemed philosopher Karl Popper pointed out in his now classic book *The Logic of Scientific Discovery* (1934), if a proposed explanation for observations is impossible to disconfirm, then we can't take it seriously as scientific explanation. This is my problem with Trent's treatment. Let us suppose that, rather than finding more hitting streaks than chance would allow, Trent had found fewer. He could then say that the reason for this is that batters crumble under the stress of thinking about the streak and perform worse than they would normally. If Trent found no difference, he could then say that batters are psychologically unaffected by their circumstance. The point is that these sorts of attempted explanation can be used to explain anything, and, given our present store of knowledge about player psychology, they are impossible to evaluate. Again, Trent's proposals may be correct, but we can't judge them, so we can't take them as seriously as Trent appears to.

In contrast, the first three proposed explanations can be disconfirmed, so we can take them more seriously. Trent claims to have disconfirmed the third, but we need to know about April and September. But the real issue I have is with his dismissal of the first two, because he did not apply the logic in their case that he correctly applied for his "hot weather" proposal. Let me begin with the first. A batter does not have to face a bad pitching staff in consecutive games for his odds of a hitting streak to increase. Let us suppose that a batter faces worse pitching than average during only 10 of 30 games in May and makes up for it by facing worse pitching than average during 20 of 30 games in June. We use the same exact logic that Trent used correctly for the "hot weather" proposal; his odds of having a batting streak, which would occur during June, would be greater than another batter that faced worse pitching than average during 15 games in May and 15 games in June. The same explanation goes for hitter-friendly and hitter-unfriendly ballparks, and it is strengthened in this case because of well-supported known differences in ballpark effects. If a player's home field were hitter-friendly and, during a stretch of time, many of his road games were in hitters' parks, he could easily have 20 or more games in this context in a given month.

I have no idea whether either of these two explanations for Trent's findings is correct. But the difference between these and his psychological proposals is that we could test these two and not those he favors. Given the importance of Trent's original findings, I would obviously like to see that happen. And I would very much like it if we remain very careful about not taking our psychological speculations too seriously.

Charlie Pavitt
Rocvkille, Maryland

This response to Trent McCotter's article appeared originally at http://sabermetricresearch.blogspot.com.

Trent McCotter replies:

I'm glad that my article has fostered some debate on the topic of hitting streaks. Charlie Pavitt has written an excellent review, and I have also received numerous e-mails from others who read the article and had insights and critiques.

I will try to outline here some rebuttals, clarifications, and corrections concerning the article.

First, I want to state that the original intent of my article was to try to disprove the standard independence assumption that underlies the coin-toss model that is used to calculate probabilities of streaks. For a long time now, players' final season statistics (like 150 games, 600 at-bats, 200 hits) were used to extrapolate what kinds of hitting streaks were likely to have happened. It works fine, so long as the games are essentially randomly distributed. By randomly permuting the games 10,000 times for each player during the period 1957–2006—and getting so many fewer streaks than we have seen in real life—I think there is strong evidence that the independence assumption underlying the coin-toss model does not work in the context of hitting streaks.

Once I had shown the poor results of the independence test, I tried to come up with explanations for why we have seen so many more hitting streaks than occurred in the random permutations.

I'll now address several of Charlie Pavitt's arguments on that topic. He says I've too quickly dismissed the effects of facing bad opponents. It's very difficult to test the effect of facing bad pitching because there is no easy way to define bad pitching. One shortcut I have used is to look at how many long hitting streaks there have been against particular teams (e.g., a batter getting a hit in 30 straight games versus the Blue Jays over the course of his career). During 1957–2006, there have been 19 hitting streaks of 30 or more games versus the league as a whole but only 5 such streaks versus a particular opponent. We expect fewer streaks, simply because you can't count the last 10 games versus Toronto and the first 20 games versus Texas as a 30-game hitting streak versus one particular opponent. But if facing bad teams were so conducive to hitting streaks, it seems that we would have seen more hitting streaks against bad teams—those bad teams would continually be boosting their opponents' averages.

Pavitt also says that I too quickly dismissed the effect of playing at certain hitter-friendly ballparks. I went through all 19 of the 30-game hitting streaks during 1957–2006. Over those streaks, 50.2 percent of the games comprising the hitting streaks were played at the batters' home ballparks, and 49.8 percent were played at road ballparks. Batters get more at-bats when they're on the road (since their team always gets to bat in the ninth inning), but batting averages are higher at home ballparks. In the end, it clearly has balanced out. Thus, players who have had 30-game hitting streaks don't seem to have received any advantage either by playing more games at home (where they have a higher batting average) or by playing more games on the road (where they get more at-bats). If playing at a hitter-friendly ballpark greatly helped long hitting streaks, it seems like we'd see a higher percentage than 50.2 percent of the games making up the streak to have been played at the hitter-friendly home park. In other words, long hitting streaks during 1957–2006 don't seem to be centered around stretches where the player was playing more games at home or on the road than they do at any given stretch of the season.

Pavitt also mentions that I didn't include any data about hitting streaks beginning in April or September. I exclude April because the season's beginning date frequently changed during 1957–2006, and it often wasn't until mid-April. So there just weren't as many games being played in April as there were in May, June, July, or August. I exclude September because streaks that begin in September have a much lower chance of actually making it to 20 or 30 games, simply because the player will run out of games to play. So comparing April or September to the months of May, June, July, and August wouldn't give us any insight.

Pavitt's final critique is that several of my "psychological" explanations for extra hitting streaks aren't testable. I agree that testing these things is difficult, simply because that's the nature of testing humans, who can adjust on the fly. However, just because something may be difficult—or even impossible—to verify doesn't mean that we should exclude it as a possible factor. For instance, the placebo effect with drugs is a psychological explanation that seems difficult to refute; we accept it as valid mostly because we've eliminated other explanations. In the baseball world, there is a common thought that batters tend to take fewer walks as their hitting streaks increase. This is tough to test, but not impossible; maybe it's just a result of multiple effects that naturally vary at-bats throughout the season. I just don't see the problem with including psychological factors in a study that deals with human behavior.

I also wanted to include some quick answers to questions that repeatedly came up:

I looked only at single-season streaks for the entire project, so multiseason streaks are not included.

I excluded all 0-for-0 batting lines, *except* where the player had a sacrifice fly. Per the MLB rules, 0 for 0 with a sacrifice fly will end the hitting streak, even though the batter had zero at-bats.

And here is one correction to the original article: The y axis of the chart on page 66 reads from 0 percent to 8 percent but should read from 0 percent to 80 percent. Thus, for example, we saw an extra 40 percent—not 4 percent—in 18-game hitting streaks.

Frazee's Friendship with Lindbergh

In their discussion of Ban Johnson's often contentious relationship with Harry Frazee, the authors of "History versus Harry Frazee: Re-revising the Story" (*BRJ* 2008) express their doubts that it stemmed from a false belief on Johnson's part that Frazee was a Jew. To support their view, they question how anyone could have thought that Frazee was Jewish since he was a friend of Charles Lindbergh. They ask whether, after his famous flight, Lindbergh would "really have chosen to stay at the home of someone perceived to be a Jew." The answer is that, yes, not only would Lindbergh have stayed at the home of a Jew when he returned to America from France, but he actually did. He wrote his book on his flight during the summer of 1927 at the Long Island home of Harry Guggenheim, the scion of one of the most prominent Jewish families in America. Lindbergh once again used Guggenheim's home when he was courting his future wife and during part of his honeymoon. Despite Lindbergh's subsequent views that Jews were trying to lead the United Stated into World War II, his friendship with Guggenheim, an aviation enthusiast, continued until Guggenheim's death in 1971.

The relationship between Lindbergh and Guggenheim is well documented in many sources, including A. Scott Berg's Pulitzer Prize–winning biography *Lindbergh* (1998).

Steven A. King
New York

"When Fans Wanted to Rock, the Baseball Stopped"

Sports, Promotions, and the Demolition of Disco on Chicago's South Side

Christopher J. Young

WHILE the winter chill still held Chicago in its grip, longtime White Sox fan and season ticket holder Dan Ferone informed Chicago White Sox management that he had decided to cancel his season tickets. Soon afterward, Mike Veeck, promotions director of the Chicago White Sox and son of club owner Bill Veeck, wrote to Ferone trying to entice him to come back. He explained that management had tried "to make Comiskey Park more than a baseball stadium with an infield and an outfield. We have tried to make the Chicago White Sox more than a baseball team with uniforms, bats, and balls." It was their goal, Veeck told Ferone, "to give Chicago baseball fans more than nine innings of a baseball game." In fact, their "game plan" was to make a Sox game "fun, exciting, and memorable." In short, they hoped "to give our customers the best entertainment in town for their money."[1]

During the 1979 season Mike Veeck proved as good as his word. Comiskey Park became ground zero for Veeck-led promotions. One such promotion was Disco Demolition Night, which took place on July 12, 1979. Ironically, the idea emerged in the wake of a "Disco Night" promotion two years earlier. Following that event, Jeff Schwartz, sales executive at WLUP, and Mike Veeck concocted the idea to have an anti-disco night. The idea reemerged in 1979 when Schwartz called Veeck to tell him that there was a new DJ at WLUP who was going to blow up disco records at a shopping mall while on the air. Immediately following this demolition of disco records, Veeck phoned Steve Dahl and asked him if he would be interested in blowing up records at Comiskey Park.[2]

The idea was to attract people to the ballpark by giving them a discount at the gate. Because the radio frequency of WLUP was 97.9, they decided that as part of the promotion they would admit for 98 cents anyone who brought a disco record to the park. The Veeck-Schwartz idea-turned-promotion coincided with another promotion that was scheduled for that night—teen night—which allowed teens in for half-price regardless of whether or not they had a record. The result was hugely successful in terms of numbers. Comiskey Park was filled beyond capacity. Some estimates put attendance *inside* the park at 50,000. And those were the people who could get in. Up to 20,000 milled about outside the ballpark.[3]

On the other hand, the promotion was a failure. While the park was packed—every owner's dream—the field itself was deemed unplayable in the aftermath of the promotion, which took place between games of a twilight double-header between the White Sox and the Detroit Tigers. As a result, the White Sox organization in general had to accept a forfeit, while Bill Veeck in particular had to endure a barrage of criticism from the press.

Disco Demolition Night was not just a cultural battle between disco and rock'n'roll; it was also a clash between the subcultures of athletic and music entertainment. When we take this perspective, the experiences of owner Bill Veeck and fan Dan Ferone are heard and become part of the story—as they should, since they, the baseball fans, were the ones that lost out that evening.

By the time disco was all the rage in the United States, especially after the 1977 hit movie *Saturday Night Fever*, it had already been part of the European discotheque scene for some time. While everyone was getting in on the disco phenomenon—from the Rolling Stones to *Sesame Street*—critics such as Dahl gathered followers dedicated to anti-disco.[4]

Newspaper reporter Toni Ginnetti described Dahl as a "24-year-old self-avowed crusader against disco music." The militia that he led in his crusade to "annihilate the forces of disco" was called the "Insane Coho Lips." Critics of disco have tended to focus on its mechanical nature. Many would have agreed with a writer for *Time*, who characterized the disco sound as a "diabolical thump-and-shriek." However, while the musical aspect of disco no doubt disturbed Dahl, when asked he tended to focus on disco as a cultural force. "The disco culture represents the surreal, insidious, weird oppression because you have to look good, you know, tuck your shirt in, perfect this, perfect that." "It is all real intimidating. Besides the heavy sociological significance," he continued, "it is just fun to be a pain in the ass to a bunch of creeps." Although Disco Demolition Night was not the first time he led his army into cultural battle, it would prove to be the most notorious.[5]

COURTESY OF THE CHICAGO WHITE SOX

White Sox owner Bill Veeck, a longtime proponent of the idea that "you can draw more people with a losing team plus bread and circuses than with a losing team and a long, still silence," endured criticism for the aftermath of his Disco Demolition Night promotion.

While the forces of anti-disco gathered, Mike Veeck looked toward the 1979 season. He assured Dan Ferone that management would strive "to make sure that when you visit Comiskey Park you'll see more than a baseball game . . . [and] that when you leave at the end of nine innings of baseball, whether we won or lost you will have had fun."[6] When Veeck's promotional acumen met with Dahl's anti-disco militancy, the result was indeed "more than a baseball game."

Mike Veeck's comments to Ferone demonstrate that the son was following in the footsteps of his already legendary father, Bill Veeck, who was labeled fairly recently as "the spiritual godfather of baseball promotions." Since the 1940s Bill Veeck had made a reputation by using promotions to improve the pennant prospects of both minor- and major-league teams. A driving point in Veeck's business philosophy was that "you can draw more people with a losing team plus bread and circuses than with a losing team and a long, still silence."[7]

Long before the promotions at Comiskey Park during the 1970s, Bill Veeck was engaged in promoting Chicago ball clubs. In the late 1950s he owned the White Sox and helped continue the excitement that was started earlier in the decade. Under Veeck's ownership in 1959, the "Go-Go White Sox" won their first pennant in forty years. Even earlier, in the 1930s and 1940s, Bill Veeck worked for the North Side Cubs. He was instrumental in beautifying Wrigley Field, including the now signature ivy that distinguishes that ballpark's outfield.[8]

Even before the first game of the doubleheader began, this veteran of baseball, Bill Veeck, began to suspect that things were going to be different. Unlike other days when people made their way to the South Side ballpark, this day a lot of people were carrying a "variety of obscene signs." Veeck's suspicions were confirmed when he saw thousands of people who were unable to get in wandering around outside of the park.[9]

Rowdy behavior that interrupted the first game of the twilight doubleheader foreshadowed what was to come. The first game had to be stopped several times because some of the attendees "began to throw records and firecrackers onto the field." This created an atmosphere that was described as "ripe for trouble" by reporters of a suburban Chicago newspaper, the *Daily Herald*. The raucous activity got too close for comfort for the Detroit Tigers' Ed Putman. He eventually had to leave the bullpen area because of the cherry bombs being thrown onto the field. Putman later told a reporter that a "cherry bomb landed so close to the back of my head that I could feel the explosion."[10] A writer for the *Chicago Tribune* reported that players from both teams "were forced . . . to play that first game under a constant bombardment of records and firecrackers."[11] Another baseball player experienced the rowdiness of the "fans." White Sox outfielder Rusty Torres said that he was at the receiving end throughout the first game. Some of the items thrown at him were lighters and empty liquor bottles. The native Puerto Rican joked that there "was one good bottle of rum, Puerto Rican rum." "The way things were going," he continued, "I wish whoever threw it had left a little in the bottle."[12]

Following the first game, Dahl, the master of demolition, and Lorelei, who modeled for radio station WLUP, were driven around the warning track before heading to center field. "We came out on the field, and I did a lap around the warning track in the Jeep," Dahl later recalled. "I was bombarded by beer and cherry bombs. Lovingly. That's how they show their love at White Sox Park." Following this display of affection, the disk jockey for "The Loop" and his radio show co-host, Garry Meier, pepped up the crowd in anticipation of the climactic explosion of disco records. Lorelei recalled that the view from centerfield was surreal—an adjective used by many eyewitnesses. She described feeling like she was "in the middle of a beehive. All I could hear was buzzing all around me." A fan who had seats along the third-base line that evening remembered that the crowd was so loud that "you couldn't hear yourself think." After leading his followers in a chant of "disco sucks," Dahl, as promised, blew up the disco records, which was meant to be a "symbolic cooling down of disco fever."[13] Whether it had that effect on disco remained to be seen. When the smoke lifted it became clear that Dahl's followers were anything but cooled down by the anti-disco rite.

COURTESY OF THE CHICAGO WHITE SOX

Comiskey Park. In February 1979, Mike Veeck, White Sox promotions director, had written a disillusioned fan to explain that the club was trying "to make Comiskey Park more than a baseball stadium with an infield and an outfield." And so it was on the evening of July 12, as the overflow crowd rioted and shut down the ballgame.

In the wake of the explosion 5,000–7,000 people stormed the field. Not since 1925 had Comiskey Park experienced such a scene.[14] Commander Dahl tried to rein in his troops, but to no avail. White Sox owner Bill Veeck stood at home plate and hopelessly pleaded with the crowd to return to their seats. Harry Caray tried futilely to get the people off the field by singing "Take Me Out to the Ball Game." Normally, at a ballgame, Caray's rendition would bring a crowd to its feet in a happy sing-along of the classic song, but this was not a normal situation, and this was not his normal audience. The baseball legend and the legendary song fell on deaf ears as the haters of disco tore up the playing field, stole bases, and destroyed a batting cage. While this was going on a bonfire continued to burn in center field.[15]

Finally, the Chicago police arrived—dressed in riot gear. Their appearance was met with applause by those who had remained in their seats. On seeing the police carrying nightsticks, the rowdy crowd on the field quickly dispersed. Close to forty people were charged with disorderly conduct. The number of reported injuries varied. Some newspapers claimed that no one was injured, while others reported that six people were wounded. The highest casualty estimate put the number at well over thirty. Chicago Police Lieutenant Robert Reilly, who was head of park detail, remarked that that evening at Comiskey Park was "as bad as the night the Beatles were here."[16]

While the buzz in the ballpark intensified and then finally broke loose with the storming of the field, baseball fans tried to flee a scene that looked to be quickly descending into a riot. Dan Ferone, who had decided to keep his season tickets after all, described the atmosphere as one of "panic and fear." Another fan, Cynthia Lonergan, told reporters that she "was afraid of being crushed." Records were being thrown from the bleachers like Frisbees. While the teams were ushered to the clubhouse for their safety, the fans were not so lucky. One fan remembered that between "the games when the nonsense started, a record album hit a buddy, Ron Battaglin, right between the eyes, vertically. Blood everywhere. Beer everywhere, too. He toughed it out with the help of the nectar of the gods." When sixteen-year-old Brian Pegg settled into what he thought were great seats—roughly 20 seats from the field along the third-base line, between the dugout and the bullpen—he did not realize his memories of this evening would not be from the ballgame. Instead he remembered the firecrackers and records that were being thrown down from the upper deck. One M-80 blew up just above the head of an elderly man, and a 45-rpm record lodged itself in a woman's shoulder blade.[17]

Anti-disco fanatics jumped turnstiles, scaled two-story fences, and climbed through the open windows of the old ballpark before the festivities began. Those who eventually wanted to flee when they felt things were getting out of hand, or when they had heard the second game was canceled, found that it took some time before they could find an unlocked exit. Bob Young remembered that the main gate was the only remaining exit available to those who wanted to leave.

In an effort to calm the crowd on the field, White Sox radio announcer Harry Caray broke out into a rendition of "Take Me Out to the Ball Game." He later described the crowd as "not typical baseball fans."

So what was meant to keep thousands from entering ended up trapping those inside who wanted to escape. The *Chicago Tribune* reported that the gates were closed once 50,000 people were in the park. Mike Veeck acknowledged that the gates had to be closed. When calculating attendance, Veeck says that the "simple rule of thumb" is to "take the advance and multiply by two-thirds to see how many will show up. Where we thought 25,000 to 30,000 we had 50,000 in the park and at least 15,000 outside who couldn't get in because we had to close the gates."[18]

Not surprisingly, the second game was not able to begin at its scheduled time. In fact, over an hour after the second game was scheduled to start, the field was deemed unplayable. While initially it was stated that the game would be postponed, in the end, the promotion cost the White Sox and their fans a game by forfeit.[19]

In the next day's press, Bill Veeck was roundly criticized. One reporter stated that last night was "a night when Veeck's circus atmosphere came crashing down around him." An editorial in the *Daily Herald* commented that the "king of the promoters" and the "master showman" was "lucky that the worst that happened is that his team forfeited a game as a result." Taking a harder stand, the editors at the *Chicago Tribune* held Bill Veeck personally responsible for the "hucksterism that disgraced the sport of baseball." Veeck, according to the editorial, endangered fans and players by creating an environment that included drunken teenagers and flying records. Bill Gleason of the *Chicago Sun-Times* simply stated that it was "the most disgraceful night in the long history of major league baseball in Chicago."[20]

Privately Veeck told his son that sometimes promotions "work too well." And he told reporters that having only "one fiasco" after being in the business for four decades was "not that bad." However, he acknowledged that he had heard of neither the radio station nor Steve Dahl. For the papers the next day, he admitted that he could have done more research. "I didn't investigate as carefully as I obviously should have," Veeck said. Nonetheless, he continued, "I don't think this has tarnished baseball, but it didn't brighten my escutcheon as a promoter." Rather than pass the promotional disaster onto his son, he accepted full responsibility. Nonetheless, Mike Veeck was surprised with how he had misread the situation. "I'm into music and this was my kind of concept," the younger Veeck told *Chicago Tribune* reporter Richard Dozer. "But the mistake I can't get over," he continued, "is that I didn't read it right." He said he could not believe how passionate people felt about the disco issue. "When I was younger," Mike Veeck explained, "I marched against the war but I never thought anyone would demonstrate for a cause like this."[21]

The responses of both Veecks illustrated the gulf between those who were at Comiskey Park on July 12 for baseball and those who were there for Disco Demolition Night. While some were there for both, accounts reveal that there was a sharp difference between the two groups. In the reporting from the time and in more recent reminiscences many people commented on the drug use that was going on. One fan quipped, "It wasn't Winstons they were smoking." And the umpire crew chief that night, Dave Phillips, later described the scene as looking like "a small Woodstock drug fest." Moreover, others have commented on how even before they entered the park they knew this game would be different. They said that the types of people going in made it feel like one was entering the park for a rock concert rather than a ballgame.[22]

While some baseball fans like Bob Young and Dan Ferone opted to leave the park, others let out their frustrations on the anti-disco fanatics. Phil Allen, a Steve

Dahl fan, but who was present that evening as a Sox fan, said that in the section where he and his brothers were sitting, the fans were singing "Na Na Na Na, Na Na Na Na, hey a**holes, sit down." Another person said that in "the upper deck we were throwing beer on the jerks, to no avail."[23]

A number of people commented on the differences between those who were there to demolish disco and those who were there for a ballgame. The *Chicago Tribune* said that Disco Demolition Night—and all that came with it—had "little to do with why baseball fans come to Comiskey or any other park and even less to do with the game of baseball." Even though he was the target of the *Chicago Tribune* editorial, Veeck would have concurred with the editors. Like them, he believed that those involved in the mayhem were not "real baseball fans."[24]

So many people showed up at the ballpark that evening for their 98-cent admission that eventually ticket holders were not even admitted into the park. Those who arrived early enough to get admitted were not pleased with what they experienced. Terry McArdle told reporters that he had gone to Comiskey Park to see a game. "It was really sad," he said, "that most of the people out there had no consideration for the sports fans." Announcer Harry Caray believed he understood the reason. He reportedly said that "the people that caused the trouble were not typical baseball fans."[25]

On the morning following Disco Demolition Night, it was apropos that Sports and Business shared a section in the *Chicago Tribune*. Fitting as well were the two headlines on the front page of the section: one announced, "When fans wanted to rock, the baseball stopped" and the other declared, "Sox promotion ends in a mob scene." Inadvertently, the arrangement of this section of the Chicago newspaper suggests what went wrong the night before.

No one would deny that major league baseball is business. And the White Sox of the 1970s were owned by one of the shrewdest businessmen in baseball. However, when two subcultures are brought together into one venue the end result is ultimately going to be unsatisfying for one side. The Veecks had hoped to bring people to the ballpark, whether it was a season ticket holder or the person who likes to take in an occasional game. If one judges success by the number of people in the ballpark, then Disco Demolition Night, as a promotion, was extremely successful—it filled the ballpark beyond capacity. Conversely, the promotion was also a failure. The promotion brought together at Comiskey Park people who arrived for different reasons. While rock fans and baseball fans appreciate the memory of the evening, the fact remains that some ticket holders were never allowed into the park, and those that were in the park lost out on a second game.

COURTESY OF CHRISTOPHER J. YOUNG

A golf ball retrieved by umpire Dallas Parks and presumably thrown on the field during the chaos that followed the first game of the scheduled doubleheader on July 12, 1979.

Disco Demolition Night demonstrated the limits of promotions for sporting events. David Israel of the *Chicago Tribune* said the following day that he was not surprised by what occurred. "It would have happened any place 50,000 teenagers got together on a sultry summer night with beer and reefer." Nonetheless, Israel continued, "it was a nuisance. And it really had no place at a ballpark."[26]

Israel's sentiment was echoed by many in the days that followed Disco Demolition Night. Even so, promotions have remained a regular feature of minor- and major-league baseball. Perhaps, White Sox pitcher and Texan Rich Wortham's assertion after Disco Demolition Night can be taken by promoters as a suggestion forged by experience: "This wouldn't have happened if they had country and western night."[27] ■

Notes

An earlier version of this article appeared as "Disco Demolition Night: Doubleheader Turns Disaster in Comiskey Park," *Illinois Heritage* 7, no. 3 (May/June 2004), 6-9.

1. Mike Veeck to Daniel Ferone, 21 February 1979, private collection, Chicago.
2. Jim Kirk, "25 Years Later, Disco Debacle Recalled Fondly," www.chicagotribune.com (7 July 2004); Mike Veeck, interviewed by Mark Liptak, www.whitesoxinteractive.com (19 October 2004).
3. In 1969 the capacity of Comiskey Park was 44,492. In 1989 the capacity was 43,931. While 50,000 was a lot, it was not the largest crowd. The largest crowd was on May 20, 1973, when 55,555 showed up for Bat Day and a doubleheader between the White Sox and the Twins; see Philip J. Lowry, *Green Cathedrals: The Ultimate Celebration of All 271 Major League and Negro League Ballparks Past and Present* (Reading,

Mass.: Addison-Wesley, 1992), 131; Richard Dozer, "Sox Promotion Ends in a Mob Scene," *Chicago Tribune*, 13 July 1979; Bob Gallas and Tom Jachimec, "5,000 Disrupt Sox Ball Game," Arlington Heights (Ill.) *Daily Herald*, 13 July 1979; Teamworks Media, "Disco Demolition 25th Anniversary: The Real Story," WTTW Chicago, 12 July 2004 (one hour); Greg Couch, "For the Record," www.suntimes.com (9 July 2004); Dave Hoekstra, "The Night Anti-disco Fans Went Batty at Sox Park," www.suntimes.com (9 July 2004).

4. Rickey Vincent, Funk: *The Music, the People, and the Rhythm of the One* (New York: St. Martin's Griffin, 1996), 207, 209.
5. Toni Ginnetti, "Outburst spotlights DJ's Cause," *Daily Herald*, 14 July 1979; Frank Trippett, Time, 23 July 1979. Earlier Dahl had taken his fight to Hanover Park and Lynwood. While the near-riot brought attention to the radio station, Dahl began to experience cancellations of previously scheduled appearances; see Edie Cohen, "Dahl May Find Forums Lacking," *Daily Herald*, 14 July 1979. Before the promotion, Mike Veeck opined about disco to *Chicago Sun-Times* sports columnist Bill Gleason. He said: "It's awful music that had to be forced upon us by the so-called tastemakers. I say 'had to' because of the extreme lack of taste in disco. It couldn't have happened by itself" (Bill Gleason, "The Disco Is Here to Stay Despite Efforts of the Sox," *Chicago Sun-Times*, 11 July 1979).
6. Mike Veeck to Ferone, 21 February 1979, private collection, Chicago.
7. Jerome Cramer, "So, You Want to Own a Minor League Baseball Team," www.forbes.com (15 September 2003), quoted in "Bill Veeck," by Steven P. Gietschier, in *American National Biography*, ed. John A. Garraty and Mark C. Carnes (New York: Oxford University Press, 1999), 22:314.
8. Gietschier, "Bill Veeck," 313–15.
9. Richard Dozer, "Veeck Protests Sox Forfeit, but Accepts Responsibility," *Chicago Tribune*, 14 July 1979; see also Brian Hewitt, "Fans Riot at White Sox Park," *Chicago Sun-Times*, 14 July 1979.
10. Gallas and Jachimec, "5,000 Disrupt Sox Ball Game"; Gallas, "Sparky Won't Play 'Disco' Makeup," *Daily Herald*, 13 July 1979.
11. David Israel, "When Fans Wanted to Rock, the Baseball Stopped," *Chicago Tribune*, 13 July 1979.
12. Gallas, "Sparky Won't Play 'Disco' Makeup."
13. Lorelei, www.whitesoxinteractive.com (18 March 2004); Phil Allen, ibid. (25 June 2003); "Discophobia Out of Control," *Chicago Tribune*, 13 July 1979; Lorelei, www.whitesoxinteractive.com (18 March 2004).
14. According to Richard Dozer, on April 26, 1925, the White Sox lost to Cleveland 7–2 in seven innings as a result of the game being shortened because the fans stormed the field; see Dozer, "Sox Promotion Ends in a Mob Scene."
15. Gallas, "Sox Pay for Disco Disaster with Forfeit," *Daily Herald*, 14 July 1979; "Anti-Disco Rally Halts White Sox," *New York Times*, 13 July 1979; Dozer, "Sox Promotion Ends in a Mob Scene"; Tom Duffy, "Tiger Rookie Stays Cool Against Sox," *Chicago Tribune*, 14 July 1979; Gallas and Jachimec, "5,000 Disrupt Sox Ball Game"; Leon Pitt and Phillip J. O'Connor, "Fans Rampage at Sox Park—2d Game Put Off," *Chicago Sun-Times*, 13 July 1979; Phil Hersh, "Bill Veeck 'Sad and Embarrassed' by Disco Night," *Chicago Sun-Times*, 15 July 1979.
16. Gallas, "Sox Pay for Disco Disaster with Forfeit"; Dozer, "Sox Promotion Ends in a Mob Scene"; Lt. Robert Reilly quoted in "Discophobia Out of Control."
17. White Sox pitcher Ross Baumgarten stated he "didn't know people could have such little regard for other people's safety," Hewitt, "Fans Riot at White Sox Park"; see also Hewitt, "A.L. Rules Sox Must Forfeit to Tigers," *Chicago Sun-Times*, 14 July 1979. As Dan Ferone helped an elderly lady get away from her box seats he recalled being concerned about the possibility of getting hit by a flying record; Dan Ferone, conversation with author, Chicago, 2003; Pitt and O'Connor, "Fans Rampage at Sox Park—2d Game Put Off,"; Gallas, "Sparky Won't Play 'Disco' Makeup"; "Aggravated White Sox Fan Bob," www.whitesoxinteractive.com (25 June 2003); Brian Pegg, www.whitesoxinteractive.com (25 June 2003).
18. Bob Young, conversation with author, Palatine, Ill., 2003; "Discophobia Out of Control"; Gallas, "Sox Pay for Disco Disaster with Forfeit," *Daily Herald*, 14 July 1979; see also Bob Gallas, "Sparky Won't Play 'Disco' Makeup."
19. Since World War II there have only been three other American League forfeits: the last game the Senators played in Washington on 30 September 1971; in Cleveland on Beer Night on 4 June 1974; and when Baltimore forfeited a game because Earl Weaver took his team out of the game against Toronto on 15 September 1977; see www.retrosheet.org/forfeits.htm; see also Bob Pille, "Sox Swallow Forfeit," *Chicago Sun-Times*, 14 July 1979. "Anti-Disco Rally Halts White Sox"; Dozer, "Sox Promotion Ends in a Mob Scene."
20. Gallas, "Sparky Won't Play 'Disco' Makeup"; "A Promotional Gimmick That Got Out of Hand," *Daily Herald*, 14 July 1979; "Veeck Asked for It," *Chicago Tribune*, 14 July 1979. For a mocking commentary, see Mike Imrem, "Promotion Ideas Now a Dime a Demolition," *Sunday Herald*, 15 July 1979; Gleason, "The Horror at Comiskey," *Chicago Sun-Times*, 13 July 1979.
21. Mike Veeck to Seth Swirsky, 27 November 2001, in Swirsky, *Something to Write Home About: Great Baseball Memories in Letters to a Fan* (New York: Crown, 2003), 101; Gallas, "Sox Pay for Disco Disaster with Forfeit"; Hersh, "Bill Veeck 'Sad and Embarrassed' by Disco Night"; Dozer, "Veeck Protests Sox Forfeit, but Accepts Responsibility"; Gallas, "Sox Pay for Disco Disaster with Forfeit."
22. Pille, "The Fans Return Quietly to Comiskey," *Chicago Sun-Times*, 14 July 1979; Dave Phillips quoted in "The Promotion Night That Ended in Flames: From Setting Records on Fire to a Forfeit," *New York Times*, 11 July 2004; www.whitesoxinteractive.com (18 March 2004); see also Dave Phillips with Rob Rains, *Center Field on Fire: An Umpire's Life with Pine Tar Bats, Spitballs, and Corked Personalities* (Chicago: Triumph, 2004), 51–54.
23. Allen, www.whitesoxinteractive.com (25 June 2003); Anonymous, www.whitesoxinteractive.com (18 March 2004).
24. "Veeck Asked for It," *Chicago Tribune*, 14 July 1979; Lynn Emmerman and Joseph Sjostrom, "'These Weren't Real Baseball Fans'—Veeck," *Chicago Tribune*, 13 July 1979. In the days that followed, Bill Veeck said, "I abjectly apologize for having put a great many White Sox fans through an evening that was scary"; Hersh, "Bill Veeck 'Sad and Embarrassed' by Disco Night."
25. Emmerman and Sjostrom, "'These Weren't Real Baseball Fans'—Veeck"; Gallas and Jachimec, "5,000 Disrupt Sox Ball Game." Bill Gleason wrote that "the majority in the mob were exhibitionists. They came not to watch baseball but to be seen"; Gleason, "The Horror at Comiskey"; see also Pille, "The Fans Return Quietly to Comiskey."
26. Israel, "When Fans Wanted to Rock, the Baseball Stopped."
27. Ibid.

The Tale of the Three Tobins

Bob McConnell

THREE players named John Tobin played pro baseball, each at some time during the early 1930s.

John Thomas Tobin's playing record is well documented. He had a 13-year major-league career, mostly with the St. Louis Browns. He led the Federal League in hits in 1915 and the American League in triples in 1921. He finished his big-league career with 1,906 hits and a .309 batting average. He then wound up his playing career with Bloomington of the Three-I League in 1930.

The records of the other two John Tobins are a little fuzzy. Until recently, researchers thought that there was a possibility they were one and the same player. Thanks to research by Davis Barker, we now have a clearer picture of the two players.

John Martin Tobin graduated from Fordham University in 1932. According to the university website, he is a member of the Fordham Athletic Hall of Fame. He was with Winston-Salem of the Piedmont League late in the 1932 season, per a note in *The Sporting News*. The league averages listed only players in ten or more games, and Tobin was not included. He pinch-hit for the New York Giants on September 22. This earned him a place in *The ESPN Baseball Encyclopedia* (fifth edition), where his birthplace is listed as Jamaica Plain, Massachusetts, a district in Boston. He went to spring training with the Giants in 1933 but was optioned to Knoxville of the Southern Association, per a note in *The Sporting News* (March 30). He did not play in any league games for Knoxville. His trail ends at that point.

John Lawrence Tobin is the third Tobin. The middle name, Lawrence, comes from a Howe News Bureau card. Other information on the card is a little contradictory, and so we are not positive that Lawrence is the correct middle name. Tobin played in four games for Tyler of the East Texas League in 1931. A Tyler newspaper referred to him as an East Texan and listed his hometown as Texarkana. He started the 1932 season with Muskogee of the Western Association. He was beaned on May 22 and sustained a concussion. We can find no additional playing record for him that season. He spent spring training with Tyler in 1933. This clinches the fact that John M. and John L. were two different players, as John M. was with the Giants that spring. John L. did not play in any league games for Tyler in 1933, and there is no further information on him for that season.

A John Tobin played in the minors from 1934 through 1937. With one exception, all of the clubs were in Texas. It is reasonable to assume that John L. was the player. The highlight of his career was a four-home-run game on June 15, 1936, while playing for Marshall versus Jacksonville in an East Texas League Game. ■

COURTESY OF FORDHAM UNIVERSITY

Coffey Field, Fordham University, 1930s. John Martin Tobin graduated from Fordham in 1932 and was inducted into the Fordham Athletic Hall of Fame in 1980 for his collegiate baseball career. His hall-of-fame plaque indicates that he also played football. Late in the 1932 season, he played for Winston-Salem of the Piedmont League and pinch-hit for the New York Giants on September 22, going 0 for 1 in his major-league career.

Zooming In on a Great Old Photo

Mark Fimoff

WIDE-ANGLE views of early baseball games provide an unending source of fascination and speculation: What ballpark? Which teams? What year? Can we identify any of the players? Of these, for obvious reasons, the last question is usually the most difficult one to answer.

Rarely, absent a highly credible contemporary source, is such a photo published with anything approaching definitive player IDs. When such claims are made, one wonders: How can you really know who the players are?

The wonderful photo below appeared in *Brooklyn Dodgers* by Mark Rucker (2002).[1]

BASEBALL HALL OF FAME LIBRARY, COOPERSTOWN, N.Y.

The caption included these points:

- Washington Park [Brooklyn], probably ca. 1912
- Cubs were in town . . .
- If . . . 1912, Tinker, Evers, and Chance . . . would be on the field
- The pitcher, **who looks like Three-Finger Brown . . .**

Since we can neither see his face nor count his fingers, it is certainly difficult to decide whether or not the pitcher looks like Three-Finger Brown. Three years later, the same photo was used by the same author in *Chicago Aces: The First 75 Years* (2005).[2] This time there is no hesitation in the caption:

- Cubs . . . playing in
- Washington Park in Brooklyn,
- 1912
- **Mordecai Brown *is* pitching . . .**
- Johnny Evers is at second base, Joe Tinker at shortstop . . .
- Frank Chance had already left for New York

Brown is clearly the reason for including this photo in a book about "Chicago aces." But, how can anyone be so certain about this ID? Can we confirm or refute it? Let's start with a magnifying glass.

To the right we see the pitcher greatly magnified. There's his glove on his right hand, so he must be throwing with his left hand. But, as we know, Miner Brown pitched with his three-fingered *right* hand.

Furthermore, if this is a 1912 Cubs-at Brooklyn game, a bit of newspaper-article and box-score research shows that, in 1912, Brown did not pitch at all in Brooklyn—not to one batter, not one pitch.

- **CONCLUSION: Mordecai Brown is not pitching.**
  - Cubs . . . playing in
  - Washington Park in Brooklyn,
  - 1912
  - ➤ ~~Mordecai Brown *is* pitching~~ . . .
  - Johnny Evers is at second base, Joe Tinker at shortstop . . .
  - Frank Chance had already left for New York

This great photo deserves a more careful analysis. Is it possible to determine who that pitcher is? Since the given caption seems untrustworthy, let's start by confirming the teams, location, and year.

"Cubs"

The Cubs wore dark jerseys and pants on the road for three seasons, 1911, 1912, and 1913.
From the National Baseball Hall of Fame Uniform Database:[3]

Note the image of the pitcher above right. It is clear that his uniform, socks, and logo match either the 1911 or 1912 Cubs road uniforms. No other Deadball Era MLB team wore a similar uniform.

• CONCLUSION: It's the Cubs, *1911 or 1912.*

Also, we note that Frank Chance did not leave for New York until after the 1912 season. So, on that point, perhaps the caption was right the first time the photo was used in 2002—Chance could be in the scene.

➤ • **Cubs . . . playing in** *Confirmed*
• Washington Park in Brooklyn,
• 1912
• ~~Mordecai Brown *is* pitching~~ . . .
• Johnny Evers is at second base, Joe Tinker at shortstop . . .
➤ • ~~Frank Chance had already left for New York~~

"Washington Park in Brooklyn, 1912"

The Hall of Fame Uniform Database shows the following outfits for the Brooklyn club's final three years at Washington Park. Comparison to the magnification (note the socks), below right, indicates that the home team could be Brooklyn and therefore the site could be Washington Park, but this is not conclusive. Also, the cap/socks combination seems to favor 1911, but cap colors in the Uniform Database are not always perfectly accurate.

To the right is shown a bird's-eye view of Brooklyn's Washington Park.[4] Just across First Street, beyond the right-field wall, is the large rectangular Guinea Flats building. Just across Whitwell Place from the Flats, at the corner of First Street and Whitwell, is a smaller three-story building, about the same height as that of the Flats building.

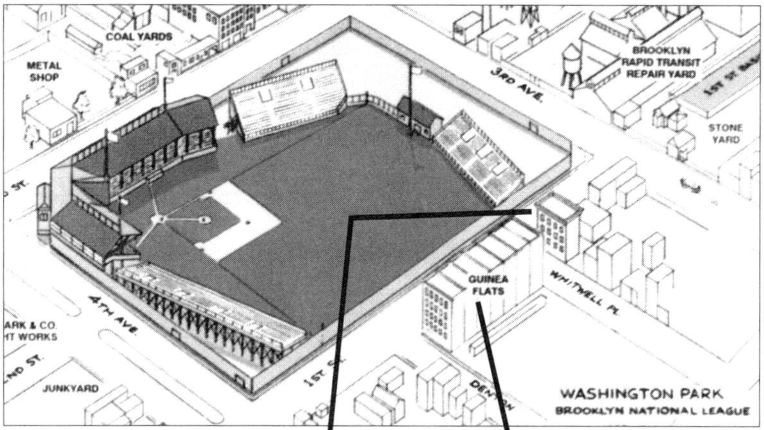

This confirmed 1915 Washington Park Federal League opening-day photo shows the smaller building, left, and the Guinea Flats building, right, beyond the right field wall.[5]

LIBRARY OF CONGRESS: LC-DIG-PPMSCA-18468

These same buildings are seen below in the photo in question.

- **CONCLUSION: This is Washington Park**
  - Cubs . . . playing in
  - ➤ **Washington Park in Brooklyn** *Confirmed*
  - 1912
  - ~~Mordecai Brown *is* pitching~~ . . .
  - Johnny Evers is at second base, Joe Tinker at shortstop . . .
  - ~~Frank Chance had already left for New York~~

It will be much easier to determine who the pitcher is if there is certainty as to the year. One thing that works in our favor is that the billboards are readable. Though one or two advertisers might keep the same design and location over a period of a few years, in most cases outfield-wall billboards changed every year. Since there were no NL games at Washington Park after 1912, and given that the Cubs uniforms are from 1911 or 1912, what is needed are confirmed photos of the right-field wall from 1911 and 1912.

An "Ajax Tire" sign in right field is seen in a cropped portion of our Washington Park photo, below left.

It is magnified and shown below, right. Note the circular tire, partially overlaid with the letters *X* and *T* between the words *Ajax* and *Tire*.

This photo is from the *Brooklyn Daily Eagle*, April 16, 1912.[6] The same circular tire, overlaid with part of the *T*, is evident.

Another photo, this one from the *Brooklyn Daily Eagle*, October 5, 1911, shows a different sign at that same right-field wall location.[7]

It's clear that the photo in question has the 1912 right-field billboard, which differs from the 1911 sign. Further comforting confirmation can be had from the following: According to box scores and accompanying newspaper articles, Cub lefties did pitch in Brooklyn in 1912 but not in 1911.

- **CONCLUSION: Photo taken in 1912**
  - Cubs . . . playing in
  - Washington Park in Brooklyn,
  - ➤ 1912 *Confirmed*
  - ~~Mordecai Brown *is* pitching~~ . . .
  - Johnny Evers is at second base, Joe Tinker at shortstop . . .
  - ~~Frank Chance had already left for New York~~

So—who was really on the field?

A lot of effort has been expended to confirm the author's original claimed location, teams, and year. This provides a firm foundation for proceeding with an attempt at identifying the pitcher. The next step is to check the Chicago-at-Brooklyn box scores for 1912.[8] These reveal that three left-handed Cubs pitchers made appearances in Brooklyn in 1912.

- Lefty Leifield—27 innings, with these lineups:
  Note that either Ward Miller or Tommy Leach played center field.

	AB
Sheckard, lf..	3
Good, lf.......	0
Schulte, rf....	2
Tinker, ss.....	5
Zimmerman, 3b	4
W. Miller, cf..	4
Saier, 1b......	4
Evers, 2b.....	3
Archer, c.....	3
Leifield, p....	4

June 7, 1912

	AB
Sheckard, lf...	3
Schulte, rf.....	5
Tinker, ss......	6
Zim'erman, 3b	5
Leach, cf......	3
Saire, 1b.......	4
Evers, 2b......	2
Archer, c......	4
Leifield, p.....	4

July 31, 1912

	AB
Sheckard, lf...	4
Schulte, rf.....	5
Tinker, ss......	4
Zim'erman, 3b..	4
Leach, cf......	3
Saier, 1b.......	3
E ers, 2b......	2
Archer, c......	4
Leifield, p.....	4

August 3, 1912

- Len "Lefty" Madden—
  1 inning, with lineup:
  Note that Cy Williams played center field.

	AB
Sheckard, lf...	5
W. Miller, rf..	2
Tinker, ss	4
Z'merman, 3b.	4
Saier, 1b	5
Evers, 2b	4
Williams, cf..	3
Archer, c	5
Madden, p	0
*C. Smith ...	1
Richie, p	2

September 19, 1912

- George Pierce—
  7 innings, with lineup:
  Note that Cy Williams played center field.

	AB
Sheckard, lf...	4
W. Miller, rf..	4
Tinker, ss....	4
Downs, 3b.....	4
Saier, 1b......	4
Evers, 2b.....	3
Williams, cf..	4
Archer, c.....	2
Pierce, p.....	2
*Good	1
Toney, p......	0

September 20, 1912

Newspaper articles indicate that, when any of the Cub lefties pitched, Frank Chance was there managing, but the above lineups show that without substitution Vic Saier played first base. Also without substitution Evers was at second, Tinker at shortstop, and Jimmy Archer was behind the plate.

- **CONCLUSION: Chance was there, but Saier played first and Archer was the catcher.**
  - Cubs . . . playing in
  - Washington Park in Brooklyn,
  - 1912
  - ~~Mordecai Brown *is* pitching~~ . . .
  - ➤ Johnny Evers is at second base, Joe Tinker at shortstop . . . *Confirmed*
  - Frank Ch~~ance had already left for New York~~
  - ➤ **Vic Saier at first base, Jimmy Archer catching**

The above lineups also reveal the following:

- When Madden or Pierce pitched, ***left-hander*** Cy Williams was always in center field
- When Leifield was on the mound, ***righties*** Ward Miller and Tommy Leach were in center.

Now, note that, when a magnified fielder has his glove hand in front of a light background, the glove is easily discerned as a dark blob. This is clear, for example, in the magnification of second baseman Evers, right.

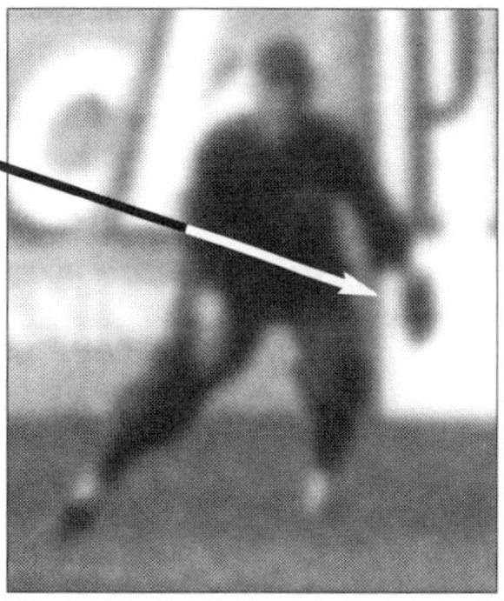

With that in mind, let's take a closer look at the center fielder.

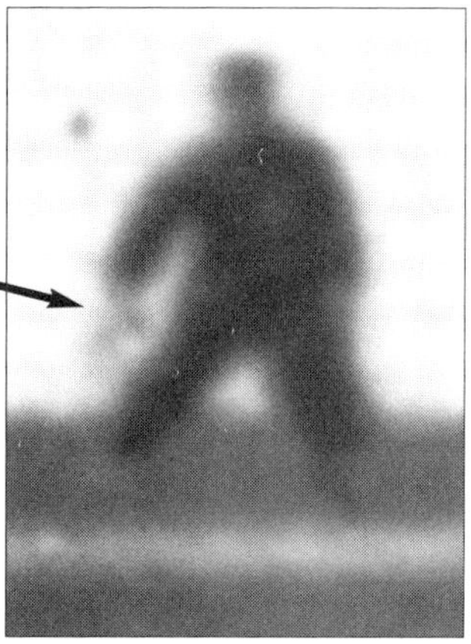

After zooming in on the distant center fielder, it is clear that he has *no glove on his right hand*. Therefore he is either Ward Miller or Tommy Leach. Checking the above lineups leads to the key finding:

• CONCLUSION: Lefty Leifield is pitching.

The lineups also indicate that when Leifield pitched, Frank Schulte played right field. So . . .

- Cubs . . . playing in
- Washington Park in Brooklyn,
- 1912
- ~~Mordecai Brown *is* pitching~~ . . .
- ➤ **Lefty Leifield is pitching**
- Johnny Evers is at second base, Joe Tinker at shortstop . . .
- ~~Frank Chance had already left for New York~~
- Vic Saier at first base, Jimmy Archer catching
- ➤ **Frank Schulte in right field**

Putting it all together:

- Cubs . . . playing in
- Washington Park in Brooklyn,
- 1912
- *Lefty Leifield* is pitching
- Johnny Evers is at second base, Joe Tinker at shortstop . . .
- Vic Saier at first base, Jimmy Archer catching
- Frank Schulte in right field

Well, maybe . . .

It's indisputable that the pitcher in the photo is not Mordecai Brown. Can we be so sure of the other conclusions, which of course are based on a presumption—the accuracy of the box scores with respect to lineups and substitutions? The records, as given in both the *New York Times* and the *Chicago Tribune*, do match. However, quoting researcher Cliff Blau on the question of confidence in Deadball Era box scores, "No, we can't be confident. . . . As for missing a player substitution, very possible."

So has a misplaced trust in circa-1912 scorekeeping provided an erroneous assumption leading to superficially clever but naïve conclusions? I don't think so. While these box scores alone do not provide absolute proof, they are entirely consistent with the accompanying articles describing the games.

Also, the pitcher's proportions do indicate a tall man, and Leifield was 6'1". Leifield pitched three complete games at Brooklyn in 1912. The Cubs' other tall lefty, 6'2" Len Madden, pitched only one inning, and George Pierce is listed at just 5'10". Therefore I stand by the identifications made here.

Note on another Washington Park photo

The National Baseball Hall of Fame has another similar image, just below, left. Comparison of the warm-up plate in that photo to the warm-up plate visible in the uncropped version of the photo that has been the subject of this article (bottom left) reveals an identical dirt pattern. That and other details indicate that both photos were taken on the same day. This additional photo yields another view of Leifield's delivery. ■

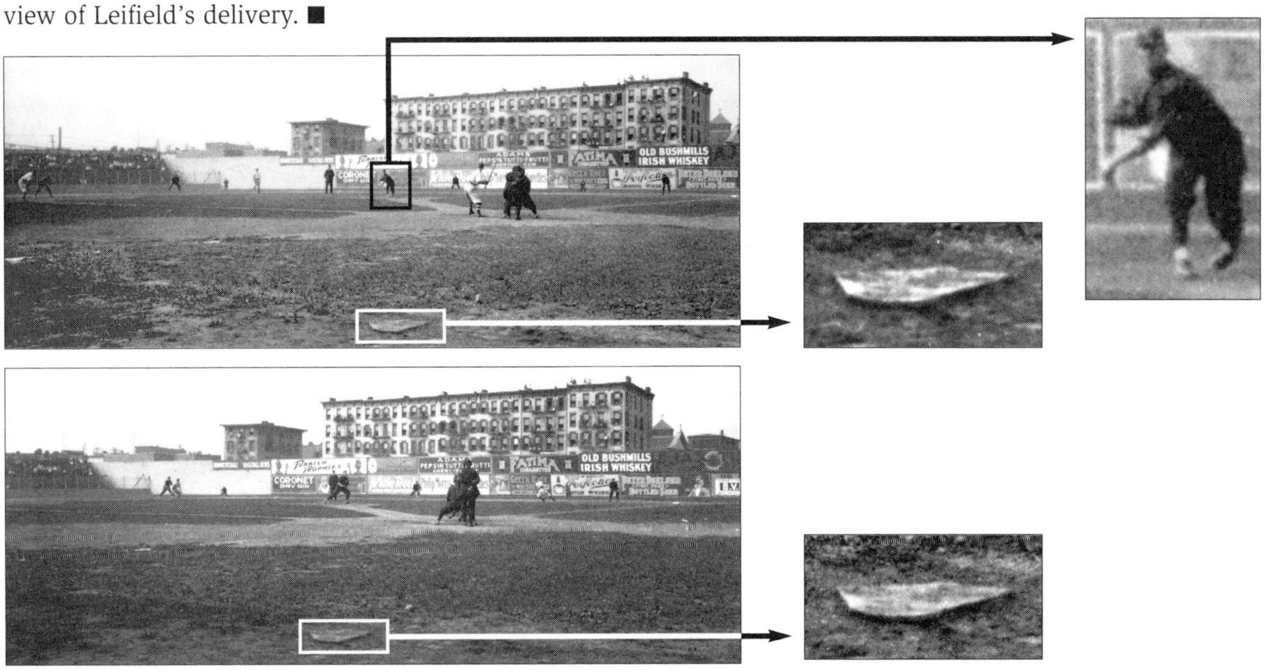

Notes

Thanks to researcher John Zinn for going through two seasons' worth of *Brooklyn Daily Eagle* microfilm to find just the right views of the Washington Park right-field fence, and to Tom Shieber at the Hall of Fame for pointing out the other Washington Park photo taken on the same day.

1. Mark Rucker, *The Brooklyn Dodgers, Images of Sports* (Charleston, S.C.: Arcadia, 2002).
2. John Freyer and Mark Rucker, *Chicago Aces: The First 75 Years* (Charleston, S.C.: Arcadia, 2005).
3. National Baseball Hall of Fame, "Dressed to the Nines—Uniform Database," http://exhibits.baseballhalloffame.org/dressed_to_the_nines/database.htm. Note corrections added to Cub uniforms for this article—1911 collar added, 1912 buttons made dark.
4. Mark Okkonen, *Baseball Memories, 1900–1909* (Sterling, 1992).
5. George Grantham Bain Collection, Library of Congress, Prints and Photographs Division.
6. *Brooklyn Daily Eagle*, 16 April 1912.
7. *Brooklyn Daily Eagle*, 5 October 1911.
8. *Chicago Tribune*, 8 June 1912, 1 August 1912, 4 August 1912, 20 September 1912, 21 September 1912.

Does Baseball Deserve This Black Eye?

A Dissent from the Universal Casting of Shame and Blame on Kenesaw Mountain Landis for Baseball's Failure to Sign Black Players Before 1946

Norman L. Macht

AT SABR's 2006 convention one speaker analyzed the commissioners of baseball and rated Judge Landis the best of all. In the question-and-answer session that followed, a member of the audience challenged the speaker: "How can you stand here in the year 2006 and praise Landis, who was so instrumental in keeping blacks out of Major League Baseball?"

Had I been the presenter, I would have replied, "How do you know that Landis was so instrumental in barring blacks?"

How do we know anything that we *think* we know? By what means do we know it? By taking somebody else's word for it? By reading it in two or three or six places and concluding that it must be true? Or by researching and analyzing the pieces objectively and independently?

What we think we know about the past is laced with uncertainty. There's very little we can be sure about. We must be open to challenging what we think we know when we come across contrary evidence, or across something that doesn't quite fit. That's not easy.

Once we form an opinion or reach a conclusion, it's natural to stop searching and therefore stop thinking. The mind stays closed and refuses to accept other findings that might discredit that opinion.

In medicine this is called confirmation bias: confirming what you expect to find in your research by selectively accepting this or ignoring that and clinging to a single explanation arrived at earlier without considering other possibilities.

Then I would have reminded the judge's critic that, yes, it's precisely because we are standing here in 2006, and Landis and baseball's club owners were operating in a different time and a different society. A historian who judges a man in the context of today's time and standards and not the standards and conditions of the time in which the subject lived commits a scholarly sin. The attempt to understand people in their context and on their terms requires that we temporarily suspend judgment. Understanding the America of the 1920s and '30s and '40s obliges us to make the effort of not judging it by the standards and values of today. Their values were their values, not necessarily ours. As Gibbon wrote of the Roman general Balisarius, "His vices were the vices of his time; his virtues were his own." This forces us to remove the halo of thinking our values are eternal. They are not, and that can be troubling to us.

There is a vast, unbridgeable distance between what we like to believe we always were as a society and what we really were. Most of us never knew that pre–World War II society, never lived there. I ask you to join me now in trying to cross that bridge, leaving behind the baggage of your values and biases and what you think you know about other people in other times.

America was a racist society in the first half of the twentieth century. A society is not a soulless abstraction. It is people; in this case, the white majority of America—our parents, grandparents, great-grandparents.

They grew up in a time when populists like William Jennings Bryan and William Allen White openly opposed any form of integration. Newspapers and popular music regularly used terms like *coons* and *darkies*. The president of Princeton University, Woodrow Wilson, addressed a group of alumni on February 8, 1903. Referring to Teddy Roosevelt's nomination of a black man to be customs collector in Charleston, South Carolina, Wilson drew laughs when he joked, "The groundhog has returned to its burrow because it feared that Roosevelt would put a coon in to replace him."

Americans went to movies where blacks, except for musicians and dancers, were cast as maids and mammies like Hattie McDaniel, fluttery caricatures like Butterfly McQueen, or slow-witted Stepin Fetchits. Joe Louis was admired by whites because he *knew his place* and was *a credit to his race*. When I was young, those phrases were in common use.

Even later, two Brooklyn Dodgers heroes, Southern-born Red Barber and Pee Wee Reese, admitted that everything in their upbringing had imbued in them the belief that the black man was inferior. Reese told author and historian Jules Tygiel, "You hear this all your life, you believe it."[1]

The Ku Klux Klan was as strong in the Midwest as in the South, dominating city halls and chambers of commerce in the 1920s. Klan dinners and dances were covered as social news on the front pages of small-town newspapers. In 1925 they almost elected one of their own as mayor of Detroit. There were Klan members in major-league clubhouses.

In 1926, New York sportswriter Joe Vila wrote:

> Stories are in circulation that certain major league managers are having trouble with their players who are hostile to members of the Ku Klux Klan. A few years ago one of the Western teams was said to have been disrupted by serious clashes on religion.
>
> According to the gossips, several managers, opposed to the Klan, have been getting rid of members who are members of the hooded order, regardless of their skill as batters and fielders. If such conditions exist they should be investigated by the bosses of Organized Baseball.[2]

In the 1930s many blacks went north in search of a better life. Northern whites who deplored Southern customs when the problem was far away were less generous in their support when the victims arrived at their doorsteps.

From Maryland to California there were lynchings every year until the 1950s. Respectable citizens who did not take part stood by and condoned them. In 1933 the governor of California went so far as to declare a lynching in his state "a fine lesson for the whole nation."

In 1937, a federal antilynching bill was filibustered by Southern Democrats in the Senate, tying up all Senate business. Editorials all over the country urged that the antilynching bill be abandoned so other business could be done, and it was. The fact is that in prewar America civil rights and equal opportunity were nowhere on this society's agenda.

From 1933 to 1945, Franklin D. Roosevelt never proposed a single civil-rights law, never supported efforts to pass a federal antilynching law, never pushed Congress, which had jurisdiction over the District of Columbia, to end any aspect of segregation there.

In 1941 it took the threat of a march on Washington to force the president to issue an order ending discrimination in employment in defense industries. Yet nobody accuses FDR of being a racist.

As late as 1948 no city was more tightly segregated than Washington, D.C.—churches, hospitals, schools, universities, hotels, restaurants, lunch counters, parks, department stores. Blacks could be served at some lunch counters but they had to stand—and the dishes they used were smashed instead of washed when they were done. Even if they could buy something in

BASEBALL HALL OF FAME LIBRARY, COOPERSTOWN, N.Y.

Despite his background—his father and grandfather were vocal abolitionists and two of his brothers were elected to Congress over Klan-backed candidates—Kenesaw Mountain Landis (1866–1944) is often supposed to have harbored a tacit racism that led him to resist integration of Major League Baseball during a period when segregation was still the status quo in much of American society.

a store, you wouldn't find any blacks working behind the counter. City and federal offices were almost all-white. Anyone could ride the streetcars and buses, but only whites could drive them. The code of ethics of the Washington real-estate board, which included all the leading banks and title companies as well as realtors, included this statement: "No property in a white section should ever be sold, rented, advertised, or offered to colored people."[3] This was the rule, not the exception, throughout the country. The Supreme Court didn't ban restrictive covenants until 1948.

We're not talking about Klansmen in sheets and hoods but the business elite of the nation. In a 1939 survey, 53 percent of Americans polled said Jews should be restricted in their lives and occupations. Resort hotels advertised that they were "restricted," which meant no Jews allowed. For blacks that had long been the reality.

Terrifying deadly riots in Chicago and Washington in 1919 had left deep scars on our ancestors, who were in no mood for any form of integration. In 1933, Ohio State University barred blacks from on-campus housing and restaurants. When the Ohio Supreme Court upheld the university's right to deny housing to a black coed, the school president, George Rightmire, said, "Knowing the feelings in Ohio, can the administration take the burden of establishing this relationship—colored and white girls living in this more or less family way?"[4]

This was Ohio—not the deep South.

Knowing the feelings in Ohio, could you blame Cincinnati Reds owner Powell Crosley and Cleveland Indians owner Alva Bradley for not putting "colored and white" boys together in "this more or less family way" in their clubhouses?

The mood of America—including its baseball fans—in May 1940 was illustrated by an editor at the *Philadelphia Record* deciding, against the advice of the sports department, to begin a campaign urging the city's two major-league teams to sign Negro players.

One month later in the "Press Box" column in *The Sporting News*, there appeared this interesting item:

"That Philadelphia A.M. sheet has stopped its agitation to get Negro players in the majors because of the reactions of its white readers."

On July 16, 1942, a letter from General Eisenhower's adjutant general went to the Red Cross in London directing that black and white army personnel be segregated as much as possible. It said, "It is believed that to avoid friction between white and Negro soldiers, care should be taken so that men of the two races are not needlessly intermingled in the same dormitory or at the same table in dining halls."[5]

That same year the Missouri legislature killed a civil-rights bill that would have given blacks equal access to public parks, theaters, and restaurants.

In 1943 race riots in Detroit forced the postponement of a game at Briggs Stadium. Federal troops were called in and stayed for six months. There were similar riots in Harlem and Los Angeles that summer.

In August 1944 there was a weeklong transit strike in Philadelphia. What was it about? The upgrading of eight Negroes to jobs formerly held exclusively by whites. Ten thousand union members shut down the city, the nation's third-largest war production center, because they didn't want blacks taking white drivers' jobs. Blacks were fit only for menial jobs—janitors and mechanics and the like. Roosevelt sent in 5,000 troops and averted a major riot, but 300 storefronts were smashed in the black North Philadelphia neighborhood.

If you were the 81-year-old Connie Mack, with your life and assets invested in the Athletics, would you have stood up to those strikers and risked your business and personal safety by telling them that blacks were equal to whites and you were going to sign black players who would take white players' jobs?

I don't think so.

The same thing was true in Washington, where there was a wartime shortage of motormen and conductors. The transit company advertised for workers—white only—in cities as far as 200 miles away, despite the availability of qualified blacks in the city. Both the union and the CIO claimed that race riots would occur if blacks were hired for those positions.

When the D.C. fire chief proposed that black firemen be transferred to fill the many vacancies at white fire stations, he was attacked in a resolution passed by the AF of L Firemen's Local. At this same time the CIO and AF of L were joining black sportswriters in berating Clark Griffith for not integrating MLB.

Hypocrisy thrived in those days too.

In 1937, Griffith had told *Baltimore Afro-American* sports editor Sam Lacy, "I know the time will come, but the climate isn't right. We wouldn't have the support of society." He was right. And Lacy conceded that baseball's integration was an unrealistic goal at that time. Incidentally, Griffith Stadium was the only nonsegregated public place of amusement in Washington.

BASEBALL HALL OF FAME LIBRARY, COOPERSTOWN, N.Y.

"Landis Clears Way for Owners to Hire Colored," according to a headline in the Baltimore Afro-American *in 1942, but Larry MacPhail of the Dodgers insisted that club owners observed "an unwritten law . . . on the subject of the racial issue."*

Negro Leagues star Leon Day later said, "They couldn't have signed any black players in the 1930s even if they wanted to. It would have been suicide for the club owners and murder for the players."[6]

This was the society that Kenesaw Mountain Landis, born in 1866, grew up in and lived in. Now that we've placed him in his time, let's look at the charges leveled against him. Landis was a racist because

- he was solely or primarily responsible for preventing blacks from playing in the major leagues;
- as the czar of baseball, he had the power to force club owners to sign Negro Leaguers.

Let's first look at the background of the man. There is no documentation of anything racist Landis ever did or said in or out of baseball. In researching his biography of Landis, David Pietrusza looked long and hard to find something. He found nothing. On the contrary, Landis's family influences point the other way. His grandfather and father were outspoken abolitionists. Two of his brothers were elected to Congress in Indiana over Klan-backed candidates at a time when the Klan was strong and active there, and very few politicians dared to speak out on the issue of prejudice. They remained fierce opponents of the Klan all their lives.

When Landis was criticized by some congressmen for remaining as a federal judge after his appointment as commissioner in 1921, he was praised by black preachers in Chicago for his leniency and fairness toward black youths brought before him. This editorial appeared in a black newspaper:

> *The Chicago Advocate*, speaking for the entire race, wishes to extend to Judge Landis their appreciation for his fair and impartial justice handed out regardless of race or creed. . . . We, the Negroes of this portion of the country, are thoroughly satisfied with the decisions of Judge Landis, and have no fault whatever to find with them. All of the Negroes ever convicted by him have been proven guilty beyond all reasonable doubt.

Landis was 54 years old at that time. If he was a racist, he either had a lot of people fooled or he became one overnight and pretty late in life.

What about this myth that Landis was an all-powerful dictator who could bully or force club owners to sign black players? How do you think that would go over in cities torn by riots and strikes, and in clubhouses torn between pro- and anti-Klansmen? In truth, Landis had no authority to tell any club owners whom to sign or how to spend their money.

If Landis was really so powerful, he would have abolished the one aspect of baseball he truly hated and fought—the farm system. But he couldn't. In 1948, when a rule restricting control of bonus players was passed, Jim Gallagher, general manager of the Cubs, said the new rule did something that Landis had tried and failed to accomplish.

"For 25 years," Gallagher said, "Commissioner Landis struggled to loosen the regulations by which major league clubs could control the careers of players for periods as long as nine years. He succeeded in reducing this term of control, which was made by slow advancement in the farm system and subsequent options by major league clubs, to six years."[7]

That was as much as this so-called czar could do in 25 years of trying. As for the charge that Landis prevented blacks from playing in the major leagues, there is no evidence that he ever stopped any club owner from signing a black player. None. Ever.

More than once he said there was not and never had been any rule barring blacks. And there wasn't.

But of course, if you are bent on condemning him, you have to call him a liar. You have no basis for it, but it might make you feel better to believe it because it enables you to identify a villain and close the case—and your mind.

More than once Landis said, "If [anybody] wants to sign one or 25 Negro players, it is all right with me. That is the business of the manager and the club owners. The business of the Commissioner is to interpret the rules and enforce them."

When he said it on July 17, 1942, the *Afro-American* ran the headline "Landis Clears Way for Owners to Hire Colored." Sports editor Art Carter made it clear that it was up to any owner "willing to blaze the trail in breaking down the bar against colored players."

Larry MacPhail of the Brooklyn Dodgers responded, "Judge Landis was not speaking for baseball when he said there was no barrier; there has been an unwritten law tantamount to an agreement between major league clubs on the subject of the racial issue."

An agreement between major-league clubs—that's the key. Landis never stopped anybody. No club owner had ever tried to sign a black player. In the words of feminist Carrie Chapman Carr, "No written law has ever been more binding than unwritten custom supported by popular opinion." And that's the way it was.

Unlike stores and restaurants and theaters, baseball clubs were interdependent. The owners' report of 1946 pointed out, "The individual action of any one club . . . could conceivably result in lessening the value of several major league franchises."

Horace Stoneham might have felt that New Yorkers would accept a black player in 1938 or '40 or '42 (in 1954, Milton Gross reported in the *New York Post* that Stoneham admitted he had tried to sign a black player three years before the signing of Jackie Robinson), but what would happen when the Giants took the field in Philadelphia or Cincinnati or St. Louis? Nobody knew.

The club owners were like the businessmen who ran the theaters and restaurants and stores and hotels. Their business depended on the goodwill of their customers, many of whom were just like those white strikers who considered colored people inferior and a threat to take the white man's job. What would happen if black players drew too many black fans? And if a black player got into a fight on the field or argued with an umpire—who knew what might spark a riot in the bleachers? We can sit here now and smugly say their fears were groundless, and maybe they were, but they were real at the time—make no mistake about that. Remember, most of us weren't there as witnesses 65 or 70 years ago, when America was a very different place.

Racism had nothing to do with Major League Baseball not signing black players in prewar America—and everything to do with it. But it was not the racism of club owners Connie Mack and Clark Griffith and Spike Briggs and Tom Yawkey and Bill DeWitt and Don Barnes and the Comiskeys and Ruppert and Stoneham and Wrigley and Crosley and Bob Quinn and Bill Benswanger and Branch Rickey—and Landis—but the racism of their customers, our parents and grandparents and great-grandparents.

Yes, I included Branch Rickey in that list. In his thoroughly documented biography of Rickey, Lee Lowenfish points out that Rickey's home was St. Louis. He had been there for 30 years. He didn't want to leave. Had Cardinals owner Sam Breadon not fired him in 1942, he would have stayed in St. Louis and there might have been no signing of Jackie Robinson. Rickey knew that St. Louis was too much of a Southern city to risk integration in the 1930s and early '40s. Sportsman's Park had a colored-only seating section for as long as Rickey was there. It was the last major-league park to be desegregated—after he left. Members of Rickey's family told Lowenfish that he just couldn't have broken the color line in St. Louis. So you cannot honestly label all the other owners as racists and not include Rickey, whose thinking was essentially the same as theirs—economic, risk-averse, uncertain of the social consequences.

When Branch Rickey moved to Brooklyn, Judge Landis was still commissioner. In early 1943, Rickey revealed to the Dodgers board of directors his plans to scout Negro Leaguers. He didn't talk about being ready to sign them when and if Landis died or resigned or was fired. That was significant; he knew Landis was not the barrier. Rickey was anticipating the end of the war, when American society might have changed enough to accept the integration of the major leagues—maybe. He couldn't have been encouraged by the race riots in Detroit, New York, and Los Angeles that summer

Judge Landis died on November 25, 1944. Nobody rushed to sign black players now that his supposed ban was no longer there. Club owners didn't fall all over themselves outbidding each other for the biggest Negro League stars. A whole year passed before Branch Rickey signed Jackie Robinson to a Montreal contract—after the war ended. Ten years after Landis and his mythical ban were gone, half the major-league clubs still had no black players.

In many baseball histories you read the shame-filled aside that, well, of course it was the national game except that African Americans were not allowed in. Well, blacks weren't allowed in any other part of white American life in those days. The fact is that Major League Baseball was not the shame of the nation, reactionary, behind the times. Baseball led the nation, integrating ten months before Harry Truman became the first president to send a civil-rights message to

BASEBALL HALL OF FAME LIBRARY, COOPERSTOWN, N.Y.

Jackie Robinson's breaking of the color barrier in baseball in 1947 might never have happened had Cardinals owner Sam Breadon not fired Branch Rickey in 1942. Sportsman's Park in St. Louis was the last major-league park to be desegregated and in the 1940s would have been a difficult venue in which to introduce integration into Major League Baseball.

Congress, a year before integration of the armed forces, three years before the first black player was taken in the NBA draft, and way ahead of the nation's political mood. Washington was still sharply segregated. Throughout Jackie Robinson's first year with the Dodgers, there was not a single mention in any Washington newspaper of any statement by any congressman—from anywhere—that was critical of the segregation policies still in effect in the capital. Baseball does not deserve this black eye. It deserves recognition for leading—dragging—the rest of America a little closer to the ultimate goal of equality of opportunity.

And you can look it up. ■

Notes

This article is adapted from a research presentation given at the 2007 SABR annual convention.

1. Jules Tygiel, *Baseball's Great Experiment: Jackie Robinson and His Legacy* (New York: Oxford University Press, 1983).
2. Joe Vila, *New York Sun*, 1926.
3. Harry S. Wender, survey, *Washington Post*, 8 May 1949; Kenesaw M. Landis (commissioner's nephew) and Tom P. Barrett, *Segregation in Washington: A Report*, November 1948 [Chicago, 1948].
4. William J. Baker, *Jesse Owens: An American Life* (New York: Free Press, 1986).
5. Harry C. Butcher, *Three Years with Eisenhower: The Personal Diary of Captain Harry C. Butcher, USNR, Naval Aide to General Eisenhower, 1942 to 1945* (London: Heinemann, [1946]).
6. Sam Lacy and Leon Day, interviews with author.
7. Jim Gallagher, *The Sporting News*, 7 July 1948, 6.

Landis, Baseball, and Racism—A Brief Comment

Richard Crepeau

IN HIS essay "Does Baseball Deserve This Black Eye?" Norman Macht raises a number of questions. First is the question embedded in the title, a question he doesn't address until his concluding comments. Second, he asks how it is known that Judge Landis was instrumental in barring blacks from baseball. This second question occupies much more of Macht's attention than the first. In addition Macht devotes considerable effort to demonstrating that the United States was a racist society through the first half of the twentieth century. To expend this much effort on a truth that has now reached axiomatic status seems odd, but there is a logic to Macht's approach.

Before addressing these issues let me just mention two points of fact raised by Macht that I would question as proof of anything. First, to blame baseball's failure to desegregate on the customers—or, as Macht would have it, "our parents, grandparents, and great-grandparents"—is ludicrous. The customers no more controlled the racial makeup of baseball than they controlled the rules of the game, the price of tickets, the salaries of players, or the profits of the owners.

Second, that baseball led the nation by integrating before either Truman's civil-rights legislation or the desegregation of the NBA is, although true, a diversionary claim. Macht's claim conveniently ignores the fact that the NFL was the first professional sport to desegregate, that African Americans were playing intercollegiate sports all through its history, and that President Roosevelt's Executive Order 8802, by which he created the Fair Employment Practices Commission, was issued in 1941, well before the desegregation of baseball.

But I digress.

What Macht offers as one of his main arguments supporting Landis is that the commissioner was a product of his times. He was immersed in a racist culture and therefore his racism, and indeed that of baseball, should not be used to condemn either Landis or baseball. This is a dubious proposition on several counts.

From what Macht tells us, and from several other sources, including Landis's major biographer, David Pietrusza, it is clear that Commissioner Landis was a bulwark against change. His denials of any rule or ban on African Americans in baseball was a convenient way of saying, I can do nothing to change things because there is nothing to change. At the same time Landis denied there was what Larry MacPhail called "an unwritten law tantamount to an agreement between major league clubs on the subject of the racial issue."[1] It seems to me that the hypocrisy of Landis's public posture is clear and that for whatever reason Landis was ducking the issue.

BASEBALL HALL OF FAME LIBRARY, COOPERSTOWN, N.Y.

Larry MacPhail, president of the Dodgers (1938–42), and his successor Branch Rickey. General manager of the Yankees when Rickey signed Jackie Robinson, MacPhail has been described as ambivalent or outright opposed to the move, a stance that may have led to Rickey's distancing himself from MacPhail shortly thereafter.

When desegregation did come, the existence of such an agreement became clear, as MacPhail and the other owners mounted considerable resistance to Branch Rickey's signing of Jackie Robinson. This is well documented by Jules Tygiel, Lee Lowenfish, and others.[2] The slow pace of desegregation is also a clear indication of resistance among the owners.

As the leader of a major public institution, Organized Baseball, Judge Landis resisted attempts to move that institution to desegregate. One can argue that he was simply a man of his times and therefore his behavior is understandable. One can also argue that those who defended institutional racism at any level, which meant a vast majority of white Americans, were part of the problem.

One thing we know about Landis is that in both his judicial career and his time as commissioner he was a staunch defender of the status quo. We also know that he was a man who saw himself in tune with the will of the populace. In both roles he played to the public, relished public adulation, and loved the spotlight. For Landis to have moved to desegregate baseball would have been an action out of character.

In a changing world in which the forces attacking segregation were beginning to move forward, Judge Landis failed the test of leadership and hid behind dissembling rhetoric. He was indeed a man of his times, not a leader of them.

As for baseball, does it deserve this black eye? Did it resist social change and social justice? Did it do so while describing itself as the game of democracy, the national pastime, and the American game? Did it see itself as a vehicle for teaching democracy to American immigrants? Did it see itself as a vehicle for spreading democracy and civilization around the world? Did it see itself as democratic because it conducted its business under the rules of fair play and equal opportunity, proclaiming its purity as a meritocracy?

If you can answer all these questions in the affirmative, and I am certain from my own work that you can,[3] then Norman Macht's primary question can only be answered in the affirmative. Baseball deserves this back eye.

As for Landis, was he a racist? No more so than his contemporaries. He was the commissioner of baseball who defended the institutional racism within Organized Baseball, and he failed to seek any alteration of the status quo. In this he shared a responsibility with many. As Tygiel notes, Landis did not "single-handedly perpetuate baseball segregation."[4] As Pietrusza points out there were no owners pressing Landis to support their desire for change, and there was no rush to desegregate after Landis's death.[5]

The question about Landis should not be whether he was racist but whether, as commissioner of baseball, he provided leadership for justice and equality. ■

Notes

1. David Pietrusza, *Judge and Jury: The Life and Times of Judge Kenesaw Mountain Landis* (South Bend, Ind.: Diamond Communications, 1998), 419.
2. Jules Tygiel, *Baseball's Great Experiment: Jackie Robinson and His Legacy* (New York: Oxford University Press, 1983), passim; Lee Lowenfish, *Branch Rickey: Baseball's Ferocious Gentleman* (Lincoln: University of Nebraska Press, 2007), passim.
3. Richard Crepeau, *Baseball: America's Diamond Mind* (Lincoln: University of Nebraska Press, 2000), chap. 2.
4. Tygiel, *Baseball's Great Experiment*, 32.
5. Pietrusza, *Judge and Jury*, 427.

The Gentlemen's Agreement and the Ferocious Gentleman Who Broke It

Lee Lowenfish

I DOUBT that any thoughtful person would disagree with Norman Macht's contention that "what we know about the past is laced with uncertainty." Another way of making the point comes in the opening epigraph to L. P. Hartley's 1953 novel, later a film, *The Go-Between*: "The past is a foreign country. They do things differently there." Though it is true that it is almost impossible to ever fully light the dim, dark abyss that is the past, those of us who want to wear the mantle of historian successfully must engage in acts of historical imagination and make at least educated guesses. So it seems to me particularly unsatisfying that Norman Macht defends Commissioner Landis's racial policies because "most of us weren't there as witnesses 65 or 70 years ago, when America was a very different place." By that line of argument we might conclude that only someone who was a contemporary of Landis could appraise his administration, and I cannot believe Macht supports that conclusion. Though I also question Macht's contention that the United States of the Landis years was "a very different place" from the country of today (despite the election of the first African American president and a greater acceptance of the diversity of our population), the main contention of his I want to address is that Landis and baseball have gotten an undeserved black eye for not pushing earlier for racial integration.

Because of its unique historic place in American society, baseball has always had to live up to a higher standard than have the other sports, and therefore its failure to act on the American creed of equality has made it vulnerable to charges of hypocrisy. Macht argues that because "America was a racist society in the first half of the twentieth century" you cannot blame Commissioner Landis for not taking the lead on integrating the sport. As an individual Kenesaw Mountain Landis may not have been more conservative on the race issue than the owners he ruled over, but he had the power to lead on it, and he did not choose to employ that power. As the "czar" appointed to clean up the mess left by the Black Sox scandal, Landis had enormous powers, which he used to ban the alleged fixers of the World Series, even though a Chicago jury had ruled them innocent. Though Macht is correct that Landis could not destroy the farm system that Branch Rickey had ingeniously invented to enable his small-market St. Louis Cardinals to compete with the big-pocketed big-city owners, the commissioner did free dozens of minor leaguers from Rickey's and other clubs' systems. Though I agree that it is poor historical judgment to expect Landis to have had the racially progressive vision of, let us say, today's pro football, which mandates minority interviewing for front-office positions through the Rooney Rule (named after the owner of one of their most racially progressive franchises, the Pittsburgh Steelers), it is nonethless true that Landis could have taken more positive steps to push for racial integration. The evidence is clear that Landis did not want to take a leadership role on this issue.

Macht cites Landis's public statement in the summer of 1942 that baseball has no rule that bars players of color from being signed. He does not mention that the commissioner was reacting to the pressure of what *New York Daily News* sportswriter Hy Turkin described as being "assailed by more than a million letters, telegrams and phone calls" that landed on his desk calling for integration, a grassroots movement organized by American communist activists but obviously not limited to their backers. According to Larry Lester in an important if rhetorically overheated article in the fall 2008 issue of the new journal *Black Ball* (McFarland Press), both the Pittsburgh Pirates and the Cleveland Indians promised in 1942 to give tryouts to several Negro League players, but both franchises got cold feet and certainly were not encouraged by the commissioner to proceed.

One of the problems in producing evidence about a conspiracy of silence is that there is rarely a smoking gun to prove complicity. (In *Soul of the Game*, the HBO fictionalized 1995 movie about Josh Gibson, Satchel Paige, and Jackie Robinson, an unintended hilarious misreading of the baseball color line came when there appeared on the screen the headline "Landis Bars Negroes.") It is interesting, though, that Macht himself quotes Dodgers general manager Larry MacPhail admitting, at the very same time that Landis was denying, that there was indeed a gentlemen's agreement against signing players of color. Responding to the pressure of the especially active sports-minded communists in Brooklyn, MacPhail in 1942 told their paper the *Daily Worker* that if the Dodgers won the

BASEBALL HALL OF FAME LIBRARY, COOPERSTOWN, N.Y.

Appointed commissioner in the wake of the Black Sox scandal, Landis was granted powers that he used to ban the alleged fixers of the 1919 World Series and later to declare some minor laguers free agents. That Landis did not use the power of his office to push for integration is held against him by many baseball historians.

World Series they might play the winners of the Negro League pennant in a postseason tournament. The offer became moot when the Dodgers fell two games short of the National League pennant and MacPhail resigned from his position to reenter the military. One wonders, though, how sincere MacPhail's offer was, given his adamant opposition to integration three years later, once Branch Rickey had beaten every team to the punch by signing Jackie Robinson. When MacPhail returned as president of the Yankees in 1946, he spearheaded the secret report that warned of dangers to the "physical properties of franchises" if Robinson integrated the Dodgers—that is, too many black fans might chase away more-prosperous white fans. It also seems highly unlikely that Landis would have approved MacPhail's suggestion of a postseason series against the Negro League champs, given that Landis had long discouraged white players from competing in such off-season exhibitions.

It required a practical visionary like Branch Rickey to make integration work, and, despite all the criticisms of his bombastic style leveled by his contemporaries and by later historians, the substance of his program and its example for other efforts at desegregation remains a stirringly successful saga. I have never been a big fan of "What Would Have Happened If" history, and Norman Macht's foray into the genre is not convincing when he suggests that if Sam Breadon had rehired Rickey in St. Louis there never would have been a Jackie Robinson signing in Brooklyn. With the Negro League player market ripe for mining, Rickey, I think, would have found a way to tap it, if not in St. Louis then in another city.

Speculative "If" history might be useful regarding what might have happened if Landis had lived through the end of World War II and was faced with the fait accompli of the Robinson signing. My educated guess (and it can be only a guess, of course) is that Landis would not have made any major objection. Once New York State passed the antidiscriminatory Ives-Quinn Law during spring training 1945 and Rickey exclaimed to his wife at the breakfast table, "They can't stop me now!" there was little Landis could have done, especially with a federal Fair Employment Practices Commission statute already on the books.

Macht is correct that Branch Rickey shared the fears of all the baseball owners about what might happen "if a black player got into a fight on the field or argued with an umpire—who knew what might spark a riot in the bleachers?" But it did not stop him from going on with his grand plan to add talented African American prospects to the products of his latest burgeoning farm system in Brooklyn. Rickey's fear of black overreaction, though, explains why he took such pains to stress to Jackie Robinson that he must be a symbol of probity and modesty in his role as racial pioneer. Later historians and black activists have been critical of Rickey's cautious handling of the issue and Robinson's buying into the program, yet there should be no trimming of the historical record to dilute praise for Rickey's leadership on the issue.

What is incontrovertibly true is that Rickey shrewdly planned for the racial revolution, trying to defuse the opposition from both whites and blacks by "attacking prejudice on its blind side," as he would put it in a remarkable series of interviews on Pittsburgh public television in 1959, during which he also pithily defined prejudice as "strong opinion without cause." He understood that the legacy of racism was deep among owners and players alike, and therefore he sought a pioneer whose ability on the field was so outstanding and his demeanor off of it so impeccable that he could not be resisted by both those who wanted a winning team and those who wanted to do the right thing after a million African Americans had served their country in World War II.

To me, then, the issue is not the black eye that Landis allegedly has received but rather the garland that baseball deserves for setting the standard, however reluctantly, for the integration of American society that was to begin, however haltingly, in the years ahead. In this area I wholly endorse Norman Macht's conclusion that baseball "deserves recognition for leading—dragging—the rest of America a little closer to the ultimate goal of equality of opportunity." ■

Response by Norman Macht

THE PRIMARY purpose of my paper was to try to root out the baseless myth embedded in the minds of many SABR members that Judge Landis blocked major-league club owners from signing black players. It may be axiomatic that the past cannot be judged by the standards and mores of the present, but there are people in SABR who still do it.

I appreciate the support for my position expressed by Richard Crepeau and Lee Lowenfish. Nothing they have written disproves my thesis. Much they have written, such as the quotes from Tygiel and Pietrusza cited by Crepeau, backs it. Lowenfish points out the fiction of the "Landis Bars Negroes" headline in an HBO movie.

Crepeau blames Landis for failing to exercise leadership in the cause of integration. But not leading a cause is not the same as blocking it. He characterizes Landis as "a man who saw himself in tune with the will of the populace," playing to the public. This implies that for "Landis to have moved to integrate baseball" would have been out of tune with the will of the populace, which is what I was trying to say. It follows that, if the public was truly demanding integration, and Landis played to the public, he would have been promoting it.

Crepeau calls it "ludicrous" to think that the customers' attitudes might affect club owners' decisions in putting their product—their teams—before the public. But everything from rowdyism to gambling and the Black Sox affair was viewed by baseball moguls as to how it would affect attendance.

Crepeau accuses Landis of ducking the issue (which, again, is not the same as "barring Negroes"). But black sportswriters didn't see it that way when he made his 1942 statement. The *Baltimore Afro-American* of July 25, 1942, ran the headline "Landis Clears Way for Owners to Hire Colored." Sports editor Art Carter said Landis made it clear that it was up to any owner "willing to blaze the trail in breaking down the bar against colored players."

My two respondents disagree on my second contention: that baseball deserves recognition for leading the way in integration, not castigation for taking so long. Lowenfish agrees; Crepeau cries foul.

Both cite the Fair Employment Practices Order of 1941, which is irrelevant, since it covered only the defense industry and did nothing for blacks trying to drive streetcars in Philadelphia and Washington, or work with white firemen, or clerk in downtown department stores.

Lowenfish believes that baseball has always had to live up to a higher standard than do other sports. But I don't think this was ever true. (For a long time there were no other professional team sports.) Standards weren't all that high in the nineteenth century. Gambling and game-fixing went on long before 1919. Club owners' subterfuges, syndicate ownerships, and rules violations were common practices. A higher standard? Though baseball fans wish it were true, the current steroids mess is further proof that it still ain't so.

Crepeau condemns "baseball" for how he says it saw itself—as an engine for democracy and justice and civilization, while remaining all-white. I think that's a stretch. Baseball owners saw it as a bottom-line business first and last, notwithstanding the hypocritical use of pompous flag-waving and self-serving oratory by some tycoons and politicians.

The record is clear that baseball was far ahead of the rest of the country in the area of integration, and Lee Lowenfish is right to credit Branch Rickey with leading the way. ■

The Possible Effect of Steroids on Home-Run Production

Alan M. Nathan

IN A RECENT paper entitled "On the Potential of a Chemical Bonds: Possible Effects of Steroids on Home Run Production in Baseball,"[1] physicist Roger Tobin develops a systematic analysis showing how performance-enhancing drugs (PEDs) taken by an already highly skilled player could produce a dramatic increase in home-run production. Tobin starts by looking statistically at home-run production during the "steroid era" (1994–2003) compared to earlier eras. The number of home runs hit by a player is the product of balls in play and home runs per balls in play (HRBiP). Tobin argues that the former involves skills and strategies that are not likely affected by PEDs. He therefore takes HRBiP as his metric for comparing home-run production in different eras. In figure 2 of his paper, he shows that, for elite home-run hitters in the pre-steroid era (Aaron, Ruth, Mays, Killebrew, Robinson), HRBiP was approximately 0.10, whereas for hitters in the steroid era (Bonds, Sosa, McGwire, Griffey, Palmeiro) the number jumped to 0.15, a 50 percent increase.

Tobin then investigates whether it is plausible that such a large increase can be attributed to PEDs. In section 2, entitled "What Do Steroids Do?" he presents lots of evidence from the scientific literature justifying his starting assumption for the remainder of the analysis. Namely, he assumes that the main effect of steroids vis-à-vis home-run production is to increase the batter's muscle mass by 10 percent. Since I have no expertise in this area, I will simply take it as a reasonable starting point. Tobin next develops section 3, entitled "How Much Can More Muscle Enhance Home-Run Production?" This section is really the heart of the paper and the one I will discuss at length. Tobin's chain of reasoning involves two distinct steps:

1. Increased muscle mass results in higher bat speed and therefore higher batted-ball speed;
2. Higher batted-ball speed results in longer fly balls and therefore higher HRBiP.

Step 1 involves partly biomechanics and partly physics. Step 2 involves partly physics and partly statistics. Tobin arrives at the following conclusion:

It is plausible that a 10 percent increase in muscle mass can lead to a 50 percent increase in HRBiP for the elite home run hitters.

In the present paper, I will discuss the steps in the analysis chain, first presenting Tobin's argument and then my own. Although Tobin and I may disagree on some details, I will end up agreeing with his essential conclusion.

MUSCLE MASS AND BATTED-BALL SPEED

Tobin initially argues that a 10 percent increase in muscle mass leads to the batter supplying a 10 percent greater force to the bat, resulting in a 5 percent increase in bat speed. The argument is essentially one of energy conservation, where the work done by the batter in applying a force to the bat over a fixed distance is converted to kinetic energy of the bat. Since kinetic energy is proportional to the square of the velocity, a 10 percent greater force leads to a 5 percent increase in bat speed. In a "Note added in proof," Tobin revises his estimate downward to 3.8 percent, based on Robert K. Adair's argument that the work provided by the muscles is converted to kinetic energy that is shared between the bat and some fraction of the body mass of the batter, mainly the arms.[2] The essential point is that both the bat and the batter's arms are moving. Therefore not all of the work provided by the body muscles goes into kinetic energy in the bat, and a fraction must also go into kinetic energy of the body. In an unpublished article that I have posted on my website,[3] I have estimated that only about half the kinetic energy goes into the bat. With the additional assumption that half of the batter's pre-steroid weight is muscle, Tobin and I both agree that a 10 percent increase in muscle mass can lead to about a 3.8 percent increase in bat speed.

From a purely physics point of view, the easiest part of the analysis is to estimate how an increase in swing speed affects batted-ball speed. Suppose a pitched ball crosses the plate at 85 mph, a reasonable value for a good fastball given that the ball loses about 10 percent of its speed between pitcher and batter. Suppose also that the pre-steroid batter swings the bat at 70 mph at the sweet-spot location. Then, if we assume a perfect head-on collision, the resulting batted ball will exit the bat at about 100 mph. If such a ball is slightly undercut, giving it backspin, and is launched at an angle of 30 to 35 degrees, it will travel close to 400 feet. Suppose now the post-steroid batter swings the bat 3.8 percent faster, or 72.7 mph. Then the batted-ball speed will increase to about 103 mph,[4] a 3 percent increase and a number Tobin agrees with in his "Note added in proof."

So, Tobin and I both conclude that a 10 percent increase in muscle mass can result in a 3 percent increase in batted-ball speed, a number that is on very solid footing. We next examine how such an increase will affect home-run production.

Figure 1. Distribution of fly-ball distances both before (solid) and after (dashed) an increase of 3% in average batted-ball speed.

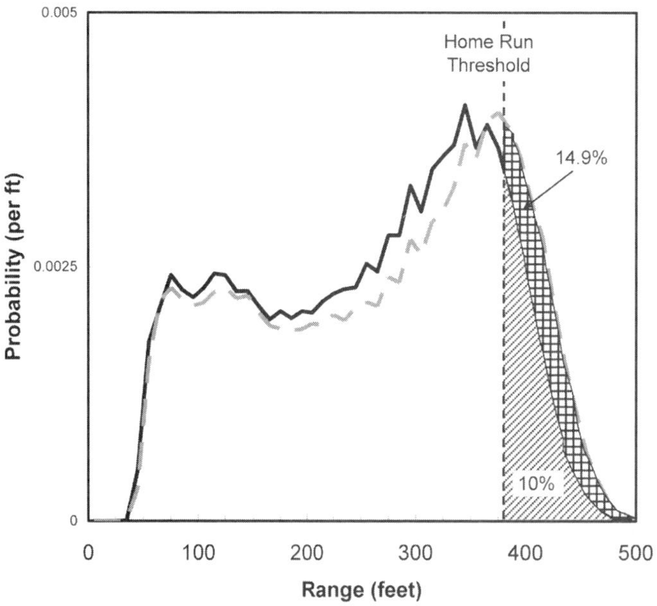

BATTED-BALL SPEED AND HOME-RUN PRODUCTION

To estimate how a 3 percent increase in batted-ball speed affects home-run production, an aerodynamics model is needed to determine the additional distance traveled by a fly ball. When we use statistical information on the distribution of fly-ball distances relative to the fence, we can estimate the change in HRBiP. Unfortunately, that statistical information is not readily available, so Tobin resorts to a numerical simulation. For a given aerodynamics model,[5] he assumes a normal distribution of batted-ball speeds and launch angles to calculate a distribution of fly-ball distances. He defines a home run to be a fly ball that has a height of at least 9 feet at a distance of 380 feet from home plate. He then adjusts the parameters of the normal distributions until the distribution results in 0.10 HRBiP, the baseline number for elite batters. The resulting fly-ball distribution is shown as the solid curve in figure 1. He then repeats the calculation with the mean batted-ball speed increased by 3 percent, as expected for a 10 percent increase in muscle mass, resulting in the distribution shown by the dashed curve in the figure. He finds HRBiP increase to 0.149, an increase of nearly 50 percent.

Given the importance of figure 1 for the conclusion of the analysis, it is worthwhile discussing it in more detail. The figure shows that the distribution of fly-ball distances is smooth and continuous, whereas a home run is a binary event on the tail of that distribution. For elite home-run hitters, the slope of the distribution at the home-run threshold (380 feet) must be very steep to achieve simultaneously the 10 percent HRBiP figure and the known rarity of very long home runs—say, those in the vicinity of 500 feet or greater. The steepness of the slope means that there must be a lot of near misses, so that a small change in the mean of the fly-ball distribution can have a large effect on the fraction falling above the home-run threshold.

There is an alternate way of reaching the same conclusion, using data compiled on actual home-run distances for the 2007 MLB season.[6] By inspecting the distance of the landing point from the nearest fence, one can estimate that each additional foot of fly-ball distance increases the home-run probability by 4 percent. Combining that with the aerodynamics "rule of thumb" that each additional mph of batted-ball speed increases the fly-ball distance by 5.5 feet, along with the previously estimated mean increase of 3 mph in batted-ball speed, and one arrives at a 66 percent increase in home-run probability, a number even larger than Tobin's estimate. Adair has conducted a similar analysis. Based on his detailed study of home-run statistics, he estimates that each additional percent of fly-ball distance increases home-run probability by about 7 percent.[7] If we use 380 feet as the baseline home-run distance, a 3 mph increase in batted-ball speed leads to a 4.3 percent increase in batted-ball distance and therefore a 30 percent increase in home-run probability. Putting together all these independent analyses, I find that an increase in HRBiP in the range 30–70 percent is completely plausible.

SUMMARY AND CONCLUSIONS

I find that the conclusion reached by Tobin, that a 10 percent increase in muscle mass can lead to a large increase in home-run probability, is well supported by my own analysis. In fact, Tobin puts the increase in the range 30–70percent, depending on the details of the underlying assumptions. Obtaining a precise number is not really the point of the paper, but rather that a modest increase in muscle mass can lead to a very large increase in HRBiP. On that, we both agree. ■

I thank Professor Roger Tobin for many interesting discussions, for a critical reading of this paper, and for providing the figure, and Greg Rybarczyk for providing the 2007 home-run data. And I thank my mentor Professor Bob Adair for his seminal contributions to our understanding of the science of baseball.

Notes

1. The paper is published in *American Journal of Physics* 76 (2008): 15–20. A copy can be downloaded for personal use at http://webusers.npl.illinois.edu/~a-nathan/pob/Tobin_AJP_Jan08.pdf.
2. The argument is presented in Adair's book *The Physics of Baseball*, 3d ed. (New York: HarperCollins, 2002). See the discussion in chap. 6, "The Optimum Bat Weight". Note particularly figure 6.1 (page 117) and the formula on page 139.
3. See http://webusers.npl.uiuc.edu/~a-nathan/pob/swingspeedmass.pdf.
4. In Tobin's paper, the factors multiplying vbat and vpitch in equation 1 are approximately 1.2 and 0.2, respectively.
5. Tobin recognizes that there is uncertainty in the so-called drag and lift coefficients that are needed to carry out the trajectory calculation. However, the uncertainty does not alter his principal conclusion.
6. See www.hittrackeronline.com.
7. Adair, 97.

Offensive Strategy and Efficiency in the United States and Dominican Republic

Robert J. Reynolds and Steven M. Day

ACCORDING to a well-known baseball saying in the Dominican Republic, "You don't walk off the island."[1] It means that, for a ballplayer looking to advance to Major League Baseball, it is better to try to hit the ball than draw a walk, even at the possible expense of making an out. This may explain a common perception among baseball fans in the United States that players from the Dominican Republic are "hackers" who make too many outs and contribute little offensively. Yet players from the Dominican Republic are highly prized in MLB. In the 2008 season, only the United States fielded more MLB players. Players born in the Dominican Republic represented almost 10 percent of the total. Dominicans are excluded from the amateur draft, and, while that offers MLB clubs a financial incentive that may contribute to the high rate at which Dominicans are recruited into MLB, that they are signed at all is an indication of their skill compared to that of the U.S. alternatives. If the performance of Dominican players were seriously substandard, it would make no sense to recruit them at all, no matter how inexpensive they were.

Is it true that ballplayers from the Dominican Republic have a different strategy at the plate from that of players born in the United States? If so, to what extent does this impact their offensive effectiveness? If these players employ ineffective strategies at the plate, why do major-league clubs recruit so heavily from the Dominican Republic?

We address these questions in a comparison of batting statistics for MLB players from the Dominican Republic and the United States. If Dominican players are systematically employing a different approach at the plate in comparison to U.S. players, the trend should be easy to demonstrate.

To quantify and describe the offensive strategy of the two groups, we examined the proportions of these plate-appearance events: walks (BB), sacrifice flies (SF), hit by pitch (HBP), and at-bats (AB). (We do not include sacrifice hits and catcher interference, as they are not included as a divisor when calculating OBP.) By measuring the rates among these events, we can infer the possibility of a systematic difference between the respective plate strategies employed by hitters from the two countries.

To characterize the efficiency of the respective plate strategies, we use on-base percentage (OBP) and introduce the statistic plate-appearance base average (PABA) as a plate-appearance analog to slugging percentage (SLG). PABA is calculated as the sum of the bases achieved in three categories—hitting (TB), BB, and HBP—divided by the total number of plate appearances: (TB + BB + HBP) / TPA. Just as OBP provides the success rate of getting on base per PA, PABA provides an average number of bases achieved by the batter per PA.

PABA is similar to bases per plate appearance and runs created (RC), though these latter include stolen bases, and advancing other players through sacrifices. Because of these additions, bases per plate appearance and RC do not provide an isolated measure of a player's efficiency at the plate. As the objective of the current work is to examine proximal hitting outcomes, PABA is the measure of choice among these three.

Using these measures collectively allows us to answer three important questions that are at the heart of offensive strategy:

1. With what frequency do the players attempt to hit and with what frequency do they walk?
2. With what frequency are they successful in those hitting attempts?
3. On average, how many bases do these players earn through their efforts at the plate?

METHODS

Hypotheses

The general hypothesis of this study was that players from the Dominican Republic are more aggressive at the plate, and consequently less efficient, than players from the United States. Specifically we hypothesized that, in comparison to U.S. players, Dominican players display no differences in the rates of SF and HBP; spend more PA opportunities on AB and fewer on BB; maintain a lower AVG and SLG; and maintain a lower OBP and PABA.

Data

The data for the study were taken from the 2007 version of the Lahman Database. This database has complete seasonal player statistics through the 2006 season along with demographic information—the most important being, for our purposes, country of birth. More information about this database can be found on the website of the Baseball Archive (www.baseball1.com).[2]

Batting statistics were compiled for every player in MLB who played in the majors in any of the seasons from 1990 through 2006, had at least one plate appearance, and was identifiable as being born in either the Dominican Republic or the United States.

It is common practice in sabermetric research to exclude individual player-seasons that fail to reach a minimum threshold of playing time, usually measured in PA. This is to ensure that an individual player has had enough chances at the plate to reduce the variability surrounding his performance and to enable him to show his "true" ability. Since the analysis in the current work is not concerned with batting statistics for individuals, we have not chosen to impose such restrictions here. As the unit of analysis is the individual plate appearance, each plate appearance can be considered an independent trial; that is, the outcome of any single plate appearance is not dependent on the plate appearances that precede it. This means that the significance of plate appearances that come from players who total only 20 PA is no less valid than the significance of the first 20 PA from players who total 500 or more. This is the same approach used when calculating league-total or team-total batting statistics: Add up all the statistics for all players who made a plate appearance and calculate averages as usual.

After assembling the player-seasons, we pooled the data into groups by national origin, one for the United States and one for the Dominican Republic. The United States was chosen as the comparison group because, as baseball's birthplace, it offers a sensible benchmark against which to compare the style of play of other nations. The large number of players from the United States also affords statistical estimates that are more precise.

Because most pitchers are notoriously poor hitters, all of the player-seasons from pitchers were excluded from the analyses.

Statistical analyses

To calculate the frequency of plate-appearance events, we divided the number of events by the total number of PA. In this way the various measures may be considered standardized rates of offensive events, allowing for direct comparisons between groups.

AVG, SLG, and OBP were calculated according to standard methods. As mentioned in the introduction, PABA was calculated as (TB + BB + HBP) / TPA.

Difference scores between groups were then calculated for all PA-event rates and offensive statistics, by subtracting the scores of the Dominican players from those of the U.S. players.

To ensure that the differences were not due to chance alone, statistical significance was tested at the 0.05 level using z-scores from the normal approximation to the binomial distribution.[3] In this context statistical significance indicates that the differences—however small—are likely systematic and not the result of random variation in the data.

It should be remembered that the 1994 season was prematurely ended by a players' strike, in August, resulting in the loss of approximately 25 percent of the regular-season games. For this reason, the statistics from 1994 are highly suspect. The 1995 season started late, resulting in a season of 144 games, about 11 percent fewer than the 162 games that is the norm in the period we study. Statistics for both seasons have been retained for the sake of continuity, but we stress that inferences should not be drawn on the basis of either season alone, and especially not on the 1994 season alone.

RESULTS

Sample characteristics

The sample contained 2,404,312 plate appearances from 8,569 player-seasons contributed by 1,706 unique players between 1990 and 2006.

The data indicate that the amount of average playing time Dominicans receive (as measured by PA per player) has varied over time but has increased in the last few seasons. In general the average PA per player was higher for the United States in the 1990s, but since 2000 the Dominican Republic has seen more average playing time per player. Table 1 below summarizes this trend.

Table 1. Average Plate Appearances Per Player, DR and US, 1990–2006

	1990	1991	1992	1993	1994	1995	1996	1997	1998	1999	2000	2001	2002	2003	2004	2005	2006	All
DR	306	271	224	239	249	223	211	248	282	290	294	277	312	350	333	300	324	282
US	277	270	277	283	224	260	289	296	291	291	287	280	290	279	281	288	299	280

Strategy at the plate

Figure 1 shows the difference, between U.S. and Dominican players, in the accrual rate of the four components of plate appearances (BB, SF, HBP, AB), and figure 2 shows the difference in batting statistics (OBP, SLG, AVG). Lines in the top half of the graphs represent differences in favor of players from the United States—U.S. players scored higher than Dominican players. Likewise, lines below the zero line (in the lower half of the graphs) represent the Dominican players outperforming the U.S. players.

Looking first at SF and HBP (figure 1), we see that the differences were minuscule, never exceeding 3 events per 1,000 PA. Significance testing revealed that in most seasons these differences were statistically insignificant. In those seasons where the differences were significant, they were still not large enough to alter significance in the difference scores for AB and BB. We therefore conclude that the differences in SF and HBP are immaterial and that any differences in AB come at the expense of BB and vice versa.

Figure 1. Difference in PA Events, US and DR, 1990–2006

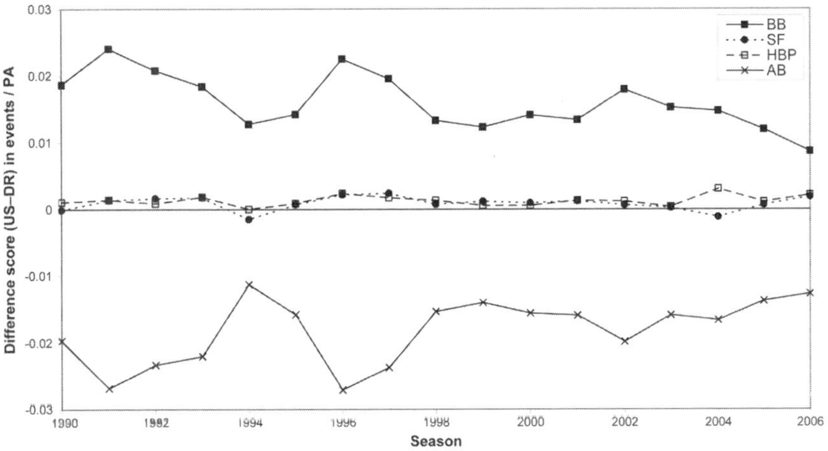

Figure 2. Difference in Batting Statistics, US and DR, 1990–2006

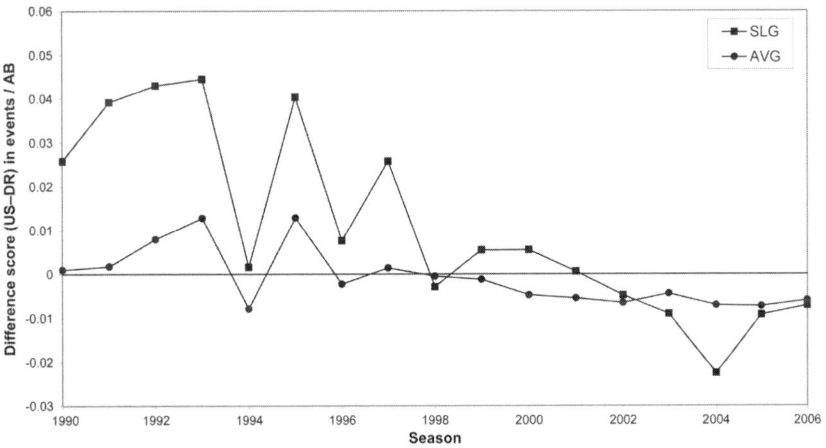

The difference scores for BB and AB show that the Dominican players consistently walk less often and try to hit more often than do Americans. This difference ranged between 12 and 24 events per 1,000 PA through the 1990s but since 2002 has been on the decline. Despite this trend, the differences were statistically significant in every season at the level of $p < 0.001$. So, although the Dominican players walk more often than they used to, they still walk significantly less often and try to hit significantly more often than do the U.S. players.

The difference scores in figure 2 show that the U.S. players hit for higher average than did the Dominican players from 1990 through 1995 (1994, the strike-shortened season, is disregarded). Then, from 1996 through 1999, the two groups of players were largely tied in AVG. From 2000 onward, the Dominican players consistently hit for higher average than did the U.S players. Interestingly, significance testing revealed that only in the most extreme seasons (1993, 1995, 2004, and 2005) were the differences significantly different from zero.

Looking at SLG in figure 2, we see that, in the early 1990s, U.S. players had a dramatically larger SLG (as many as 45 more bases per 1,000 AB in 1993). By 1999 the differences declined sharply, until 2002, when the Dominican players finally overtook the U.S players. However, from 1998 onward, only the 2003, 2004, and 2005 seasons were significantly different from zero.

Offensive efficiency

The actual scores (not differences) for OBP for both the Dominican and the U.S. players are displayed in figure 3. The OBPs for the two countries were highly significantly different ($p < 0.001$ in most years) until the 2000 and 2001 seasons, when they show a short-lived convergence. In 2002–4 the differences again gained significance in favor of the U.S. players. In 2005–6 the difference in OBP declined once more, as the Dominican players improved their OBP faster than did the U.S. players. The difference in 2006 shrank to just 0.002, a mere 2 extra times on base per 1,000 PA.

Overall the OBP for both groups improved over the study period, though the improvement of the Dominican players was greater, bringing them to parity with the U.S. players.

Figure 4 shows the scores for PABA for the two groups. Since hitting provides most of the bases in the numerator of PABA, its pattern is similar to that of SLG seen in figure 2. The U.S. players lead initially, but over time the Dominican players catch up, as the groups reach parity in the early years of the first decade of the twenty-first century. The differences began as highly significant in the early 1990s and continue to be so until 2001. In 2006, both groups achieved nearly 500 bases through action at the plate for every 1,000 plate appearances they made.

DISCUSSION

The data presented in figures 1 through 4 present an interesting picture when considered collectively. They reveal that, despite an initial handicap and an apparently inferior offensive strategy, the Dominican players have improved their hitting to the point that they have overtaken the U.S. players in AVG and SLG and are now at parity with the U.S. players in OBP and PABA. In other words, Dominicans walk less and try to hit more, but when they do try to hit they are more successful in terms of frequency and base production. Their hitting is so successful that they make up for the on-base opportunities and number of bases they would have achieved if they had walked more and tried less often to hit. This in turn allows Dominicans to get on base at the same rate and earn the same number of bases per plate appearance.

Table 2 summarizes the hypotheses of the study and the results found.

Table 2. Summary of Hypotheses and Findings

Hypothesis	Result
No difference in rates of SF and HBP	Confirmed
DR has more AB and fewer BB than US	Confirmed
DR maintains lower AVG and SLG	1990s: Confirmed
	2000s: Rejected
DR maintains lower OBP and PABA	1990s: Confirmed
	2000s: Rejected

Figure 3. On-Base Percentage (OBP), US and DR, 1990–2006

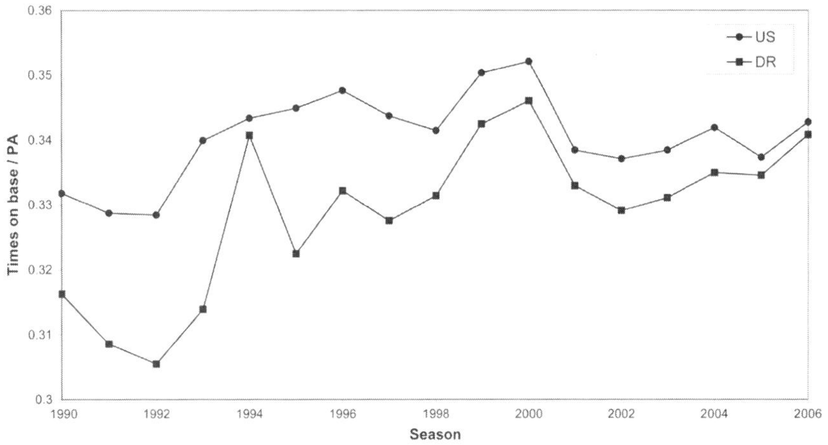

Figure 4. Plate-Appearance Base Average, US and DR, 1990–2006

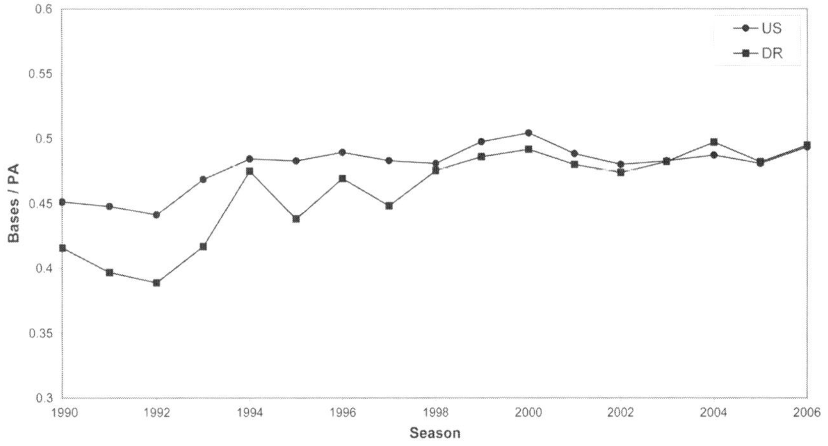

Limitations

One limitation of the study is the potential for misclassification. Players were selected as being born either in the United States or in the Dominican Republic. However, some may have moved to the other country at a very young age, meaning that their country of relevant baseball development would be misclassified in this study. It seems likely that such crossover is too rare to alter the results. In any event, thorough biographical detective work could eliminate misclassification were it a major concern.

Another potential limitation stems from the small size of the Dominican group. The statistics for this group can be more easily influenced by outliers in the performance data than can the statistics for the U.S. group. For example, the sudden shift in the SLG-difference score in favor of the Dominican Republic (figure 2) and the resulting spike in PABA (figure 4) seen in the 1998 season is due in large part to Dominican Sammy Sosa's 66 home runs that year. In contrast,

Mark McGwire's 70 home runs in the same season had little effect on the U.S. group's composite score. However, the trends are generally consistent before and after 1998, suggesting that the results are fairly robust to such unusual performances. Were every data point skewed by outliers, the difference scores year to year would be erratic, bouncing wildly up and down. Instead, the trends are clear and subject to a consistent amount of variation.

This study is also limited in the conclusions that can be drawn from it. Though the methods used here provide a clear picture of offensive strategy and offensive efficiency, it does not provide insight into the real-world impact that these achievements have on their teams' performances. A more detailed analysis of the base-out and score situations could provide insight in this regard, but it is outside of the scope of the present work.

CONCLUSIONS

The results here indicate that, during the period 1990–2006, Dominicans consistently preferred trying to hit over trying to walk. In the 1990s, comparisons between Dominican and U.S. players showed gaps in performance, but in recent years Dominicans have elevated their success rate at hitting (AVG) so as to bring their OBP up to match that of the U.S. players. Furthermore, Dominicans have elevated the number of bases they accrue per hit (SLG) so that they achieve the same number of bases per plate appearance (PABA) as do players from the United States, demonstrating that their hitting-intensive approach to offense does pay off—at least in terms of bases achieved. Thus the characterization of Dominican players as underperforming "hackers" is largely no longer deserved.

Despite its limitations, this analysis provides a thorough and focused way of comparing different groups of players with respect to offensive style. Use of OBP and PABA provides a compact method to evaluate the total offensive batting efficiency of players. MLB clubs could use analyses such as these to search for fertile ground from which to draft new players, or to improve their own players' batting strategies. In future research, this methodology could be applied to compare leagues, teams, or any two clearly defined and logically comparable groups. ■

Notes

1. Michael Lewis, *Moneyball: The Art of Winning an Unfair Game* (New York: Norton, 2003).
2. Sean Lahman, *Baseball Archive Database, 1871–2006*, www.baseball1.com.2007.
3. Marcello Pagano and Kimberlee Gauvreau, *Principles of Biostatistics*, 2d ed. (Pacific Grove, Calif.: Duxbury, 2000).

Players Being "Clutch" When Targeting 20 Wins

Phil Birnbaum

IN A BLOG post of March 23, 2008 ("Do Players Turn 'Clutch' When Chasing a Personal Goal?" sabermetricresearch.blogspot.com), I speculated about the anomaly, discovered by Bill James, that there are more 20-game winners than 19-game winners in the major leagues. That is the only case, between 0 and 30, where a higher-win season happens more frequently than a lower-win season.

Here, once again, are some of the win frequencies. For instance, there were 123 seasons of exactly 19 wins since 1940. (All numbers in this study are 1940–2007.)

Wins	Seasons
16	311
17	221
18	185
19	123
20	144
21	92
22	54

In the earlier post, I suggested that the bulge at twenty wins appears to be about 29 "too high." So we'll proceed as if there are an extra 29 twenty-win seasons to be explained.

I did a little digging to see if I could figure out what caused this to happen. I think I have an answer, and it's a bit of a surprise.

EXTRA STARTS

The first thing I looked at was whether pitchers with 18 or 19 wins late in the season would be given an extra start near the end of the season to try to hit the 20 mark. So, for each group of pitchers, I checked what percentage of their starts came in September or later:

16-win pitchers	17.53% of starts in September
17-win pitchers	17.77% of starts in September
18-win pitchers	18.36% of starts in September
19-win pitchers	18.49% of starts in September
20-win pitchers	18.47% of starts in September
21-win pitchers	18.15% of starts in September
22+-win pitchers	18.18% of starts in September

So it looks like there's a positive relationship between September starts and eventual wins, and a little bulge that happens in the 18–20 range. Maybe those pitchers are getting extra starts, or, as Greg Spira suggested,[1] perhaps the other pitchers miss a start in favor of a minor-league call-up, while the pitchers with a shot at 20 are given all their usual starts. The bulge appears to be about a quarter of a percent.

If we assume that, if not for targeting 20 wins, the 19–20 pitchers would have been 0.25 percent lower without the special treatment, that's 23 of their 9,229 combined starts. If half those starts led to a 19-game winner becoming a 20-game winner, that's an extra 11 pitchers in the 20-win column. It seems reasonable—it's fewer than 29, anyway, which is the number we're trying to explain.

RELIEF APPEARANCES

Greg also suggested, in the previous post, that pitchers with 19 wins may be given an extra late-season relief appearance to try to get their twentieth win. I checked Retrosheet game logs, and Greg is right—there has been some of that going on.

I found all September relief appearances for eventual 20-game winners where they had at least 18 wins at the time of the relief appearance and they got a decision (Retrosheet game logs won't list a reliever unless he wins or loses, but that doesn't matter for this study). Here they are:

1951	Early Wynn gets his 18th win (in relief)
1951	Mike Garcia gets his 19th win
1956	Billy Hoeft gets his 20th win
1957	Jim Bunning gets his 20th win
1964	Dean Chance has 19 wins but loses
1966	Chris Short gets his 20th win
1991	John Smiley gets his 19th win
1997	Randy Johnson gets his 20th win

So that accounts for seven 20-game winners who would otherwise have won only 19 games.

But what about 19-game winners? Those guys may get extra relief appearances too. I checked, and there are fewer of them.

1956	Lawrence Brooks has 18 wins but loses
1962	Art Mahaffey has 19 wins but loses
1964	Bob Gibson gets his 19th win
1964	Jim Bunning gets his 19th win
1974	Ken Holtzman has 19 wins but loses

(Bob Gibson's appearance was in the last game of the 1964 season, so he couldn't have been going for 20.)

And here are the late-season relief decisions for the eventual 21-game winners:

1940	Bobo Newsom, 20th win
1940	Rip Sewell, 20th win
1946	Howie Pollet, 18th win
1947	Johnny Sain, 21st win
1959	Sam Jones, 18th win, loss at 20 wins
1960	Warren Spahn, loss at 17 wins
1960	Ernie Broglio, 19th win
1965	Mudcat Grant, loss at 21 wins

So it looks like pitchers do get extra relief appearances in pursuit of high win totals (or *did*—most of these guys were pre-1970). There were four 19-game winners created this way, seven 20-game winners, and six 21-game winners.

The difference between 19 and 20, here, is three players—a lot fewer than I would have thought. But three is something, again, when there are only 29 to explain.

CLUTCH PITCHING

Maybe, when going for their 20th win, a player will bear down and pitch better than usual. I found all starting pitchers with exactly 19 wins and looked at how they did in the start(s) that would give them their twentieth win.

In 490 such starts, they went 227-142 (.655). I couldn't get their ERA or runs allowed from the Retrosheet game logs, but I did get the average number of runs their team allowed in those games. It was 3.63.

That doesn't mean much without context. Here are the results for some other win totals:

17 wins	3.72 runs allowed, .658, 670–348 in 1385 starts
18 wins	3.54 runs allowed, .652, 487–260 in 982 starts
19 wins	3.54 runs allowed, .655, 367–193 in 704 starts
20 wins	3.62 runs allowed, .615, 227–142 in 490 starts
21 wins	3.53 runs allowed, .676, 138–66 in 273 starts
22 wins	3.34 runs allowed, .774, 82–24 in 148 starts

Now we have something: Immediately after hitting the 20-win mark, the starters suddenly became a lot less likely to win. Instead of a winning percentage of maybe .660, which you would have expected (remember that, the more wins, the better the pitcher, so that the winning percentage should increase down the list), they wound up at only .615. That's .045 points in 369 decisions, or about 17 wins—almost half the 35 wins we're trying to explain!

By this measure, it looks like this half of the anomaly is not too many 20-game winners relative to 19-game winners, but that poor performance at 20 causes a logjam, preventing the 20-game winners from getting to 21.

But: If you look at runs allowed, the performance at 20 wins doesn't seem all that bad. It should be around 3.54, and it's at 3.62. That's .08 runs for each of their 490 starts—about 40 runs. How did these pitchers win 17 fewer games while allowing only 40 extra runs? Forty runs is 4 games, not 17 games.

The answer: run support. Here is the pitchers' run support for each category:

17 wins	4.39 run support
18 wins	4.41 run support
19 wins	4.45 run support
20 wins	4.05 run support
21 wins	4.46 run support
22 wins	4.48 run support

The 4.05 is not a typo. When starting a game with 20 wins, pitchers got four-tenths of a run less support than they should have. That's huge. Over 490 games,

COURTESY OF THE SEATTLE MARINERS

In 1997, Randy Johnson of the Seattle Mariners won his twentieth game in relief. He is one of eight pitchers with a 20-win season that includes at least one relief appearance in September.

it's almost 200 runs. That wipes out 20 wins, which keeps twenty 20-win pitchers from getting to 21 wins.

I have no idea why this should happen. I suppose it's possible that, seeing how the ace already has 20 wins, the manager might play his bench for this meaningless September game. But how often would that happen? No way it would be enough for 0.4 runs per game, would it?

By the way, it looks like these 20-game winners beat Pythagoras in these starts. They finished only 17 games below expectation, while losing 240 runs (40 pitching, 200 hitting). Assigning blame in proportion over those 17 extra games, we'll say that 3 of the extra losses came from pitching, 14 from run support.

I find it something of a relief that it was run support, and not (positive) clutch performance on the part of their pitchers, that caused the effect—it wasn't the case that they pitched better when close to a (selfish) goal. Going for their twnetieth win, pitchers did not appear to do any better or worse than when going for their eighteenth, nineteenth, or twenty-second wins. And they pitched only marginally better than when going for their twenty-first.

It's human nature that pitchers want to win 20 for personal reasons, but at least the evidence is that they try just as hard every other game of the year.

CONCLUDING

To summarize these results: We were looking for 29 "extra" 20-game seasons. We got:

- 11 from extra starts
- 3 from extra relief appearances
- 3 from pitchers' own poorer performance in subsequent games
- 14 from poor run support from their teammates in subsequent games.

That adds up to 31 games, which is close enough to our original estimate of 29.

It's interesting that about half the effect comes from 19-game winners getting extra chances to hit 20 and that the other half comes from 20-game winners being unable to rise to 21.

And, to me, the biggest surprise is that almost 40 percent of the 20-game-winner effect came from that huge hole in run support. In other words, a big part of the surplus of 20-game pitchers is probably just random luck.

The higher the performance level, the harder it is to achieve it. There should be more .270 hitters than .275 hitters, more .275 hitters than .285 hitters, and so on.

In 1940, Rip Sewell of the Pittsburgh Pirates won his twentieth game in relief. He is one of eight pitchers with a 21-win season that includes at least one relief appearance in September.

But, surprisingly, there's an exception: Significantly more players hit .300 to .304 in a season than .299 to .296.

That finding comes from Bill James's study "The Targeting Phenomenon"[2] (subscription required, but the essay is *The Bill James Gold Mine 2008*, 67).

For pitcher wins, Bill found a similar exception that's even more striking. More pitchers win zero games than 1. More pitchers win 1 game than 2. More pitchers win 2 games than 3. And so on, all the way up to 30 wins. But there's one exception –20. Significantly more pitchers finish with 20 wins than with 19.

Why? Because, Bill argues, players care about hitting their "targets."

"[Brooks Robinson] had a miserable year in 1963, and went into his last at-bat of the season hitting exactly .250—147 for 588. If he made an out, he wound up the season hitting under .250—but he got a hit, and wound up at .251. He said it was the only hit he got all season in a pressure situation. . . .

"[P]layers WANT to wind up the season hitting .250, rather than in the .240s. They tend to make it happen."

The implication is that there's a kind of clutch effect happening here, where the player somehow gets better when the target is near. But if that's true, wouldn't that point to baseball players being selfish? Studies have shown very little evidence for clutch hitting when the *game* is on the line. If players care more about hitting .300 than winning the game, that doesn't say much for their priorities.

(Although, in fairness, it should be acknowledged that the opposition is probably trying harder to stop Brooks Robinson from driving in the game-winning run than it is to keep him from getting to .250. For the record: Robinson's final 1963 hit drove in the third run in the ninth inning of a 7–3 loss to the Tigers.)

The study also finds that, while this kind of targeting happens for batting average, RBIs, wins, and (pitcher) strikeouts, there's no evidence for targeting in SLG, OBP, OPS, saves, or runs scored. For ERA, there's some evidence of targeting but not enough to say for sure.

Also, Bill finds that targeting seems to have started around 1940. He argues that this coincides with a jump in fan interest in players' statistical accomplishments.

These are very interesting findings, and I wouldn't have expected as much targeting as seems to have actually occurred. But I'm a bit skeptical about clutchness and whether players really can boost their performance in target-near situations. I wondered if, instead of clutch performance, it might be something else. Maybe, if a player is close to his goal, he is given additional playing time in support of reaching the target.

That is, if a pitcher has 19 wins late in the season, perhaps the manager will squeeze in an extra start for him. Or if a player is hitting .298, maybe they'll let him play every day until he gets to .300, instead of resting him in favor of the September call-up. If and when he reaches .300, then they could sit him (as, I think I remember reading, Bobby Mattick did for Alvis Woods in 1980).

To test the extra-start theory, I looked at pitchers since 1940, grouping them by number of wins. I then looked at their winning percentage, number of starts, and the number of seasons in the group:

Wins	Pct.	Starts	Seasons
16	.606	32.3	311
17	.613	33.0	221
18	.648	33.3	185
19	.650	34.4	123
20	.667	34.9	144
21	.673	34.7	92
22	.691	35.9	54
23	.705	35.9	34
24	.707	38.5	23

So, reading one line of the chart: 20-win pitchers had a .667 winning percentage and an average of 34.9 starts that year. There were 144 seasons in the group.

Looking at the numbers, we do see a bit of an anomaly. More wins normally means more starts, except that pitchers with 20 wins had more starts than pitchers with 21 wins. And, there's a big jump between 18 and 19, more than you'd expect given the other gaps in that win range.

Suppose we wanted to smooth out the number-of-starts column. We might adjust them like this:

Wins	Starts	
17	33.0	
18	33.3	
19	~~34.4~~	33.8
20	~~34.9~~	34.3
21	34.7	
22	35.9	

Now we have a smooth increasing trend. To get it, we had to remove 0.6 starts from each of the 19- and 20-win groups.

One possible interpretation: When a pitcher has 19 wins near the end of the season, he's given an extra 1.2 starts. Half the time, that gives him an extra win, and he goes to 20 (which now shows 0.6 extra starts). The other half, he fails to get the win, and stays at 19 (which also shows 0.6 extra starts).

Another way to look at this is through the winning-percentage column: Pitchers with 19 wins have almost the same winning percentage as the 18-win guys, which means more losses. And the 20-win guys, at .667, are only .006 away from the 21-win pitchers, which suggests more wins. That's exactly what happens if you take a bunch of 19-win guys, give them an extra start, and reclassify them.

So what do you think of this as an explanation? Does the *average* 19-win late-September pitcher really get 1.2 extra starts? That seems too high to me, although I don't really know. And, some of the effect might be not from extra starts but from leaving the pitcher in the game longer when he's losing or tied, long enough for his offense to bail him out and give him the win.

Now look at the last column, the number of seasons. If we were to smooth out that column, we might do it this way:

Wins	Seasons	
17	221	
18	185	
19	~~123~~	151
20	~~144~~	115
21	92	
22	54	
23	34	

The difference is 29 pitchers in the 19-win row, and 29 pitchers in the 20-win row. Assume those 29 pitchers moved from 19 to 20 because of the extra start. If you figure that these pitchers generally win half their starts, that means about 58 pitchers were given that one extra shot.

So: 58 pitchers in the 68 baseball seasons since 1940 means about a little less than one pitcher a year getting that extra start. There are normally only about two 19-win pitchers a year, so that means about half of them would have to get the special treatment.

Again, that seems high. However, in support of this theory, the effect diminishes after 1980. In fact, there are now *fewer* pitchers winning 20 than 19:

Wins	Seasons
17	97
18	84
19	43
20	41
21	25
22	12

There's still a bit of an effect, but not as much—in line with Bill's idea that, these days, managers are less likely to pitch an ace on short rest (or leave him in longer in a tie game) just to help him reach a personal goal.

There are probably other things that might be causing this that I haven't thought of.

In any case, it wouldn't be too hard to figure out a decent answer: Just head to Retrosheet and look at 19- and 20-game winners. See if their days of rest varied late in the season, which would mean the extra-start theory is correct. Check whether they were left in the game longer than normal. And check whether they pitched better in late-season games, which would mean the clutch theory is correct.

And you can do the same thing for hitting, for players around .300. Is it just a matter of opportunities, or is there some clutchness too? If it is the latter, that would be a very significant finding. It would suggest, perhaps, that:

- clutch hitting does exist, and either
- it shows up only for personal goals, or
- it shows up only when the situation is not clutch for the other team.

Maybe I'll look into this myself, if nobody else does. ■

Notes

A version of this article appeared originally as a post at Sabermetric Research (27 March 2008), http://sabermetricresearch.blogspot.com/2008/03/players-being-clutch-when-targeting-20.html.

1. Greg Spira, Sabermetric Research, 26 March 2008, https://www.blogger.com/comment.g?blogID=31545676&postID=6993388544957206639.
2. Bill James Online, www.billjamesonline.net/ArticleContent.aspx?AID=164&code=James01017. Subscription required, but the essay also appears in *The Bill James Gold Mine 2008* (Skokie, Ill.: Acta Sports, 2008), 67.

The 100 Top-Fielding MLB Pitchers, circa 1900–2008

John A. Knox

HOW IMPORTANT is the subject of pitchers' fielding? Just ask Jim Leyland, manager of the 2006 Detroit Tigers, who lost the World Series. Five errors—four of them throwing errors—committed by four different pitchers, one in every one of the five games of the series, led to seven unearned runs for the opposing St. Louis Cardinals. In the close-fought Games 4 and 5, these unearned runs provided the ultimate difference between victory and defeat. The pitchers' errors delivered the Cardinals a key assist to the world championship, totaling Detroit's chances and leaving Leyland and Tigers fans understandably put out.

On the premise that any facet of the game crucial enough to lose a World Series is worth closer scrutiny, I embarked on a study of fielding by pitchers. This subject is apparently something of a terra incognita even in sabermetric circles. At Baseball-Almanac.com, comprehensive fielding records provide all-time leaders in fielding percentage for every position—except pitcher. The SABR archives list only one article on the subject, Jim Kaplan's "The Pitcher as Fielder" (1987). This valuable discussion is narrative, however, rather than analytic and is now more than two decades old. The Fielding Bible (Dewan 2006) omits discussion of pitchers as fielders; an online follow-up by Dewan analyzes fielding data for pitchers only for the period 2003–5.[1] In a detailed discussion (written in 2002) of the best all-time fielders at each position, ESPN's Rob Neyer omits pitchers except to briefly "hazard a wild guess."[2] Such wild guesses presumably entered into Rawlings's "Summer of Glove" in 2007, during which the best fielders at each position in the half-century-long Gold Glove era were selected.

Why is there a paucity of research on fielding by pitchers? Dewan says he omitted pitchers from *The Fielding Bible* because he "ran out of time," not because of a belief that fielding by pitchers was irrelevant or could not be quantified.

A reviewer of this article suggests that pitchers' fielding excellence may be difficult or unrealistic to contemplate because pitchers are generally encouraged to leave the fielding to other players. This has not always been the case in baseball, however, and in recent times pitchers such as Greg Maddux have clearly not gotten the memo about standing aside when the ball is in play. An analogy with stolen bases may be in order: Just because slow-of-foot players are discouraged from stealing, this doesn't mean that the excellence of the fleet-of-foot cannot be discussed, quantified, and ranked. Similarly, I will assume in this paper that the best-fielding pitchers are not significantly thwarted in their ability to field, any more than fast runners are chronically dissuaded from stealing. Over the course of a long career, a talent that benefits the team will usually be expressed, and it can then be analyzed.

Moreover, as noted in the opening vignette regarding the Tigers, a pitcher's ability to field cannot be an insignificant talent if poor fielding by pitchers can lose a World Series. Is it a coincidence that longtime Braves manager Bobby Cox regularly acquires good-fielding pitchers such as Maddux, Tom Glavine, Mike Hampton, Tim Hudson, Derek Lowe, and Javier Vazquez but does not acquire equally stellar pitchers who are not good fielders (e.g., Randy Johnson)? This is implicit evidence that fielding by pitchers is valued to an extent by at least some managers.

Sabermetrics can shed light on this little-explored corner of baseball and afford us something better than a wild guess at the best-fielding MLB pitchers of all time. In this article, I make a first attempt to satisfy this need, using statistics to devise ranked lists of the top 100 best fielders on the mound since 1900. I hope that this work, though admittedly less sophisticated than the work of experienced sabermetricians, will provide a stepping stone for more-sophisticated analyses on the subject.

My results contain a considerable surprise: They identify a virtuoso pitcher-fielder whose career efforts in a combination of categories rise well above those of all others. Yet this pitcher, though eligible, never won a Gold Glove and is rarely mentioned in discussions of the best-fielding pitchers. Before I reveal his identity and that of the other pitchers on the lists, however, I will discuss the data-analysis methods used in this study.

DATA AND METHODS

In this study I confronted three key data-analysis questions: which data to use, which variables to use to measure fielding prowess, and which pitchers to analyze.

Data

I obtained all fielding data on MLB pitchers from Baseball-Reference.com. To avoid confusion, where possible I use the same acronyms for statistics that are used on the site. While Baseball-Reference.com is fairly comprehensive, at the time of writing the database was lacking in some respects relevant to this study, particularly with regard to career nine-inning range factor (RF9) and career league-average nine-inning range factor (lgRF9) at the pitcher position. I explain below how I circumvented these omissions.

Measures of fielding

Given the paucity of research on pitchers' fielding, there is not much work available on creative sabermetric approaches to the topic, such as there is for the study of, say, catchers or first basemen (James 2001, 355–57). Dewan applied his plus/minus system (Dewan 2006) to pitchers for 2003–5, but his approach seems impossible to implement currently with pitchers from earlier eras.[3]

There are two schools of thought regarding fielding. Adapting a famous line from Robert Browning's poem "Andrea del Sarto," one of them might be summarized as "the fielder's reach should exceed his grasp"—that is, range is considered primary. The other school of thought looks for "the faultless fielder"—that is, sure-handedness is emphasized. Most traditional discussions of fielding focus on one or the other of these two attributes. Gold Glove awards, in particular, seem to be biased toward range. It seems reasonable to assume, however, that a combination of range and sure-handedness is optimal. In this study, I opted for a combination of four slightly innovative statistical measures of pitchers' fielding, each normalized to a 0–100 scale.

Rezeroed normalized relative clean-fielding rate (RCFR). Following James's mention of "relative error rate" (James 2001, 878), I obtained a pitcher's career-averaged fielding percentage (FP) and then divided it by the league-averaged fielding percentage (lgFP) averaged over his career. This "relative clean-fielding rate" was then normalized to 100 percent.

However, fielding percentages among competently fielding pitchers are clustered together, even across different eras. To obtain a less skewed spread, I then subtracted the minimum value obtained for all pitchers in the study and then renormalized that result. This was done to facilitate combination of different statistics into a rating scheme. Note that all of these machinations do not change the order of ranking compared

COURTESY OF THE ATLANTA BRAVES

Greg Maddux, whose reputation as one of the best-fielding pitchers ever to play in the majors is well established, ranks twelfth for sure-handedness and second for range. In his 23-year career, he won 18 Gold Glove awards.

to what would be obtained via a measure as simple as career FP − lgFP; only the values are changed.

This statistic has somewhat more year-to-year volatility for active pitchers than is optimal, a function of the relatively small number of total fielding chances per year for today's pitchers.

Relative nine-inning range-factor rate (RRF9R). As with RCFR, I obtained a pitcher's career-averaged nine-inning range factor, divided it by the league-averaged nine-inning range factor averaged over his career, and then normalized the result.

Unfortunately, Baseball-Reference.com does not provide career RF9 and lgRF9 for about 20 percent of all pitchers eventually included in the analysis, representing every decade of the sport and several of the best-fielding pitchers of all time. Using range factor without the nine-inning adjustment was not an option; relief pitchers in particular would have been significantly slighted.

As an imperfect alternative, *season* RF9 and lgRF9 (which are available for all pitchers) were summed over each pitcher's career and then averaged. Since this is not equivalent to a career statistic based on total number of chances, a correction was made by omitting from the averages any years in which the pitcher handled fewer than ten chances.

This "fix" was beta-tested on the RF9 of 232 pitchers in the study for whom career RF9 *are* available. (I did not test it on lgRF9 because of a lack of data availability.) The season-averaged RF9 had an average percent error versus the career RF9 equal to a minuscule 0.045 percent. The largest errors were 5.44 percent and 5.32 percent (Hoyt Wilhelm and Greg Maddux), but they are anomalies; the fix resulted in only 8.6 percent of all pitchers tested having an absolute discrepancy greater than 1 percent versus the career RF9. These estimation errors are presumably not much greater than the inescapable error due to missing data. I therefore concluded that using averages of season RF9 and lgRF9 would be an acceptable substitute for all values of career RF9 and lgRF9.

The greatest error with this fix is a probable slight overestimate of RRF9R for pitchers with long careers spanning periods of rapidly changing lgRF9, which I dub the "Nick Altrock effect." Since other factors (see below) tend to penalize the earliest pitchers, however, this exaggeration serves as a crude corrective.

Double play–error ratio (DP/E). James (2001, 876–77) observes that the ratio between double plays and errors is a "peripheral quality index" of baseball. Although James is comparing different leagues and age levels, it seems reasonable that comparisons of individuals at the same position in MLB would reveal that high-quality fielders maximize this ratio as well. This metric will mimic fielding percentage to an extent, as we will see, but it also rewards those pitchers who have an additional knack for turning double plays.

A second reason for including DP/E, one that flies in the face of Jamesian argumentation, is that is's a measure of "clutchness." As we have seen with the Tigers in October 2006, pitchers' errors—especially throwing errors—often give the opposing team two extra bases and unearned runs. Conversely, a pitcher-related double play leads to two outs and is, at least in an anecdotal sense, a "rally killer." According to James (2001, 637), the most commonly occurring pitcher-related DP is the 1-6-3 twin killing, followed far behind by 3-6-1 and 1-4-3: two throwing situations and one catching situation in which the risk of a ball going into the dugout is not negligible. The pitcher who can turn the DP in such make-or-break situations gets a huge boost; the pitcher who cannot and who, worse yet, commits an error on such plays loses all the benefits, and he furthermore gives his opponents an extra out plus one or two extra bases. Such large differences in outcomes can separate successful MLB pitchers from those on the waiver wire (see, for example, Kaplan 1987 for a story about Ed Halicki). This differential effect is captured at least to a small extent in DP/E and seems to be worthy of inclusion as a measure of pitchers' fielding abilities.

Double plays turned per nine innings (DPd9). In this measure of fielding, the number of double plays turned by a pitcher is divided by the total number of innings pitched and then multiplied by 9. In practice, DPd9 is a kind of mirror image of DP/E. It leans toward the range side of the ledger by rewarding pitchers who turn double plays even when they pitch relatively few innings (e.g., relief pitchers and starters who rarely pitch into the late innings). I have not seen this metric used or discussed in any studies.

By using metrics such as range factor and double plays, this analysis is likely biased toward ground-ball pitchers. No attempt has been made to correct for ground-ball versus fly-ball pitchers; I did not have access to historical statistics that would permit the development of a correction factor. But I also chose not to pursue a correction, since the best-fielding pitchers should rightly be those who have the most opportunities—or intentionally create the most opportunities—to demonstrate their abilities by inducing ground balls. A fly-ball pitcher with great fielding skills who rarely makes fielding plays has chosen to emphasize one talent (getting outs with fly balls) over another (getting ground-ball outs, some of them through his own fielding) and will deservedly get short shrift in this analysis. His rewards lie elsewhere.

To a lesser extent, strikeout pitchers may also be penalized by this analysis; as with fly-ball pitchers, they make the choice to retire batters without their glove. This is briefly explored statistically in the next section.

Taken together, these four measures of fielding prowess should afford a comprehensive, if fairly traditional, view of pitchers' fielding. In the results section, I justify the use of all four measures and employ different linear combinations of them to create three different rankings of the best-fielding pitchers.

Initial choice of pitchers

Ideally, I would have analyzed the fielding statistics of all pitchers in the history of Major League Baseball. Unfortunately, time constraints prevented such a comprehensive study. Instead, I limited this study to a list of 287 pitchers who satisfied a combination of the criteria outlined below. To be included, pitchers had to have met the following two criteria:

1. at least 1,500 innings pitched
2. at least 50 percent of all innings pitched from the year 1900 onward

They also had to have satisfied one or more of the following four criteria:

3. career FP of at least .960 *and* at least 10 points higher than career lgFP
4. career FP of at least .960 *and* 7–9 points higher than career lgFP, and RF9R significantly above 1
5. Gold Glove recipient
6. top 45 in most career assists, top 44 in most career putouts, or top 48 in most career double plays, as listed in *The SABR Baseball List and Record Book* (SABR 2007, 302–4).

The first criterion is the accepted minimum threshold for pitcher fielding records. Criterion 2 was imposed to focus on the directly comparable modern era of fielding. As noted by James, the number of errors plummeted during the first decade of the twentieth century "as gloves grew in size and padding" (James 2001, 72). League fielding percentages at the pitcher position soared from the low .900s throughout the 1890s to the .940s by 1903–4, and with few exceptions the career lgFP of veteran pitchers has remained between .940 and .960 ever since (as will be seen in figure 1). As a result, the modern age of fielding at the pitcher position dawned very shortly after 1900. Instead of imposing a rigid cutoff date for consideration, I opted to draw the line after players who did more than half their pitching during the nineteenth century.

Criteria 3 and 4 give priority to pitchers who were significantly better fielders than their peers and who also posted a FP of at least .960. This minimum FP threshold was chosen because it is near the historical high for career-averaged lgFP (see below). This rewards pitchers who rose above their poorer-fielding eras if they cleared the .960 threshold. Criteria 5 and 6 dispense with the FP threshold and differential, including instead those pitchers with a reputation or long record of fielding achievement.

Admittedly, this approach eliminates from consideration a few relatively excellent fielders of the 1880s and 1890s: for example, Kid Nichols (.952 FP in a .917 era) and Dave Foutz (.925 FP in a .881 era). In the end, I decided that it was a little too much of a stretch to include nineteenth-century pitchers.

While not completely comprehensive, the multiple qualifying criteria of this approach cast a wide net and presumably omit very few fine fielders from the subsequent analysis. This is, at least, a more systematic approach than the "wild guess" or conventional wisdom of Neyer, Kaplan, or the Rawlings finalist-selection committee.

RESULTS

The career statistics for the 287 MLB pitchers selected via the criteria outlined above were analyzed using the four measures of fielding described above (pages 50–52). First I discuss aggregate statistics and trends for the whole group, and then I turn to individual rankings of the 100 top-fielding pitchers.

Aggregate trends over time

Out of the 287 pitchers considered, 203 (71 percent) were right-handers and 84 (29 percent) were left-handers. This suggests a somewhat higher proportion of southpaws in the study than in the general population or in the rank-and-file MLB pitching population.

Among pitchers from 1900 through 2008, Kirk Rueter, who won 130 games, ranks first in sure-handedness, range, and overall fielding. He never won a Gold Glove.

The decade of first appearance on the mound for each pitcher is chronicled in table 1. All decades of the twentieth century are represented substantially, with the greatest concentration from the 1950s onward.

Table 1. Temporal Distribution of Pitchers Considered in Fielding Analysis

Decade	Number of Pitchers Considered Who First Appeared During Decade	Percentage
1890–99	8	2.79
1900–9	21	7.32
1910–19	24	8.36
1920–29	22	7.67
1930–39	17	5.92
1940–49	16	5.57
1950–59	34	11.85
1960–69	33	11.50
1970–79	35	12.20
1980–89	39	13.59
1990–99	33	11.50
2000–7	5	1.74

Figure 1 illustrates the evolution of fielding by pitchers over time, by plotting career-averaged lgFP as a function of the midpoint of each pitcher's career. A peak, along with a clear differential between the better-performing National League pitchers and less-successful American League pitchers, is evident in the years bracketing the 1930s. A noticeable dip in career-averaged lgFP occurred in the 1960s and 1970s. This fielding slump may have been a consequence of the introduction of artificial turf, or—recalling James's observation that various measures of quality-of-play decrease after expansion (James 2001, 878)—it may have been due to the leagues' formation of new teams; or it could have resulted from both of these factors. From the 1980s to the present, fielding percentages have generally risen slowly back toward the 1930s peak.

The evolution of range factor is less complicated. The trend of career-averaged lgRF9 among the pitchers analyzed is nearly monotonically downward (figure 2), peaking near 3.25 in the early 1900s and descending thereafter to below 1.70 today. As noted by James (2001, 877), the number of fielding plays by pitchers decreases consistently as one moves upward from Little League to the major leagues. Figure 2 shows this has also been the case as one moves forward in time in MLB from the early 1900s to the early 2000s. Interestingly, the NL–AL differential in career-averaged lgRF9 during the early to mid twentieth century seems less obvious than in career-averaged lgFP.

Figure 1. Career-Averaged lgFP for the 287 Pitchers in the Analysis, Plotted at the Midpoint Year of Each Pitcher's Career

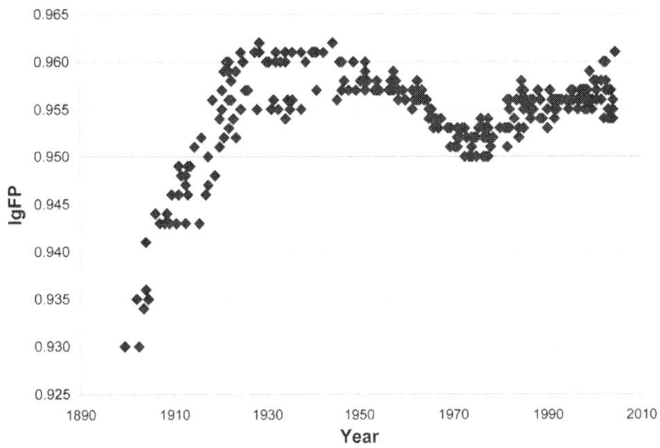

Figure 2. Career-Averaged lgRF9 for the 287 Pitchers in the Analysis, Plotted at the Midpoint Year of Each Pitcher's Career

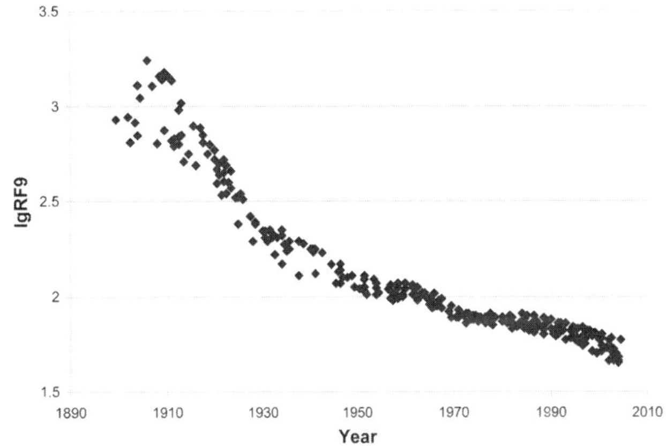

Statistics of fielding measures

Before normalizing the results and compiling scores, it is instructive to look at the range of raw values for career-averaged FP, RF9 (approximated for all pitchers, as described above, pages 50–52), DP/E, and DPd9 for the pitchers examined. Table 2 lists some relevant details.

Rawlings finalists and perennial Gold Glove winners Jim Kaat and Bob Gibson do not show up among the leaders in any of the categories—a hint of some surprises to come.

One question that arose during this study was: Are different measures of fielding independent of each other, or are they duplicative, measuring the same attributes? As a simple test of independence, I calculated correlations between the normalized RCFR, RRF9R, DP/E, and DPd9. The results are presented in table 3.

Table 2. Descriptive Statistics for Four (Non-normalized) Measures of Career Fielding by Pitchers

	FP	RF9	DP/E	DPd9
High (best of best)	.9903 (Don Mossi, 1954–65)	4.6134 (Nick Altrock, 1898–1924)	9.3333 (Don Mossi, 1954–65)	0.2487 (Kirk Rueter, 1993–2005)
Low (worst of best)	.9147 (Joaquin Andujar, 1976–88)	0.8881 (Sid Fernandez, 1983–97)	0.2169 (Al Orth, 1895–1909)	0.0241 (Sid Fernandez, 1983–97)
Mean	.9681	2.2600	1.7064	0.1077
Median	.9695	2.1493	1.5000	0.1003
SD	0.0113	0.5642	1.0210	0.0391

Table 3. Correlation r of (Normalized) Measures of Fielding

	RCFR	RRF9R	DP/E	DPd9
RCFR	1	−0.13	+0.53	−0.04
RRF9R	−0.13	1	+0.05	+0.64
DP/E	+0.53	+0.05	1	+0.49
DPd9	−0.04	+0.64	+0.49	1

These correlations range from negligible (for RRF9R-DP/E and RCFR-DPd9) to moderately high (for DPd9 – RRF9R, RCFR – DP/E, and DP/E – DPd9). Even so, no one factor explains more than 41 percent of the variance of another factor. (Very high correlations are obtainable with this data set; for example, the correlation between year and lgRF9 is a robust $r = -0.94$.)

Perhaps most importantly, the intuitive notion that sure-handedness (proxied by RCFR) and range (proxied by RRF9R) are largely independent, complementary measures of fielding is supported by this statistical analysis. The two variables are weakly negatively correlated ($r = -0.13$), confirming that, in fact, when a pitcher's reach exceeds his grasp, he makes a few more errors as a result.

These correlations also confirm that DP/E reinforces the measure of sure-handedness, but it is not a carbon copy of RCFR and exhibits virtually no relationship with range. Conversely, DPd9 reinforces the measure of range, but does not duplicate RRF9R and bears almost no relationship to sure-handedness. Also, despite both being based on double-play statistics, DP/E and DPd9 do not overlap overmuch.

In summary, this statistical analysis provides some encouragement for including all four measures in the calculations and rankings that follow, giving priority to RCFR and RRF9R as the dominant measures of fielding.

Individual rankings

What is the best way to bring together different measures of ability into one overall rating? My approach in this paper was to normalize each fielding measure on a 100-point scale and then combine them into a 100-point maximum score, weighting each of the four fielding measures independently.

To accommodate both schools of thought regarding fielding, I made several different calculations to derive the scores and ranks that appear on my list of the 100 top-fielding pitchers. Following are the three separate equations used:

1. **Range-Biased Score** = 60% RCFR + 30% RRF9R + 5% DP/E + 5% DPd9
2. **Sure-Handedness (SH)-Biased Score** = 60% RRF9R + 30% RCFR + 5% DP/E + 5% DPd9,
3. **No-Bias Score** = 45% RCFR + 45% RRF9R + 5% DP/E + 5% DPd9

The weighting percentages used in the two biased scores are admittedly arbitrary. The 60-30-10 breakdown emphasizes one facet of performance without overwhelming the other. The choice of small percentages for DP/E and DPd9 arose from analysis of the correlations and the strikingly non-normal distribution of the two statistics (see table 2). Overweighting DP/E and DPd9 would arguably exaggerate the importance of a very few plays each season. (The statistical analysis also afforded the opportunity to test indirectly the hypothesis that strikeout pitchers are penalized by the scoring process. The correlation between the number of strikeouts per nine innings and the no-bias score is −0.22, indicating that strikeout pitchers score somewhat lower than pitchers who obtain few strikeouts. The correlation is not especially strong, however, implying that the analysis is not overly slanted against strikeout pitchers.)

The no-bias score is the one that I will focus upon the most. In table 4, I rank the top 100 pitchers using the no-bias calculation, giving the score for each pitcher and also providing the rank for each pitcher based on my sure-handedness–biased and range-biased calculations.

Table 4. The 100 Top-Fielding MLB Pitchers (at Least 1500 IP) Since Approximately 1900, as Calculated Using Equations 1–3

Names of players active as of May 2009 appear in boldface.

Rank	Name	Score (No Bias)	SH-Biased Rank	Range-Biased Rank
1	Rueter, Kirk	86.89	1	1
2	Maddux, Greg	80.75	12	2
3	Shantz, Bobby	77.28	11	3
4	Petry, Dan	77.08	8	6
5	Gumbert, Harry	76.28	18	4
6	**Ortiz, Russ**	75.78	5	18
7	Gura, Larry	75.36	4	22
8	Jones, Randy	74.82	23	9
9	Tewksbury, Bob	74.61	14	13
10	Nagy, Charles	74.45	20	11
11	Lemon, Bob	74.32	37	5
12	Rhoden, Rick	74.32	2	42
13	Altrock, Nick	74.16	25	8
14	Fitzsimmons, Freddie	74.13	26	7
15	Mossi, Don	73.70	3	49
16	Radke, Brad	73.69	7	35
17	**Halladay, Roy**	73.32	19	19
18	**Hernandez, Livan**	73.22	24	15
19	Terrell, Walt	73.05	15	27
20	Caldwell, Mike	72.88	17	23
21	Fryman, Woodie	72.78	6	58
22	Mathewson, Christy	72.57	13	37
23	Wise , Rick	72.51	9	44
24	Morton, Carl	72.38	21	28
25	Walsh, Ed	72.08	32	17
26	Stottlemyre, Mel	72.06	39	14
27	Mays, Carl	72.00	43	12
28	Reuschel, Rick	71.87	28	20
29	**Lowe, Derek**	71.57	41	16
30	**Glavine, Tom**	70.83	34	33
31	Alexander, Pete	70.69	16	56
32	Hill, Ken	70.52	45	25
33	Horlen, Joe	70.36	42	29
34	Garber, Gene	70.33	55	21
35	Miller, Stu	70.22	47	30
36	Herbert, Ray	70.01	40	36
37	Stieb, Dave	69.40	56	34
38	**Moyer, Jamie**	69.38	38	46
39	Suggs, George	69.33	29	53
40	**Rogers, Kenny**	69.17	129	10
41	Staley, Jerry	69.13	74	26
42	Splittorff, Paul	68.94	31	60
43	**Hudson, Tim**	68.87	70	32
44	**Oswalt, Roy**	68.78	36	57
45	Wood, Wilbur	68.74	27	76
46	Howell, Harry	68.74	61	39
47	Wilson, Jim	68.46	22	103
48	Nolan, Gary	68.44	10	139
49	Mussina, Mike	68.42	35	76
50	Rommel, Eddie	68.16	91	31
51	**Buehrle, Mark**	68.13	73	40
52	**Garland, Jon**	68.11	60	47
53	McLish, Cal	68.09	54	51
54	Reynolds, Shane	68.08	44	65
55	Smith, Bob	68.08	46	64
56	Cantwell, Ben	67.82	118	24
57	Davis, Curt	67.38	94	41
58	Joss, Addie	67.30	57	69
59	Monbouquette, Bill	67.16	30	108
60	Jansen, Larry	66.86	67	67
61	Candiotti, Tom	66.85	72	63
62	Warneke, Lon	66.84	33	114
63	Gubicza, Mark	66.82	103	43
64	**Vazquez, Javier**	66.61	63	79
65	Brewer, Tom	66.58	131	38
66	Forsch, Bob	66.54	53	90
67	Walters, Bucky	66.25	90	61
68	Trachsel, Steve	66.23	79	74
69	Auker, Elden	66.23	104	50
70	Brown, Lloyd	66.21	96	54
71	Barnes, Jesse	66.14	82	73
72	Niekro, Phil	66.14	69	83
73	Abbott, Jim	66.11	66	86
74	Tanana, Frank	65.90	50	111
75	Purkey, Bob	65.89	126	45
76	Dauss, Hooks	65.84	75	84
77	Burdette, Lew	65.84	101	59
78	Tapani, Kevin	65.74	48	117
79	Sullivan, Frank	65.71	64	99
80	Nehf, Art	65.57	87	82
81	Donahue, Red	65.54	59	107
82	Buhl, Bob	65.37	84	91
83	Brecheen, Harry	65.35	58	115
84	Coveleski, Stan	65.31	78	94
85	Osteen, Claude	65.20	89	88
86	Bush, Joe	65.03	85	96
87	Smith, Frank	64.83	98	87
88	Wright, Clyde	64.75	128	68
89	Tudor, John	64.75	86	101
90	Schumacher, Hal	64.73	137	66
91	Quinn, Jack	64.67	100	92
92	McGregor, Scott	64.57	62	133
93	Burkett, John	64.55	52	146
94	Rixey, Eppa	64.53	80	113
95	Reed, Ron	64.51	65	132
96	Ferrell, Wes	64.48	76	119
97	Kison, Bruce	64.44	117	85
98	Sutcliffe, Rick	64.35	95	104
99	Smith, Zane	64.22	132	81
100	Brett, Ken	64.20	109	98

DISCUSSION AND CONCLUSIONS

The most shocking and compelling conclusion drawn from the foregoing analysis is that Kirk Rueter was the Mozart of fielding pitchers; in the "no bias" rating, his numerical lead over second-ranked pitcher Greg Maddux is as large as the gap between numbers 2 and 9! (And this analysis is actually biased toward Maddux, because of the overestimate in Maddux's RRF9R noted earlier; without that bias, Rueter's lead over Maddux would be 1.72 points larger.) Yet Rueter never won a Gold Glove and is mentioned infrequently as one of the better fielding pitchers of his time. Below, to dispel any notion that this result is a statistical fluke, I examine the case for Rueter's fielding brilliance, as well as the surprising absence or presence of some names on the top-100 list.

The case for Rueter

Kirk Rueter excelled at every phase of fielding. His career FP of .988 ranks as sixth-best all-time.[4] Rueter's RF9 of 2.70 is third among all those in this study who pitched during the past three decades. Even better, Rueter's DP/E ratio of 53/7 = 7.57 is second only to Don Mossi's 9.33; after Russ Ortiz (7.00), no other pitcher's DP/E is within half of Mossi's record. But Rueter shines brightest in the overlooked statistic of DPd9, in which he ranks first all-time, outpacing the renowned fielders Bob Lemon and Bobby Shantz. No other pitcher among the 287 examined excelled in each of the four fielding measures, not even Greg Maddux (whose career FP of .970 is solid, but hardly record-setting).

Even when biasing the results toward sure-handedness or range, Rueter remains on top. Out of all the pitchers in the study, only Rueter and Dan Petry place in the top 10 in all three calculations, and Rueter is first in all three. To displace Rueter from the top position, one must either focus almost solely on FP or on RF9 and ignore double plays. The bottom line is that for a wide range of reasonable interpretations of all-around fielding prowess by pitchers, Kirk Rueter is king.

Why was Rueter's virtuoso performance overlooked during his career? First, he had the bad luck to coincide with the second-best-ever fielding pitcher, Greg Maddux, who exhibits the best relative range among all pitchers in this study. Rueter's exceptional year of 2001, in which he fielded 1.000, had an RF9 of 2.81, and turned 11 DPs (the most by an MLB pitcher in a quarter-century), captured little attention when compared to Maddux's Gold Glove performance of .986 FP, 2.82 RF9, and 3 DPs.

Furthermore, "style points" seem to matter in impressions of pitchers' fielding. The "Mad Dog" attacked grounders like a rabid canine. In contrast, on the mound Rueter, listed at 6-foot-3 and 195 pounds but seemingly closer to a Rick Reuschel weight of 235 pounds, was never confused with a Baryshnikov or a Bob Gibson. He simply got the job done in the field better than anyone else, usually in short outings (Rueter averaged about 5.7 innings per start for his entire career), which prevented him from setting single-game fielding records. All of these factors combined may have led to the egregious omission of Kirk Rueter from the pantheon of the very best fielders in the history of Major League Baseball. The primary result of this paper, aside from quantifying fielding by pitchers, should be the establishment of Rueter's claim to the throne.

COURTESY OF THE TORONTO BLUE JAYS

Roy Halladay, who ranks second behind Russ Ortiz as the best-fielding pitcher among active players, has never won a Gold Glove. His consistency at fielding his position is a plausible contribution to his placing among the top finishers for the Cy Young Award four times.

The case for Maddux and Shantz, and a curious phenomenon

Kirk Rueter's exceptional brilliance as a fielder should not detract from the praise correctly lavished on Greg Maddux (18 Gold Gloves) and Bobby Shantz (8 Gold Gloves). Conventional wisdom and this statistical analysis agree that Maddux and Shantz are among the best-ever fielding pitchers. (This, in turn, lends more credence to the conclusions drawn regarding Rueter.) Both Maddux and Shantz exemplify extraordinary range, but they committed more errors than the sure-handed Rueter.

Although this study has not addressed the fine-grained detail of season fielding performances, one fascinating nugget unearthed from a comparison of these three pitchers deserves discussion. Shantz, Maddux, and Rueter did something extremely unusual at the very ends of their careers: their RF9 values shot through the roof at ages when nearly all other fielders at all positions are losing range.

In Bobby Shantz's last three years in MLB, in 1962, '63, and '64, or from age 36 to 38, his RF9 values were

4.02, 3.52, and an incredible 5.02. These values should be compared to an estimated career RF9 for Shantz of "only" 3.00, and his previous high of 3.69 at age 31. Shantz's 5.02 may be the highest pitcher RF9 since the early 1900s, even without adjustment for lgRF9. Even more spectacularly, 5.02 is just 0.01 shy of Ozzie Smith's career-average RF (but not RF9) at shortstop! Shantz deservedly won the Gold Glove in these three years; the pitching Gold Glove probably should have been permanently named after him for his miracle fielding season of 1964.

Somewhat similarly, in his last two years Maddux returned to mid-career form in terms of RF9: 3.18 in 2007 and 3.43 in 2008 at age 42, the latter his highest RF9 since 3.57 in 1999. These values exceed his phenomenal career RF9 of 3.13. In his last seven games in the majors, Maddux stepped up his fielding performance even more, gobbling up grounders to the tune of a 3.54 RF9.

Kirk Rueter posted career-best RF9 in each of his last two years in the big leagues in 2004 and 2005, at ages 33 and 34. Compared to a career RF9 of 2.70, Rueter's RF9 suddenly soared from 2.34 in 2001 and 2.63 in 2002, to 3.26 in 2004 and 3.86 in 2005.

What is responsible for this counterintuitive trend in range factor? Rueter was losing effectiveness as a pitcher, with climbing ratios of walks-plus-hits per inning pitched (WHIPs) of 1.529 and 1.658 in 2004–5. According to the ESPN website, Rueter's ground-ball/fly-ball ratio skyrocketed from 1.02 in 2001 to 1.60 in 2004, but came back down to 1.15 in 2005. Therefore, more and more balls were jumping off the bats, back to the mound, and into Rueter's glove. A similar phenomenon could have been at work at the end of Maddux's career, to an extent, although his ground-ball/fly-ball ratio actually decreased to just above 1.00 in 2007–8. No such explanation suffices for Shantz, whose ERAs and WHIPs stayed well below career and league averages in 1962–64. One alternative explanation is that these masters of fielding were intentionally using their gifts with the glove to prolong their tenures as major-league pitchers.

The case against Kaat and Gibson

Where are Jim Kaat and Bob Gibson on the top-100 list? Along with Maddux, they were the finalists for the Rawlings "Summer of Glove" award for best-fielding pitcher, the recipients of 25 Gold Gloves between them (16 to Kaat, 9 to Gibson).

So it is shocking that of the 287 pitchers analyzed in this study, Kaat comes in at a miserable number 272, Gibson even worse at number 277. Why are both Kaat and Gibson in the *lowest* 16 of nearly 300 good-fielding pitchers in this study? Neither pitcher posted a career FP equal to the lgFP over their eras. Their range factors were near league norms. They turned a fair number of double plays, but at less than half the per-inning rate of Kirk Rueter. Whatever it was that inspired the voters to give 25 Gold Gloves to Kaat and Gibson does not turn up in this analysis, but it is blindingly obvious in the case of Maddux and Shantz and their 26 Gold Gloves.

My best explanation is that "flashbulb memories" of spectacular plays in crucial games cemented Gibson's reputation. Kaat's acumen for the finer aspects of fielding (see Kaplan 1987) overshadowed his actual day-in-day-out performance on the field. The ritual awarding of Gold Gloves regardless of statistical performance (e.g., Kaat's eighth Gold Glove year of 1969: .826 FP, 1.41 RF9) also probably played a role in solidifying conventional wisdom, regardless of performance. This statistical analysis, however, makes a strong case *against* Jim Kaat and Bob Gibson being two of the best-fielding pitchers of all time.

Other surprising omissions

In any list of the best in baseball, there is always one player who just misses the cut. In major league baseball, that man is always Tommy John. As fate would have it, Tommy John placed number 105 in the no-bias score calculation, just 0.27 points behind Ken Brett. Consistently on the cusp via his consistency, and now having missed the biggest cut of all (his last non–Veterans Committee chance to be voted into the Hall of Fame), John deserves an Irving R. Thalberg Award for lifetime almost-great achievement under trying circumstances in all baseball endeavors, including fielding.[5]

Among relatively recent pitchers with exceptional range, Fernando Valenzuela (number 116; .963 FP, 2.42 RF9), Mike Hampton (number 121; .960 FP, 2.48 RF9) and Kevin Brownvi (number 176; .951 FP, 2.63 RF9) are often mentioned. Neither Hampton nor Brown, however, posted FP values significantly better than league averages. These three pitchers place number 78, number 52, and number 71, respectively, in the range-biased score calculation, about 20 points behind the leaders.

One surprising inclusion

Among the best-fielding pitchers is the only career-long pure reliever on the list: Gene Garber (number 34, .967 FP, 2.62 RF9). Garber's appearance is surprising for at least two reasons: (1) unless RF9 is used, relievers' range factors are misleadingly low, and they are probably overlooked as a result; and (2) Garber's unorthodox 180-degree pivoting delivery and sidearm throwing style sent chills up the spines of 1980s-era Braves fans whenever he had to field a batted ball. Yet the statistics indicate that "Geno" was the all-around best-fielding pure reliever of his time, at least among those with at least 1,500 innings under their belts. (Mike Marshall, Clay Carroll, and Kent Tekulve all posted similarly impressive fielding statistics, but failed to pitch enough innings to qualify.) Stu Miller (number 35) is the other reliever on the list.

Current pitchers on the list

Twelve of the 100 top best-fielding pitchers are currently active. Of particular note are the following:

> **Roy Halladay** (number 17), second-best among actives, whose consistency has never garnered a Gold Glove but is a plausible factor in his four top-five finishes in the Cy Young.
>
> **Livan Hernandez** (number 18), who rates at the top in Dewan's plus/minus scheme, although his performance sagged in 2008.
>
> **Kenny Rogers** (number 40), a member of the 2006 World Series–losing Tigers, whose exceptional range (number 10 in range-biased score; 2.73 RF9) has likely been instrumental in his snagging of five Gold Gloves. His season fielding percentages, however, have often been in the low-to-mid .900s—for example, .912 in his Gold Glove year of 2006. Ironically, Rogers's 2008 performance (.987 FP, 3.94 RF9, 11 DPs) at age 43 arguably ranks among the best fielding seasons in all of MLB pitching history, but it did not rate a Gold Glove; Mike Mussina's efforts (.976 FP; 1.84 RF9; 4 DPs) did.

Summary and future work

A four-variable ranking scheme has been applied to the fielding statistics of 287 MLB pitchers spanning the last eleven decades of Major League Baseball. This scheme is based on functions of fielding percentage differential versus league averages; nine-inning range factor versus league averages; the ratio of double plays to errors; and the number of double plays turned per nine innings. The results reveal longtime San Francisco Giants pitcher Kirk Rueter to be the most accomplished all-around fielding pitcher in the modern history of baseball, by a considerable margin. Perennial Gold Glove recipients Greg Maddux and Bobby Shantz follow Rueter, lending confidence to the ranking scheme. The results lead to a variety of conclusions and speculations about the fielding abilities of individual pitchers, many of them counter to prevailing wisdom. Along with the Rueter revelation, another surprising conclusion is that the accolades heaped on Jim Kaat and Bob Gibson for their fielding prowess are not even remotely justifiable via this analysis.

This work is admittedly more of a pilot study than a definitive work on the subject. Future work should examine all pitchers instead of a subset, since a few high-RF9/mediocre-FP pitchers may have been missed in this analysis who would rate in the top 100 of a range-biased ranking. A further improvement would be to apply more sophisticated approaches to the fielding of pitchers, perhaps Dewan's plus/minus scheme or a variant of the Win Shares method of James. An application of eigenvector analysis might also be able to identify truly independent variables for measuring fielding. I hope that any future efforts will be compared and contrasted to the methods and results of this paper. ■

Notes

I thank Charlie Pavitt, Barry Flanagan, Stephen Jascourt, Pam Knox, David Knox, and Satya Patel for their assistance and comments.

1. Baseball Examiner (http://www.baseballexaminer.com/statoftheweek/5-12-06.htm). In volume 2 of *The Fielding Bible* (Skokie, Ill.: ACTA, 2009), Dewan does discuss pitcher fielding, but this source was published too late for me to incorporate his discussion into this present article.
2. Rob Neyer, ESPN (http://sports.espn.go.com/espn/print?id=1410373&type=columnist).
3. Baseball Examiner (www.baseballexaminer.com/statoftheweek/5-12-06.htm).
4. *The SABR Baseball List and Record Book* (SABR 2007) incorrectly ranks Rueter as seventh by placing Jim Wilson above Rueter. The statistics found at Baseball-Reference.com indicate that Rueter leads Wilson by a microscopic .00000515.
5. As James (2001, 885) observes, Tommy John was a mathematics major in college—and so is possibly the only pitcher mentioned in this article who is also qualified to peer-review it.
6. Kevin Brown is the only pitcher examined who did not qualify by fulfilling at least one of my criteria 3 through 6. His name arose instead during initial discussions with Jim Charlton about this manuscript, and I was loath to leave him out.

Other Sources

Dewan, John. *The Fielding Bible.* New York: ACTA, 2006.

James, Bill. *The New Bill James Historical Baseball Abstract.* New York: Free Press, 2001.

Kaplan, Jim. "The Pitcher as Fielder." In *The National Pastime*, ed. John Thorn. New York: Warner Books, 1987.

SABR. *The SABR Baseball List and Record Book.* Edited by Lyle Spatz. New York: Scribner, 2007.

Catcher ERA—Once More with Feeling

It's Tough to Be a Rookie

Tom Hanrahan

DO CATCHERS in general do a better job of handling the pitching staff as they gain major-league experience? In a previous study published in *By the Numbers* ("Catchers—Better as Veterans," spring 2000), I concluded that the answer to this question was a resounding *Yes!* The two sets of data used were the team ERA (adjusted for league average) of all clubs where the same primary catcher was used in consecutive seasons, from 1946 through 1987, and the number of previous major-league games the catcher had caught prior to each year. In this study, I found that the team ERA dropped significantly as a catcher went from being a rookie to having spent four to seven years with the same club. The effect was particularly strong when dealing with rookie catchers with very little experience (fewer than 50 MLB games caught). Virtually every team (16 of 17) that kept these catchers had a better ERA by the time they gained more experience.

Some students of the game pointed out a potential flaw in my methodology. I attempted to "hold all other things equal" by comparing catchers in rookie seasons to their later years while with the same team, assuming that changes in the pitching staffs, while not inconsequential, would be random enough. However, it is possible that teams employing a rookie catcher might be in a "rebuilding" year more often than is typical, and thus employing an untried or subpar pitching staff at the same time. To make a quick check of this, I recorded team records for the year before a rookie catcher's being used. These teams (for the rookie catcher in the database) averaged only about 76 wins (per 162), which does suggest a tendency to rebuild when a rookie catcher is brought in. The team records of the catchers' rookie years wouldn't appear to be of much analytical value, since that would be influenced *by* the catcher (or so the theory goes). Well, now what? I decided what I needed to do was to compare specifically pitcher–catcher pairs on the same team as the catcher matured. This ought to show any influence the catcher has on the pitcher over time. And that is the subject of this article.

THE UPDATE

First, I updated my original study. Actually, a gentleman named Jerry Swenson did all of the research (read: grunt work) for me. The database now includes the years 1988 through 2003, adding 47 percent more players to the file, increasing the number of catcher-years from 560 to 835. The additional years used did not change the original conclusions: Team ERA improved significantly from the catchers' rookie seasons to their prime years. Figure 1 shows two curves, the original and the new (combined) relative change in team ERA versus how many games a catcher had spent with a team. The one noticeable difference found when adding the more recent data is a lessening of the poorer ERAs when a catcher was well past his prime (> 1,000 games caught). However, there isn't as much data in this area (many catchers are not playing full-time by this point), so it could be just random noise.

Figure 1. Team ERA by Catcher's Experience

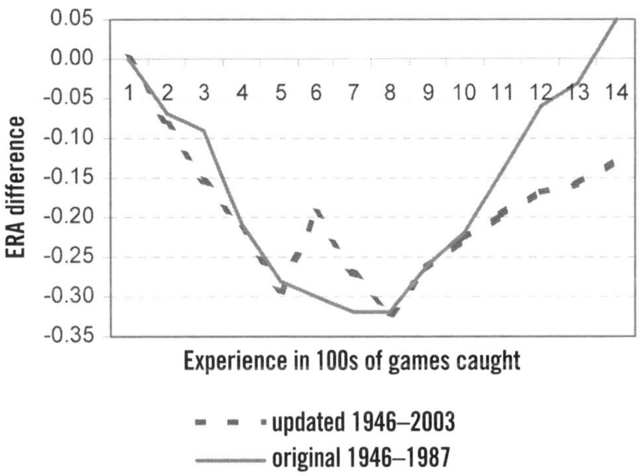

PITCHER–CATCHER PAIRS: THE DATA

In the original study, I identified 16 catchers who, after having caught fewer than 50 games in the major leagues, had a full-time rookie year and then stayed with a team through their prime years. This was a set of catchers who burst on the scene and were good enough to continue playing. From Jerry Swenson's research of recent years, this set of catchers now numbers 26.

I found all of the pitchers who tossed at least 100 innings in these catchers' rookie seasons. I then looked for any other seasons where the same pitcher threw at least 100 innings in a year when the catcher was in his prime with the team. I defined "prime" largely by the findings in the previous study, as when the catcher had four to seven years with the team. I could then compare the individual pitchers' ERA in different years, all with the same catcher. I also entered data for all of the pitchers who threw at least 100 innings in the year prior to the catcher's rookie season (when they were obviously throwing to a different receiver). All of these data were entered into a file that contains 26 catchers, 90 catcher-pitcher pairs, and a total of 233 paired seasons. A list of names, teams, and years appears at the end of this article. Of course, there are many more cases of pitchers throwing to rookie or veteran catchers—but, again, this data is only for those pitcher-catcher pairs who played for the same teams.

FROM ROOKIE TO PRIME BACKSTOPS

First, I will compare the seasons when the catchers were raw rookies to their time as veterans of four to seven years' service.

Example: In 2000, Ramon Hernandez had his first full year in MLB, catching 142 games for the Oakland A's. He had caught only 40 games previously. In 2000, there were five pitchers who threw at least 100 innings for the A's. Only two of these also threw 100 innings in 2003 (and 2004—while our research stopped initially at 2003, I since updated any numbers with data from the 2004 campaign), which would be "rookie year plus 3 (and plus 4)": Mark Mulder and Tim Hudson. Hudson's ERA in 2000 was 4.14, and in 2003–4 combined it was 3.07. Mulder put up a 5.44 ERA in 2000 and a 3.84 ERA in 2003–4. So, Hudson and Mulder were both more effective when Hernandez was a veteran receiver with the A's.

Overall results:

- There were 39 qualifying pitcher–catcher pairs. Of these, 22 have lower ERAs with the veteran catcher.
- Pitchers throwing to the catchers as veterans had a composite ERA that was 0.40 lower than when the catchers were rookies.
- Assuming a normal distribution, this 0.40 difference is well beyond the bounds of chance (greater than 2 sigma).

There was a significant amount of variation in the data. A few points stand out. In 1961, after a decent first season in the bigs, Chris Short put up a disastrous 5.94 ERA for the Phillies in Clay Dalrymple's initial season as Philadelphia's primary catcher. Short would later post ERAs consistently in the 2s with Dalrymple in 1964 through 1967. Another large jump was exhibited by Sandy Koufax, who in 1958 managed only a 4.48 ERA throwing to a young Johnny Roseboro. Of course, a few years later, Roseboro was privileged to

NATIONAL BASEBALL HALL OF FAME LIBRARY, COOPERSTOWN, N.Y.

Johnny Roseboro, Roy Campanella's successor as Dodgers catcher. Roseboro caught many gems pitched by Sandy Koufax, including two of his four no-hitters, although in the late 1950s, when both batterymates were still young, the numbers put up by Koufax were generally mediocre.

catch numerous gems from Sandy's amazing arm; certainly the move to Dodger Stadium helped as well. Conversely, the largest increase in ERA from rookie to veteran catcher was the combo of Luis Tiant and Carlton Fisk. Luis put up a brilliant 1.91 ERA in Fisk's rookie year (1972) but was much less effective in the later 1970s.

One problem area I saw is that Steve Carlton was famous for having his own personal catcher (Tim McCarver) late in his career with the Phillies, so it is questionable whether he can be used in this dataset. There may be other similar examples (Greg Maddux?) that I have not yet studied.

At this point, some readers might be thinking that the first two pitchers mentioned here were also very young in the catcher's initial year, and of course Tiant by 1978 was who knows how old. This is true, and it could be the topic of a future study, although there certainly were counterexamples in this database. And this leads to my next line of analysis.

ROOKIES COMPARED TO THE YEAR PRIOR

Next comparison: I compared the ERAs of pitchers who had 100 innings pitched in both the catcher's rookie year and with the same team the previous year.

Overall results:

- There were 73 qualifying pitcher–catcher pairs. Of these, 22 were the same used in the previous dataset.
- Of the 73 pitchers, 47 had a higher ERA with the rookie catcher than with his predecessor.
- The composite ERA of these 73 pitchers was 0.37 higher with the rookie catcher.
- Assuming a normal distribution, this 0.37 difference is well beyond the bounds of chance (greater than 3 sigma).

This extra comparison, while not quite apples to apples, does at least answer the objection made previously: If it were true that the pitchers in the first study were improving as they naturally matured along with the catchers, then we would also expect them to have been even worse when they were a year younger. Instead, the opposite is the case. There are more data for this second comparison, since it is easier to find pitchers who threw 100 innings in consecutive years than for four or more years apart.

CONCLUSIONS

Catchers, as a whole, somehow are "worse" at helping their pitchers when they are major-league rookies. Pitchers, having worked previously with who knows what catcher, have their ERA go up when throwing to the new guy. However, after throwing to the new guy for a few years, their ERA goes way down. Maybe 40 or 50 or 60 runs per year, if you add up the effects for a whole pitching staff. No defensive player saves 50 runs a year. No catcher prevents stolen bases or passed balls, or blocks the plate, to anywhere near the tune of 50 runs a year.

The last team to win a pennant with a rookie catcher, even bending the definition of *rookie* a bit, were the 1990 Reds, for whom Joe Oliver had caught 47 games the previous season. This is 36 pennants ago. At hardballtimes.com, Matthew Namee recently published a note stating that only two teams using catchers age 22 or younger had won a World Series: Tim McCarver's Cardinals in 1964 and Mike Scioscia's Dodgers in 1981. McCarver had already spent parts of four years in St. Louis, and Scioscia was not a rookie in 1981 either.

You want an advantage for your fantasy-league team next year? Stay away from pitchers throwing to rookie catchers. Do I know *why* this happens? No. But handling pitchers in the majors does seem to be a learned skill. ■

Note

This article is adapted from an article that appeared in *By the Numbers* (November 20, 2004), the newsletter of SABR's Statistical Analysis Committee.

Database List of Players Used

Rookie Year	Catcher	Team-LG	Pitchers
1952	White	BOS-A	McDermott M, Parnell M, Nixon W
1956	Triandos	BAL-A	Moore R, Palica E, Wight B, Brown H
1958	Roseboro	LAD-N	Koufax S, Drysdale D, Labine C, Podres J, Williams S
1961	Dalrymple	PHI-N	Mahaffey A, Roberts R, Buzhardt J, Green D, Short C, Baldschun J
1962	Haller	SFG-N	Sanford J, Marichal J, Miller S
1963	McCarver	STL-N	Gibson B, Broglio E, Simmons C, Sadecki R
1966	Casanova	WAS-A	Richert P, McCormick M, Ortega P, Hannan J, Cox C
1966	Hundley	CHI-N	Ellsworth D
1968	Bench	CIN-N	Nolan G, Abernathy T, Maloney J
1969	Herrmann	CHI-A	Wood W, Horlen J, John T, Peters G
1969	Sanguillen	PIT-N	Veale B, Blass S, Moose B, Ellis D, Walker L
1970	Munson	NYY-A	Stottlemyre M, Bahnsen S, Peterson F
1972	Fisk	BOS-A	Siebert S, Culp R, Tiant L
1972	Rader	SFG-N	Barr J, Bryant J, Stone S, Marichal J
1973	Boone	PHI-N	Carlton S, Lonborg J, Ruthven D, Twitchell W
1974	Sundberg	TEX-A	Bibby J
1976	Wynegar	MIN-A	Goltz D, Hughes J, Campbell B, Redfern P
1987	Santiago	SDP-N	McCullers L, Hawkins A, Whitson E, Show E
1987	Surhoff	MIL-A	Higuera T, Nieves J, Wegman B, Bosio C
1990	Oliver	CIN-A	Browning T, Rijo J, Jackson D, Mahler R
1991	Hoiles	BAL-A	Milacki B, Ballard J, McDonald B
1991	Rodriguez	TEX-A	Rogers K, Ryan N
1993	Piazza	LAD-N	Hershiser O, Candiotti T, Gross K, Martinez R, Astacio P
1994	Wilson	SEA-A	Fleming D, Johnson R
1996	Kendall	PIT-N	Neagle D
2000	Hernandez	OAK-A	Heredia G, Hudson T, Mulder M

Greatest Catchers

A Composite Ranking Methodology

Chuck Rosciam

WHO IS THE GREATEST catcher to have ever played in the major leagues? Some might say it is Yogi Berra or Johnny Bench or Roy Campanella. The answer depends on what one uses as a measure of greatness.

There have been numerous measures used or proposed[1] and numerous lists[2] ranking the great backstops. All of these measures have merit. All have their proponents and their opponents. From my perspective, the greatest catcher is a player who excels on offense and defense far better than his contemporaries and better than all other backstops relative to their contemporaries. So, the task is to find a measure that encompasses these qualities with some objective and quantifiable scale.

A study was undertaken not to invent a new statistic but rather to merge the majority of the existing measures of performance—both offensive and defensive—into one composite value that would answer the question.

Since 1876, there have been 1,693 players whose career position was as a catcher.[3] Additionally, there have been 429 other players who have caught in one or more games, such as Cap Anson (105 games caught) and Jimmie Foxx (108). Out of these 2,122 players, how does one narrow down the list to a select group of the greatest catchers? I chose 800 (or more) games caught in a career (and games caught > 50 percent of games played) as the criterion. That translates, on average, into a rough minimum of ten years catching half of one's team's games (10 x 80). It should be noted that the average number of games behind the plate each season for starting catchers is about 100 (99.7 for 1904–60 and 108.6 after 1960). So it would take roughly eight years as a starter to qualify. Furthermore, there have been only 980 catchers (out of the 1,693) with three or more years of major-league catching service who have averaged about 55.1 games per season. Additionally, the minimum number of years of service for Hall of Fame consideration is ten. This effectively narrows the pool of catchers down to 166 to analyze, just 10 percent of all career catchers—the cream of the crop.

What measures of greatness should be used in building a composite ranking system? I chose five of the most commonly used offensive and five of the generally accepted defensive measures.

The first two offensive measures (OBP and SLG) could have been combined into the additive measure of OPS, but this dilutes the strength of either/both. I chose both runs created (RC) and win shares (WS) because both are widely used and measure different skills. (WS includes RC batting/baserunning plus fielding and pitching). The stats used for offense were the career totals (all positions), even though some players, like Gene Tenace and Mickey Tettleton, might have spent a lot of time at other positions. Both played more than 50 percent of their games as a catcher. Offensive stats while playing as a catcher could not be parsed out for the period before the 1950s, so career totals were used. On the offensive side the selected measures are:

Table 1. Offensive Measures

1 On-base percentage (OBP)
2 Slugging average (SLG)
3 Adjusted batting runs (BRA)[4]
4 Runs created per game (RC27)[5]
5 Win shares (WS)[6]

On the defensive side I chose the below five measures (table 2). Average number of games caught reflects the player's stamina throughout the season and his career. It should be noted that the individual may or may not have played other positions at the time or had been a bench-warming backup. It also gives credit to those guys whose career was spent entirely, or nearly so, at the position (e.g., Mickey Cochrane played 1,451 games behind the plate and one game in the outfield) and gives credit to someone like Ray Mueller, who caught all of 155 games for the Reds in 1944. Moreover, it demotes guys like Gene Tenace, who played 670 games at other positions (not including appearances as a designated hitter or pinch-hitter) and just 892 games as catcher. The lowest-ranking catcher for GCAvg is Greg Myers, who managed to catch only 47.1 per year (out of the 162-game schedule).

I did not include the long-used fielding percentage because a very large component is putouts, which include strikeouts and depends greatly on the pitchers whom the catcher works with. A better measure would have been to only include *independent putouts* (IPOs, putouts minus strikeouts), but that data is available only for games since the 1950s. And, any attempt to guesstimate IPOs for prior years would be just that—a guess. Therefore, I included the two key components of fielding percentage (assists and errors). I did not include passed balls as one of the measures because that too is highly dependent on the pitcher, especially if he's a knuckleballer like Hoyt Wilhelm, Phil Niekro, or Tim Wakefield.

Not included is the currently popular caught-stealing percentage (CS%), because data for that is complete only for games since the 1950s, and Palmer's *range* and *throwing* stats include stolen bases and caught stealing. I did not use catcher's earned run average (CERA) because my previous study, Keith Woolner's study, and Tom Hanrahan's study[7] all indicate that, although there is a difference between catchers in pitcher ERA and in CERA, as backstops gain experience over time, the difference in any given year is not statistically significant.

Table 2. Defensive Measures

1 Average number of games caught (GCAvg)
2 Assists per game average (A/G)
3 Errors per game average (E/G)
4 Range (Rng)[8]
5 Throwing (Thr)[9]

Before I begin to "merge" these ten measures into a single, composite measure for ranking greatness, I will display the top five catchers in each of the ten categories. This will give you an idea of the variety of values involved and the different catchers ranked under each methodology.

Table 3. On-Base Percentage

Rank	Catcher	OBP
1	Mickey Cochrane	.419
2	Wally Schang	.393
3	Gene Tenace	.388
4	Roger Bresnahan	.386
5	Bill Dickey	.382

Table 4. Slugging Average

Rank	Catcher	SLG
1	Mike Piazza	.545
2	Roy Campanella	.500
3	Javy Lopez	.491
4	Gabby Hartnett	.489
5	Bill Dickey	.486

Table 5. Adjusted Batting Runs

Rank	Catcher	BRA
1	Mike Piazza	444
2	Gene Tenace	272
3	Johnny Bench	269
4	Bill Dickey	257
5	Mickey Cochrane	250

Table 6. Runs Created per Game

Rank	Catcher	RC27
1	Mickey Cochrane	7.64
2	Deacon McGuire	7.43
3	Ed Herrmann	7.10
4	Hank Gowdy	6.87
5	Mike Piazza	6.73

Table 7. Win Shares

Rank	Catcher	WS
1	Yogi Berra	375
2	Carlton Fisk	368
3	Johnny Bench	356
4	Gary Carter	337
5	Hartnett / Piazza	325

NATIONAL BASEBALL HALL OF FAME LIBRARY, COOPERSTOWN, N.Y.

Roy Campanella, Dodgers catcher, sliding into home. Among catchers who have caught 800 or more games, he ranks second in career slugging average, at .500, behind only Mike Piazza (.545). At 118.7, the average number of games Campanella caught per season he played, he ranks third, behind only Jason Kendall and Ivan Rodriguez.

NATIONAL BASEBALL HALL OF FAME LIBRARY, COOPERSTOWN, N.Y.

Gabby Hartnett, 19 of whose 20 years in the major leagues were spent with the Cubs, combined power at the plate with better than average defense behind it to top Chuck Rosciam's composite ranking of all-time best catchers. Hartnett was inducted into the Hall of Fame in 1955.

Although win shares is grouped under offense, the WS formulas include a defensive component as well, and adjustments are made for this later on. From just these five offensive "top fives," we have 16 different catchers out of the 25 slots. This distribution alone indicates that there must be some composite measure that takes into account these different ways to look at offense.

Additionally, there is defense to consider.

Table 8. Average Number of Games Caught

Rank	Catcher	GC Avg
1	Jason Kendall	126.7
2	Ivan Rodriguez	120.7
3	Roy Campanella	118.3
4	Bob Boone	117.1
5	Ramon Hernandez	116.2

Table 9. Assists per Game

Rank	Catcher	A/G
1	Pop Snyder	1.65
2	Bill Bergen	1.53
3	Duke Farrell	1.41
4	Lou Criger	1.36
5	Red Dooin	1.33

Table 10. Errors per Game

Rank	Catcher	E/G
1	A. J. Pierzynski	0.028
2	Mike Matheny	0.034
3	Dan Wilson	0.035
4	Chris Hoiles	0.036
5	Damian Miller	0.037

Table 11. Range Factor

Rank	Catcher	RNG
1	Ivan Rodriguez	202.35
2	Ron Karkovice	161.50
3	Johnny Bench	158.53
4	Thurman Munson	158.46
5	Ed Bailey	151.60

Table 12. Throwing

Rank	Catcher	THR
1	Ivan Rodriguez	149.94
2	Charles Johnson	134.93
3	Ron Karkovice	131.92
4	Clay Dalrymple	130.00
5	Mike LaValliere	128.15

With defense included, there are now 36 different catchers occupying 50 top-five slots. Mickey Cochrane appears more often in the above ten lists than does Yogi Berra. Does this mean Cochrane is *greater* than Berra? The answer is no. What is displayed in the above ten tables is nothing more than a set of ten different perspectives of a catcher's career, expressed in a variety of stat values covering more than a hundred years of different game environments and styles of play. It's an interesting set of lists, but it doesn't answer the question fully.

Because these ten measures have completely different resultant values and different contexts, a four-step methodology was deployed to put them all into the same scale and context.

Step 1 was to convert the raw measures into the *league relationship* in which each was compared to the league-average catcher for that year. One (1.00) would be the league average, and above that would be better than the league average. Below 1.00 would be worse than the league-average catcher. This puts the raw values into a common scale and into equal context. So a catcher in an era where there were a lot of assists would not gain an advantage over one in a low-assist era. Every stat was divided by that of the league-average catcher. That would mean that a value of 2.00 in slugging meant twice the league average, irrespective of the accumulated stats or in what year or league it was accomplished. For example, Yogi Berra's slugging average (SLG) is .482, and the league average for the 19 years he played averaged .372. Dividing Berra's SLG by the LgSLG equals 1.29 (r-SLG). This is the fifth best all-time for catchers. The top five slugging averages relative to the league averages are shown in table 13.

Table 13. Slugging Converted to Lg-Related

Catcher	SLGL	SLGr	SLG
Mike Piazza	.545	.3991	.36
Bill Dickey	.486	.3601	.35
Mickey Cochrane	.478	.3681	.30
Johnny Bench	.476	.3681	.29
Yogi Berra	.482	.3741	.29

NATIONAL BASEBALL HALL OF FAME LIBRARY, COOPERSTOWN, N.Y.

Ivan Rodriguez, now in his nineteenth year of major-league service, leads catchers in two defensive categories, range factor and throwing. He ranks sixth on Rosciam's list of greatest catchers and first among active players.

Step 2 was to normalize[10] these ten relationships by scaling them all from 0.00 to 1.00 in proportion to their individual measure differences. The process used was a *z-score*. This facilitated combining the ten disparate stats into a form of some equality (apples to apples). For example, Berra's SLG-to-LgSLG relationship of 1.29 ranked fifth out of 166, behind first-place Mike Piazza (1.36) and ahead of ninth-place Carlton Fisk (1.24). But the numerical differences don't mean anything when we're trying to compare them to the numerical differences in RC27, with Piazza at 1.46, Berra at 1.36, and Fisk at 1.17. So, the *z-score* range of 0 to 1 is the answer. All measures would be on the same scale of differences. Taking the same five catchers from Table 13 and showing their SLG and RC27 values in a *league-relative* and a *normalized* state, we get:

Table 14. Slugging and RC27

Catcher	rSLGn	SLGr	RCn	RC
Mike Piazza	1.36	.997	1.46	.987
Bill Dickey	1.35	.996	1.31	.950
Mickey Cochrane	1.30	.988	1.49	.992
Johnny Bench	1.29	.986	1.29	.938
Yogi Berra	1.29	.985	1.36	.969

Once normalized, the five offensive measures could now be combined in some fashion in a third step.

In step 3, I chose to average them so that the resultant values remained between 0 and 1. The same was done with the five defensive measures. To demonstrate from beginning to end (raw and league to league-related to normalized), Gabby Hartnett's offensive and defensive values are shown in table 15.

Table 15. Hartnett's 10 Offensive and Defensive Values

Measure	Raw	lg-value	r-value	Rank	n-value
OBP	.369	.333	1.108	23rd	.859
SLG	.489	.380	1.286	6th	.984
BRA	242	100	2.420	7th	.991
RC27	6.39	4.65	1.313	12th	.948
WS	325	50	6.50	16th	.997
OFF Avg			**n-OFF**		**.956**
GC	89.65	48.17	1.861	50th	.690
A/G	.699	.605	1.156	26th	.851
E/G	.078	.089	1.159	66th	.582
Rng	127.4	100	1.274	19th	.863
Thr	111.6	100	1.116	28th	.813
DEF Avg			**n-DEF**		**.761**

Tables 16 and 17 show the top five catchers with their five *normalized stats averaged* for offense (n-OFF) and for defense (n-DEF).

Table 16. Top Five Offensive Measures

Rank	Catcher	n-OFF
1	Mickey Cochrane	.988
2	Mike Piazza	.987
3	Bill Dickey	.967
4	Gabby Hartnett	.956
5	Gene Tenace	.950

Table 17. Top Five Defensive Measures

Rank	Catcher	n-DEF
1	Jim Sundberg	.893
2	Brad Ausmus	.873
3	Damian Miller	.861
4	Ivan Rodriguez	.841
5	Gary Carter	.821

Step 4, the final step, was to weight the offense and the defense based on the strength and scope of the measures involved and on the general perception of what makes a catcher *great*. Unfortunately, this is a matter of one's own opinion and open to much debate. However, taking my cue from Bill James in the various win-shares formulas for catchers,[11] I assigned two-thirds weight to offense and one-third to defense—primarily because win shares includes a defensive component and it's included under offense. In addition, two-thirds of the time catchers earned their win shares for batting and baserunning. Others might wish to assign each weight equally or to use different percentages based on their own analysis.

Table 18 lists all 166 catchers (800 + games caught and > 50% games played as a catcher) with their years in the majors, years catching, games played, games caught, and their normalized offensive average (n-OFF),

Table 18. Normalized, Averaged, and Weighted Greatness Measures

Rank	Catcher		Career	Yrs	YrsC	G	GmC	n-OFF	n-DEF	n-RNK
1	Gabby Hartnett	HOF	1922–1941	20	20	1990	1793	0.956	0.761	0.891
2	Bill Dickey	HOF	1926–1946	17	17	1789	1708	0.967	0.731	0.888
3	Johnny Bench	HOF	1967–1983	17	17	2158	1742	0.923	0.797	0.881
4	Roy Campanella	HOF	1948–1957	10	10	1215	1183	0.911	0.790	0.871
5	Gary Carter	HOF	1974–1992	19	19	2296	2056	0.882	0.821	0.862
6	Ivan Rodriguez	Current	1991–20nn	18	18	2267	2173	0.847	0.841	0.845
7	Mickey Cochrane	HOF	1925–1937	13	13	1482	1451	0.988	0.490	0.822
8	Thurman Munson		1969–1979	11	11	1423	1277	0.829	0.804	0.821
9	Bill Freehan		1961–1976	15	15	1774	1581	0.883	0.620	0.795
10	Yogi Berra	HOF	1946–1965	19	19	2120	1699	0.930	0.515	0.792
11	Ernie Lombardi	HOF	1931–1947	17	17	1853	1544	0.913	0.479	0.768
12	Wally Schang		1913–1931	19	19	1842	1435	0.936	0.429	0.767
13	Roger Bresnahan	HOF	1897–1915	17	15	1446	974	0.947	0.402	0.766
14	Ted Simmons		1968–1988	21	20	2456	1771	0.923	0.424	0.757
15	Mike Piazza		1992–2007	16	15	1912	1629	0.987	0.283	0.753
16	Carlton Fisk	HOF	1969–1993	24	24	2499	2226	0.915	0.420	0.750
17	Gene Tenace		1969–1983	15	15	1555	892	0.950	0.321	0.740
18	Darrell Porter		1971–1987	17	17	1782	1506	0.853	0.516	0.740
19	Lance Parrish		1977–1995	19	19	1988	1818	0.698	0.820	0.739
20	Jorge Posada	Current	1995–20nn	14	14	1483	1390	0.902	0.410	0.738
21	Charlie Bennett		1878–1893	15	15	1062	954	0.835	0.511	0.727
22	Chief Meyers		1909–1917	9	9	992	911	0.820	0.517	0.719
32	Elston Howard		1955–1968	14	14	1605	1138	0.736	0.651	0.708
24	Ed Bailey		1953–1966	14	13	1212	1064	0.768	0.543	0.693
25	Tom Haller		1961–1972	12	12	1294	1199	0.791	0.479	0.687
26	Mickey Tettleton		1984–1997	14	12	1485	872	0.864	0.334	0.687
27	Sherm Lollar		1946–1963	18	18	1752	1571	0.734	0.567	0.678
28	Javy Lopez	Current	1992–20nn	15	15	1503	1351	0.808	0.382	0.666
29	Rick Ferrell	HOF	1929–1947	18	18	1884	1806	0.681	0.634	0.665
30	Mike Scioscia		1980–1992	13	13	1441	1395	0.645	0.701	0.664
31	Deacon McGuire		1884–1912	26	25	1781	1611	0.839	0.308	0.662
32	Smoky Burgess		1949–1967	18	17	1691	1139	0.871	0.243	0.662
33	Jack Clements		1884–1900	17	17	1157	1073	0.797	0.376	0.657
34	Johnny Kling		1900–1913	13	13	1260	1168	0.662	0.637	0.654
35	Jason Kendall	Current	1996–20nn	13	13	1833	1774	0.728	0.494	0.650
36	Darren Daulton		1983–1997	14	12	1161	965	0.821	0.266	0.637

Rank	Catcher		Career	Yrs	YrsC	G	GmC	n-OFF	n-DEF	n-RNK
37	Johnny Romano		1958–1967	10	10	905	810	0.816	0.272	0.635
38	Charles Johnson		1994–2005	12	12	1188	1160	0.547	0.798	0.631
39	Chris Hoiles		1989–1998	10	10	894	819	0.770	0.353	0.631
40	Terry Steinbach		1986–1999	14	14	1546	1381	0.649	0.591	0.629
41	Spud Davis		1928–1945	16	16	1458	1282	0.751	0.374	0.625
42	Duke Farrell		1888–1905	18	17	1563	1003	0.705	0.460	0.624
43	Earl Battey		1955–1967	13	13	1141	1087	0.668	0.526	0.621
44	Chief Zimmer		1884–1903	19	19	1280	1239	0.607	0.644	0.619
45	Jim Sundberg		1974–1989	16	16	19621	927	0.481	0.893	0.619
46	Ed McFarland		1893–1908	14	14	894	830	0.683	0.483	0.616
47	Hank Gowdy		1910–1930	17	16	1050	893	0.662	0.471	0.599
48	Del Crandall		1949–1966	16	16	1573	1479	0.498	0.795	0.597
49	Walker Cooper		1940–1957	18	18	1473	1223	0.750	0.288	0.596
50	Johnny Roseboro		1957–1970	14	14	1585	1476	0.581	0.615	0.592
51	Manny Sanguillen		1967–1980	13	12	1448	1114	0.589	0.569	0.582
52	A.J. Pierzynski	Current	1998–20nn	11	11	1099	1055	0.545	0.649	0.580
53	Damian Miller	Current	1997–20nn	11	11	989	958	0.416	0.861	0.564
54	Butch Wynegar		1976–1988	13	13	1301	1247	0.516	0.647	0.559
55	Wes Westrum		1947–1957	11	11	919	902	0.503	0.669	0.558
56	Jody Davis		1981–1990	10	10	1082	1039	0.443	0.752	0.546
57	Shanty Hogan		1925–1937	13	12	989	908	0.553	0.530	0.545
58	Steve O'Neill		1911–1928	17	17	1590	1532	0.548	0.537	0.544
59	Ernie Whitt		1976–1991	15	15	1328	1246	0.545	0.542	0.544
60	Andy Seminick		1943–1957	15	15	1304	1213	0.627	0.377	0.544
61	Tim McCarver		1959–1980	21	20	1909	1387	0.695	0.220	0.537
62	Jason Varitek	Current	1997–20nn	12	12	1330	1273	0.629	0.322	0.527
63	Heinie Peitz		1892–1913	16	16	1234	960	0.557	0.465	0.526
64	Paul LoDuca	Current	1998–20nn	11	11	1082	932	0.542	0.483	0.522
65	Bob Boone		1972–1990	19	19	2264	2225	0.388	0.788	0.522
66	Harry Danning		1933–1942	10	10	890	801	0.528	0.507	0.521
67	Mike Macfarlane		1987–1999	13	13	1164	1058	0.480	0.597	0.519
68	Mike Lieberthal		1994–2007	14	14	1212	1170	0.578	0.398	0.518
69	Milt May		1970–1984	15	14	1192	1034	0.500	0.545	0.515
70	Ron Hassey		1978–1991	14	14	1192	946	0.588	0.364	0.513
71	Ramon Hernandez	Current	1999–20nn	10	10	1188	1162	0.538	0.460	0.512
72	Benito Santiago		1986–2005	20	201	9781	917	0.473	0.588	0.512
73	Bob O'Farrell		1915–1935	21	21	1492	1338	0.634	0.264	0.511
74	Mike LaValliere		1984–1995	12	12	879	850	0.429	0.651	0.503
75	Ray Schalk	HOF	1912–1929	18	18	1762	1727	0.409	0.682	0.500
76	George Gibson		1905–1918	14	14	1213	1194	0.462	0.574	0.499
77	Clay Dalrymple		1960–1971	12	12	1079	1003	0.399	0.699	0.499
78	Al Lopez	HOF	1928–1947	19	19	1950	1918	0.356	0.746	0.486
79	Frank Snyder		1912–1927	16	16	1392	1247	0.425	0.608	0.486
80	Muddy Ruel		1915–1934	19	19	1468	1410	0.453	0.540	0.482
81	Brad Ausmus	Current	1993–20nn	16	16	19141	887	0.282	0.873	0.479
82	Frankie Hayes		1933–1947	14	14	1364	1311	0.584	0.249	0.472
83	Terry Kennedy		1978–1991	14	14	1491	1378	0.496	0.425	0.472
84	Hank Severeid		1911–1926	15	15	1390	1225	0.526	0.358	0.470
85	Gus Triandos		1953–1965	13	13	1206	992	0.492	0.413	0.465
86	Phil Masi		1939–1952	14	14	1229	1101	0.509	0.378	0.465
87	Johnny Edwards		1961–1974	14	14	1470	1392	0.385	0.621	0.464
88	Don Slaught		1982–1997	16	16	1327	1237	0.608	0.172	0.463
89	Bengie Molina	Current	1998–20nn	11	11	1112	1049	0.353	0.678	0.461
90	Rick Dempsey		1969–1992	24	24	1766	1633	0.440	0.498	0.459
91	Buddy Rosar		1939–1951	13	13	988	934	0.336	0.675	0.449
92	Ed Herrmann		1967–1978	11	11	922	817	0.479	0.389	0.449
93	Tony Pena		1980–1997	18	18	1988	1950	0.333	0.678	0.448
94	Joe Azcue		1960–1972	11	11	909	868	0.281	0.741	0.434
95	Ray Mueller		1935–1951	14	14	985	917	0.323	0.644	0.430

Rank	Catcher		Career	Yrs	YrsC	G	GmC	n-OFF	n-DEF	n-RNK
96	Birdie Tebbetts		1936–1952	14	14	1162	1108	0.371	0.525	0.423
97	Darrin Fletcher		1989–2002	14	14	1245	1143	0.483	0.287	0.418
98	Todd Hundley		1990–2003	14	14	1225	1096	0.537	0.176	0.417
99	Dave Valle		1984–1996	13	13	970	902	0.376	0.487	0.413
100	Gus Mancuso		1928–1945	17	17	1460	1360	0.360	0.478	0.399
101	Clint Courtney		1951–1961	11	11	946	802	0.409	0.376	0.398
102	Ron Karkovice		1986–1997	12	12	939	918	0.238	0.718	0.398
103	Steve Yeager		1972–1986	15	15	1269	1230	0.259	0.672	0.397
104	Wilbert Robinson		1886–1902	17	17	1371	1316	0.360	0.454	0.392
105	Eddie Taubensee		1991–2001	11	11	975	871	0.504	0.161	0.389
106	Dan Wilson		1992–2005	14	14	1299	1281	0.269	0.626	0.387
107	Jack O'Connor		1887–1910	21	21	1451	860	0.319	0.504	0.381
108	Mike Gonzalez		1912–1932	17	17	1042	868	0.258	0.614	0.376
109	Mike Heath		1978–1991	14	14	1325	1083	0.291	0.543	0.375
110	Lou Criger		1896–1912	16	16	1012	984	0.229	0.661	0.373
111	Bill Rariden		1909–1920	12	12	982	948	0.338	0.430	0.369
112	Bruce Benedict		1978–1989	12	12	982	971	0.231	0.638	0.367
113	Ivey Wingo		1911–1929	17	17	1327	1233	0.356	0.384	0.365
114	Greg Zaun	Current	1995–20nn	14	14	1114	956	0.450	0.181	0.360
115	Andy Etchebarren		1962–1978	15	15	948	931	0.367	0.343	0.359
116	Charlie Moore		1973–1987	15	15	1334	894	0.362	0.352	0.359
117	John Warner		1895–1908	14	14	1073	1032	0.223	0.626	0.357
118	Tom Pagnozzi		1987–1998	12	12	927	827	0.209	0.646	0.355
119	Mike Matheny		1994–2006	13	13	1305	1285	0.122	0.816	0.353
120	Jimmie Wilson		1923–1940	18	18	1525	1351	0.348	0.356	0.350
121	Michael Barrett	Current	1998–20nn	11	11	1047	878	0.420	0.201	0.347
122	Alan Ashby		1973–1989	17	17	1370	1299	0.397	0.241	0.345
123	Mike Tresh		1938–1949	12	12	1027	1019	0.233	0.548	0.338
124	Sammy White		1951–1962	11	11	1043	1027	0.231	0.549	0.337
125	Buck Rodgers		1961–1969	9	9	932	895	0.162	0.669	0.331
126	Ray Fosse		1967–1979	12	12	924	889	0.321	0.333	0.325
127	Jerry Grote		1963–1981	16	16	1421	1348	0.280	0.413	0.325
128	Rich Gedman		1980–1992	13	13	1033	979	0.373	0.223	0.323
129	Luke Sewell		1921–1942	20	20	1630	1562	0.199	0.565	0.321
130	Bo Diaz		1977–1989	13	13	993	965	0.313	0.336	0.320
131	Jim Hegan		1941–1960	17	17	1666	1629	0.197	0.567	0.320
132	Rollie Hemsley		1928–1947	19	19	1593	1482	0.233	0.489	0.318
133	Joe Oliver		1989–2001	13	13	1076	1033	0.332	0.286	0.316
134	Brent Mayne		1990–2004	15	15	1279	1143	0.285	0.362	0.311
135	Del Rice		1945–1961	17	17	1309	1249	0.225	0.472	0.308
136	Pop Snyder		1873–1891	18	18	930	877	0.231	0.460	0.307
137	Rick Cerone		1975–1992	18	18	1329	1279	0.218	0.475	0.303
138	Sandy Alomar Jr.		1988–2007	20	19	1377	1324	0.340	0.222	0.300
139	Chad Kreuter		1988–2003	16	16	944	892	0.312	0.275	0.300
140	Frank Bowerman		1895–1909	15	15	1045	826	0.220	0.459	0.300
141	Val Picinich		1916–1933	18	18	1037	935	0.360	0.177	0.299
142	Kirt Manwaring		1987–1999	13	13	1008	993	0.159	0.581	0.299
143	Mickey Owen		1937–1954	13	13	1209	1175	0.230	0.436	0.299
144	Cy Perkins		1915–1934	17	16	1171	1111	0.230	0.429	0.297
145	Joe Girardi		1989–2003	15	15	1277	1247	0.217	0.440	0.291
146	Clyde McCullough		1940–1956	15	15	1098	989	0.260	0.338	0.286
147	Bill Killefer		1909–1921	13	13	1035	1005	0.131	0.587	0.283
148	Pat Borders		1988–2005	17	17	1099	1015	0.191	0.447	0.276
149	Jeff Reed		1984–2000	17	17	1234	1071	0.321	0.184	0.276
150	Randy Hundley		1964–1977	14	14	1061	1026	0.191	0.395	0.259
151	Red Dooin		1902–1916	15	15	1290	1195	0.193	0.388	0.258
152	Eddie Ainsmith		1910–1924	15	15	1078	993	0.246	0.277	0.256
153	John Bateman		1963–1972	10	10	1017	953	0.158	0.440	0.252
154	Greg Myers		1987–2005	18	18	1108	894	0.289	0.174	0.251

Rank	Catcher	Career	Yrs	YrsC	G	GmC	n-OFF	n-DEF	n-RNK
155	Zack Taylor	1920–1935	16	16	918	856	0.121	0.475	0.239
156	Billy Sullivan Sr.	1899–1916	16	16	1147	1122	0.121	0.474	0.239
157	Bill Bergen	1901–1911	11	11	947	941	0.021	0.649	0.230
158	Buck Martinez	1969–1986	17	17	1049	1008	0.161	0.345	0.223
159	Dave Duncan	1964–1976	11	11	929	885	0.248	0.159	0.219
160	Bob Swift	1940–1953	14	14	1001	980	0.160	0.323	0.215
161	Paul Casanova	1965–1974	10	10	859	811	0.088	0.467	0.214
162	Oscar Stanage	1906–1925	14	14	1096	1074	0.162	0.300	0.208
163	Otto Miller	1910–1922	13	13	927	890	0.142	0.328	0.204
164	Malachi Kittridge	1890–1906	16	16	1215	1196	0.074	0.456	0.201
165	John Flaherty	1992–2005	14	14	1047	1032	0.143	0.280	0.188
166	Phil Roof	1961–1977	15	15	857	835	0.141	0.276	0.186

their normalized defensive average (n-DEF), and their overall normalized average (n-RNK)— weighted .667 offense and .333 defense.

From my perspective, Gabby Hartnett tops the list of greatest catchers and is one of the very best to have ever donned the "tools of ignorance." You'll note that seven of the top ten are already enshrined in the Hall of Fame. Thurman Munson and Bill Freehan should have gone in, and Ivan Rodriguez is a currently active player who may well be a first-year selection. The second group of ten (11–20) are well known for their offense but somewhat lacking in their defense, as indicated by the n-DEF rankings. However, they are all Hall of Fame–caliber backstops.

What is important is not who number 1 is, as that can change by adjusting what measures are used and how they are weighted, but rather who is in the top 10 to 20 percent and who is not.

I leave it up to the readers to add or subtract or choose their own 10 measures and to weigh the offense and defense based on their own research and analysis. However, the methodology presented here is one nice, logical way to create a merged composite ranking from all of those performance measures out there. For this old catcher, the ranking results of this research in determining the greatest catchers is sound. ■

Notes

Thanks to Tom Hanrahan and Pete Palmer for their help in this research and to Phil Birnbaum, Dan Heisman, Trent McCotter, and Nick Frankovich for their review and comments.

1. Catcher-performance measures such as Bill James's win shares, runs created, or his new loss shares; Pete Palmer and Gary Gillette's batting runs and fielding runs (in *The ESPN Baseball Encyclopedia*, 5th ed., ed. Gary Gillette and Pete Palmer [New York: Sterling, 2008]); John Thorn and Phil Birnbaum and Bill Deane's total player rating (TPR, in *Total Baseball: The Official Encyclopedia of Major League Baseball*, 5th ed., ed. John Thorn, Pete Palmer, et al. [New York: Viking, 1997]), catcher's earned-run average (CERA), OPS (on-base percentage plus slugging average), Clay Davenport's wins above replacement (WARP at baseballprospectus.com), and Charles F. Faber's baseball ratings (batting and fielding points, *Baseball Ratings: The All-Time Best Players at Each Position*, 2d ed. [Jefferson, N.C.: McFarland, 1995]).
2. Keith Carlson's article "A Comparison of Catcher Evaluation Statistics" in SABR's *By the Numbers* (February 2006) is one example of listing catchers by ranked statistics.
3. Data through 2008, with career position determined as playing the majority of one's games at that position. Data for 1954–2008 from Retrosheet.org.
4. Adjusted batting runs, as developed by Pete Palmer and published in *The ESPN Baseball Encyclopedia*, 5th ed. (New York: Sterling, 2008).
5. Runs created per game, as developed by Bill James and published in *Major League Handbooks*, various editions.
6. Win shares, as developed by Bill James and published in *Win Shares*, by Bill James and Jim Henzler (Morton Grove, Ill.: Stats Publishing, 2002).
7. Keith Woolner, "Field General or Backstop?" *Baseball Prospectus* 10 (January 2000); and Tom Hanrahan, "Catcher ERA—Once More With Feeling," *By the Numbers* (November 2004), and reprinted in this volume, *The Baseball Research Journal* 38 (Summer 2009): 59–61.
8. Range (based on stolen bases allowed per inning) as developed by Pete Palmer and published in the *The ESPN Baseball Encyclopedia*, 5th ed.
9. Throwing (based on caught-stealing percentage) as developed by Pete Palmer and published in the *The ESPN Baseball Encyclopedia*, 5th ed.
10. The formula for *normalizing* the data is the common statistical normal cumulative distribution for the mean and the standard deviation of the data (*z-score*).
11. From a sample of 100+ catchers' *win shares* broken down by their "hitting" and "fielding" components, it was determined that "hitting" constituted .667 (two-thirds) and "fielding" .333 (one-third) of the *win shares*.

Leg Men

Career Pinch-Runners in Major League Baseball

Clifford Blau

IN 1974, the Oakland Athletics signed track star Herb Washington as a "designated runner," despite his having had very little baseball experience. Keeping on the roster a player whose *only* purpose was to run was a new idea, but there have been many other real baseball players whose *main* purpose it was to pinch-run. The first was Wilson Collins in 1913 with the Boston Braves. This article gives the stories of all baseball players who did nothing but pinch-run in at least half of their career major-league games (minimum five appearances). It will attempt to show how they came to be used in that capacity. The players are presented in order of their initial major-league appearance.

Charles William R. (Sandy) Piez was the first player to spend most of his major-league career as a pinch-runner. Sandy was the first of four sons born to German immigrants, Anton and Huldah (Hormick) Piez. His birth date has usually been reported as October 13, 1892. However, with the assistance of Richard Malatzky, I discovered that he was actually born on that date in 1888 in New York City. A couple of years later, Anton moved the family to Erie, Pennsylvania, where Charles grew up. He began his professional career while at college in 1910, at first playing under an assumed name, later under his own. In his fourth year in pro ball, he attracted the attention of several major-league teams by stealing 72 bases in the Virginia League. The Giants purchased his contract midseason. John McGraw looked him over during spring training in 1914 and, rather than farm him out to a higher minor league, decided Piez could help the Giants by pinch-running for their slow-footed catchers. McGraw had used several players in that role the previous year, including Claude Cooper, Eddie Grant, and Jim Thorpe. Sandy, also nicknamed Sweet, did nothing but pinch-run until his twelfth appearance when, after running for Chief Meyers, he stayed in the game in right field for two innings, not getting to bat. His next appearance in the field came on September 16. With the Giants leading the Reds 8–0, he replaced George Burns in left and got his first at-bat. Finally, on the last day of the season, Piez started both games of a doubleheader against the Phillies, playing center field in the first game and left in the second. He hit two singles and a triple to finish his major-league career with a .625 slugging average. As a pinch-runner, he scored 8 runs in 33 games, stealing 4 bases. The following year, the Giants sent him to Rochester in the International League. Sandy managed to steal only 17 bases in 117 games in 1915 and, when offered the head coach position with the Rutgers baseball team the following year, he decided to retire as a player. Piez spent two years coaching at Rutgers, where his team went only 6–11. After his coaching career, he tried his hand at several business ventures. His final job was as a salesman for a gas-heater company. The end came unexpectedly soon for Sandy. On December 29, 1930, he was in a car driven by his brother-in-law. The car slid off an icy bridge in Atlantic City and into the ocean; while the driver escaped, Sandy drowned, leaving behind his wife Helen and a 15-year-old son, Charles Jr.

NATIONAL BASEBALL HALL OF FAME LIBRARY, COOPERSTOWN, N.Y.

Sandy Piez, the first player to spend most of his major-league career as a pinch-runner. In 37 games for the Giants in 1914, he stole four bases. At .375, his career batting average exceeds Ty Cobb's. Piez had eight at-bats—two singles and a triple.

Edward Francis Hock was born March 27, 1899, in Franklin Furnace, Ohio. His father, Adam Hock, the son of

Prussian immigrants, was a farmer, while his mother Mary Catherine (Compliment) Hock raised Eddie and his three younger siblings. When the United States entered World War I, Eddie volunteered for the navy. Hock returned home after the war and played baseball on weekends in an independent league. He attracted the attention of the St. Louis Cardinals, who gave him a brief tryout during July 1920. Eddie got into only one game and soon returned home. He began his professional baseball career in earnest the next year, playing for Richmond in the Virginia League. At the close of the season, he was drafted by the Cincinnati Reds, who assigned him to Atlanta in the Southern League for 1922. At the start of the 1923 season, the Reds kept him until early May, using him twice as a pinch-runner before shipping him to Oklahoma City in the Western League, where he would play most of the next four seasons. Hock started the 1924 season with Cincinnati again, this time staying with them until mid-June, pinch-running 10 times in 16 appearances and scoring 5 times in that capacity. When they tried to send him to the minors, he failed to clear waivers and the Pittsburgh Pirates claimed him. Ironically, the Bucs immediately sent him to Oklahoma City in partial payment for Emil Yde. Hock had been playing each of the outfield positions to this point, but in 1925 Oklahoma City converted him to shortstop, and he later moved to third. Eddie was now at his peak, leading the Western League in 1925 with 53 stolen bases, and scoring 127 runs in 1926. However, he never again played in the major leagues. He became a playing manager in 1935 and continued in this role through 1942, winning three pennants. Hock spent 22 years in the minor leagues, finishing third all-time in runs and hits, and first in singles. He stole 486 bases in his career. Eddie lived with his wife, Philomena, and two sons, Joe and Fred, in Portsmouth, Ohio. After a protracted illness, he was found drowned in the Ohio River on November 21, 1963, a suicide.

LIBRARY OF CONGRESS, LOT 13163-31, NO. 74

John McGraw, Giants manager, a forerunner of Charlie Finley in his willingness to devote a roster spot to a player whose main contribution would be to pinch-run. McGraw tapped Piez for the position in 1914. In 1925, it was Pip Koehler.

CHICAGO HISTORY MUSEUM, SDN-063357

Eddie Hock, who in 1924 pinch-ran 10 times for the Cardinals and scored five runs, although he had no base-stealing attempts. Over the next two seasons he put up impressive numbers in stolen bases and runs scored, but they were in the minors, where he ended his playing career.

Horace L. (Pip) Koehler was born January 16, 1902, in Gilbert, Pennsylvania, the third of four children of Franklin and Ida Koehler. He went to college at Penn State, where he played baseball under Hugo Bezdek, former Pittsburgh Pirates manager. Koehler also captained the basketball squad for two years. After graduating in 1923, he taught physical education at Windher High School in Wilkes-Barre for two years while playing semipro ball. The New York Giants brought him to spring training in 1925, where he made a good impression on John McGraw. Koehler was with the Giants briefly after the season started, getting in one game as a pinch-runner before being optioned to Reading in the International League. The Giants recalled him in mid-August, and he made 11 more appearances with them, 9 as a pinch-runner. Following the season, the Giants sent him to Toledo to help complete a deal for Earl Webb. While most players would have been disappointed, Pip was glad for the move because he didn't feel he was good enough to play in the majors. He spent the next eight seasons in the American Association, putting up good but not great numbers. Although he had good speed, he wasn't a big base stealer. His top figure was 20 in 1926; he was also caught stealing 13 times that year. In the winters, Pip played and coached professional basketball from 1927 to 1939 in various cities and leagues; at 5-foot-10, he was big enough to play center in those days. On the baseball field, he split his time between the outfield and infield, primarily third base. He married Corinne Ann Slater in 1929. In 1935, he became a playing manager in the Yankees organization. After he was released by the Yankees in 1940, he found a job managing Tacoma in the Western International League. He finished out his playing career in 1942 with Tacoma. In 1947, he was hired as manager of the Ogden Reds in the Pioneer League. During the following season, with the Reds in last place, he was "reassigned" to a scouting position in the Pacific Northwest region with Cincinnati. In the early 1950s, he left baseball. When Tacoma was in need of a new business manager in 1963, general manager Rosy Ryan, a former teammate of Koehler's in Toledo, hired him. Koehler worked for the club for more than a decade. In December 1986, he died at home following a heart attack.

Herman Layne was born February 13, 1901, to John G. Layne, a coal miner, and Lula Riggs Layne in New Haven, West Virginia. Apart from his baseball career, he lived there his whole life. He had two sisters and two brothers, including a twin, Harry, who also had a 13-year professional baseball career. After attending West Virginia University, Herman joined Bristol of the Appalachian League in 1922. He starred there with a league-leading .354 batting average and his contract was purchased by the Detroit Tigers. The Tigers farmed him out, and he advanced the next two years to the Sally and International Leagues. After he led the International League with 16 triples in 1926, Toronto traded him to the Pittsburgh Pirates for $30,000 and two players. Pittsburgh expected Layne to win their left-field job in 1927. However, he was beaten out in spring training by Lloyd Waner. Layne appeared in just 11 games for the Bucs, 8 as a pinch-runner, before being farmed out to Indianapolis in the American Association in early June. This must have been very disappointing to him, but he got a measure of revenge on June 30. In an exhibition game against the Pirates, Layne hit two homers to lead the Indians to victory. Following the 1929 season, he was traded to Louisville for Eddie Sicking. In his first season with Louisville, he led the American Association in triples and stolen bases. He spent three and a half seasons with Louisville. Layne returned to Indianapolis in 1933, and he finished his career in 1934 with Charleston, West Virginia, in the Middle Atlantic League. Layne's career batting average was .327, and he played for five pennant-winning teams in his 13-year career. After his retirement from baseball, Herman returned to New Haven, where he had a long and successful career in business. Herman Layne passed away on August 27, 1973 of a heart attack.

Success came quickly but proved fleeting for Dinny McNamara. Tragedy was longer lasting. Born **John Raymond McNamara** on September 16, 1905, in Lexington, Massachusetts, he was the seventh of ten children born to Dennis and Katherine (Lynch) McNamara, three of whom died before their first birthday. Nicknamed Dinny after his father, John was an all-around sports star at Lexington High School and then went on to attend Boston College. There he played center field on the baseball team and fullback for the football team for four years. Following graduation, he signed a contract with the Boston Braves and in early July made his debut as a pinch-runner, scoring a run. In fact, Dinny would pinch-run seven times in his first eight days with the Braves. After going 0 for 9 in three starts, McNamara was optioned to Providence of the Eastern League, where he finished the season. That fall, he started a job as an assistant college football coach at Fordham. When the 1928 season began, McNamara was back with the Braves but again saw limited action, pinch-running six times and making three other appearances before being returned to Providence at the end of May. Although he fielded well for Providence, his hitting was weak and he could only manage a .266 slugging average in 320 at-bats. Dinny gave up on baseball and concentrated on coaching. After five more years at Fordham, he returned to Boston College in 1934 as assistant football coach and freshman baseball coach. The following year, he was named head football coach. However, an automobile accident two years earlier had left him with emotional problems, and the strain of being head coach was too much for him. With a 3–1 record, he resigned. A lifelong bachelor, he lived out his days in Lexington, apparently never working again. A second automobile accident put an end to his life when he was hit while walking near his home in December 1963.

Robert Wayne Kahle was born on November 23, 1915, in New Castle, Indiana. He was the second son of Edward and Clara Kahle. Following high school, Bob Kahle was discovered playing semipro ball and given a tryout with the Indianapolis club of the American Association. The club's manager, Red Killefer, signed him and sent him to the lower minors for seasoning. An infielder, Kahle spent three years in the lower minors before getting his shot with Indianapolis. He did well enough there in 1937 to be drafted by the Boston Bees. However, a sore arm hindered his chance to become a regular there. In almost three months with the National League club, Bob got into just eight games, five as a pinch-runner while pinch-hitting three

Connie Mack probably saw Bob Kahle playing for Hollywood when the Athletics trained in California, but he was unwilling to pay the reported asking price of $15,000, nixing Kahle's conditional sale to Philadelphia after the 1940 season. When no other major-league club stepped forward, Kahle returned to his distinguished career in the Pacific Coast League, putting together a 29-game hitting streak in early 1941.

times. Then Boston optioned him to Hartford in the Eastern League. A shooting pain every time he swung the bat or threw the ball limited him to 10 games before he asked to be put on the voluntarily retired list (there being no disabled list then) for the rest of the season. At the end of spring training in 1939, the Bees sold him conditionally to the Yankees' farm team in Newark. After a month's trial, they decided not to keep him, and Boston turned around and sold his contract to Hollywood of the Pacific Coast League for $7,500. Killefer was the manager of the Stars, and Kahle settled down as the regular third baseman there for the next five seasons, winning the team MVP award in 1940. Another conditional sale followed that season, this time to the Philadelphia Athletics. Again, the deal wasn't completed as Connie Mack decided Kahle wasn't worth the $15,000 price. Kahle's 29-game hitting streak early in 1941 may have caused Connie to regret his decision. After the 1942 season, Kahle enlisted in the navy. He never saw action, though, except on the baseball field, as he was stationed at various Pacific Coast bases. Returning to the Stars in 1946, he found his third-base spot occupied by Hollywood's player-manager Buck Fausett. Bob was soon traded to Portland for pitcher Paul Gregory. He was the Beavers' regular third baseman that year, but early in 1947 he was sent to the Southern Association, where he closed out his playing career with Little Rock. Kahle returned to Hollywood, where he worked as a painter for Burbank Studios for 33 years. Bob maintained an interest in baseball, organizing the Little League in the Westchester section of Los Angeles. Dying of lung cancer on December 16, 1988, Bob left behind his widow Evelyn, three sons, and nine grandchildren.

Patrick Nicholas Capri was born November 27, 1918, in New York City. Pat went to New Utrecht High School and attended Brooklyn College for two years before signing a contract with the St. Louis Cardinals organization in 1938. He worked his way through their enormous farm system, spending two years with Fostoria in the Ohio State League and then playing for Williamson in the Mountain States League in 1940 and Asheville in the Piedmont League in 1941. He led the latter two leagues in double plays by second basemen and made the league all-star team in 1940 while knocking in 105 runs and scoring 98. He was on the roster of Springfield in 1942 when he suffered a knee injury. It was severe enough to keep him out of military service, and he was placed on the voluntarily retired list. That December, he married Rita Petrizzo. In 1944, he was reactivated and started the season with the Columbus Red Birds, who soon released him. He signed as a free agent with Newark, which also released him. However, the Boston Braves, fearing that regular second baseman Connie Ryan would be called up for military service, signed Capri as insurance. As it worked out, when Ryan reported to the navy in late July, the Braves made other arrangements for a new second baseman, and Capri was released in early August. He got into seven games with Boston; only in the last one did he do anything but pinch-run. Capri quickly found another spot owing to the manpower shortage; he signed with Indianapolis. Soon after he joined the Indians, though, he suffered a broken nose and missed two weeks. He closed out the season with Indianapolis, playing 20 games with a .318 batting average. However, he left baseball for good after that, working as a self-employed paperhanger. Pat lived in Brooklyn until his death in 1986.

Some pinch-runners were accepted by their teammates; others were thought to be a waste of a roster spot. Only **Joe Tepsic**, though, was accused of costing his team a pennant. Joseph John Tepsic was born September 18, 1923, in Slovan, Pennsylvania. After graduating Union High School in Burgettstown, Pennsylvania, he enrolled at Waynesboro College. When America entered World War II, he enlisted with the Marines and was bayoneted in the left shoulder by a Japanese soldier in the battle of Guadalcanal. It took him two years to recuperate; after he did, he enrolled in Pennsylvania State University, where he starred on the baseball team and the football team, besides running the hundred-yard dash for the track team. Following his second spring with the baseball team in 1946, he signed a contract with the Brooklyn Dodgers for an estimated bonus of

$17,000. It was the highest bonus the Dodgers had ever given. Part of his agreement with Brooklyn was that he would be kept on the Dodgers the remainder of the season. Due to his inexperience, however, Joe was used sparingly, appearing in just 15 games, 10 of them as a pinch-runner. With the team in a tight pennant race with the Cardinals, general manager Branch Rickey offered Tepsic a reported $1,500 to accept assignment to the minors, but he stubbornly insisted on continuing to warm the Dodgers' bench, feeling he was better than most of the players on the team. Rickey had hoped to recall veteran Chet Ross. The Cardinals and Dodgers finished the regular season tied, and St. Louis won the playoff for the league title. Many Dodgers felt that Ross could have helped them win at least one extra game down the stretch and blamed their loss on Tepsic. They voted Joe just a one-eighth share of their second-place bonus money. In 1947, the Dodgers were no longer restricted from optioning Tepsic to the minors but when they did so, he indignantly said he would quit before going down. He did in fact go home for two weeks before agreeing to report to St. Paul. His attitude continued to be a problem; despite a .302 batting average, he was demoted to Fort Worth in the Texas League "to promote harmony on the team." Playing right field, Tepsic made a good impression in the Texas League with his speed, stealing 14 bases in his first 31 games before tailing off. However, the Dodgers sent him outright to Fort Worth after the season. He went to spring training with the Montreal Royals in 1948. He stayed with the Royals briefly; his only appearance with them was as a pinch-runner. When they assigned his contract to Nashua, Joe once again threatened to quit. As a compromise, he was sent to Lancaster in the Interstate League instead. He spent the next few years drifting around the minors. In 1952, Joe realized he wasn't going to make it in baseball and left the game. He returned home, where he owned and operated a small grocery store with a lunch counter, Village Dairy Store. Now retired, he lives in Tyrone, Pennsylvania.

Jack Dempsey Cassini's chance of becoming a major-league star ended almost before it started. He was born October 26, 1919, the third of five children born to O. J. and Ida (Sprague) Cassini. His younger brother Eddie would grow up to be a minor-league umpire. At the age of 20, Jack began his professional career by tearing apart the Ohio State League. Playing 99 games for Tiffin, he compiled a .396 batting average while scoring 118 runs and had a league-leading 51 steals. Following the season, his contract was acquired by the Cincinnati Reds organization, which assigned him to Ogden in the Pioneer League. He led that league in steals in 1941 but spent the next four years in the army. After the war, the now 26-year-old Cassini was assigned to Syracuse in the International League. After a slow start there, he was sent down to the Texas League, where he finally got his timing back while splitting his time between second, third, and shortstop. When Reds manager Johnny Neun asked him during spring training in 1947 which was his best position, Cassini replied that Bill McKechnie thought it was third, Jewel Ens believed it was second, and club president Warren Giles said he should look for a front-office job. The Reds' manager didn't appreciate that bit of humor and released Cassini. Jack went back to the Texas League, which he led in runs and stolen bases. During the season, he won a race against Joe Tepsic to determine who was the fastest man in the league. Tulsa, which had given Cassini a conditional $750 signing bonus the year before, now sold his contract to Indianapolis in the American Association for $6,500. After he led the American Association in steals in 1948, the Pittsburgh Pirates purchased his contract. Jack was a candidate for the third-base job but in his month with the club he got into only eight games, all as a pinch-runner. He scored three times, including the only run on opening day. Then he went back to the American Association. Following the 1949 season, he was traded to the Brooklyn Dodgers in a deal for Danny O'Connell. Jack spent four years playing for the Dodgers' farm club at St. Paul, leading the American Association twice in steals, giving him six league titles for his career. He made the all-star team in 1952 and 1953, making it five times he was so honored in Organized Baseball. Then he was traded to Montreal, where he spent one season. After the 1954 season he was obtained by Memphis of the Southern League to be their manager. Jack played second base for the Chicks and had them a game and a half out of first on August 2 when he was hit in the face with a pitch. He suffered a broken cheekbone and blurred vision. This put him out of action for the remainder of the season and effectively ended his playing career. He spent more than twenty years after that as a scout and minor-league manager. He is now retired and living in Arizona.

Howard Edward Phillips was born July 8, 1931, in St. Louis, Missouri. After graduating from Hannibal High School in 1949, where he earned letters in baseball, basketball, football, and track, he signed a contract with the St. Louis Cardinals organization. Eddie had a fine season in 1950 with West Frankfort in the Mississippi–Ohio

Progression of Pinch-Running Records (In cases of ties, only the first player is shown.)

Year	Player	Games
1904	John McGraw	4
1909	Bill O'Hara	16
1914	Sandy Piez	33
1926	Stuffy Stewart	34
1954	Dick Schofield	38
1962	Jack Reed	40
1974	Herb Washington	92

Year	Player	Runs
1904	George Winter	2
1909	Josh Devore	4
1910	Neal Ball	5
1911	Art Fletcher	7
1916	Mike McNally	10
1922	Les Mann	12
1926	Stuffy Stewart	13
1954	Dick Schofield	17
1966	Jackie Hernandez	18
1974	Herb Washington	29

Year	Player	Stolen Bases
1909	Bill O'Hara	6
1967	Allan Lewis	14
1974	Herb Washington	29
1976	Larry Lintz	30

Valley League, scoring 119 runs in 117 games and stealing 36 bases. Promoted to the Western Association in 1951, he led the league in triples while stealing 28 bases for St. Joseph. However, he would never again steal more than eight bases in a season. Phillips advanced to the Western League in 1952 and led it in batting average. A .306 batting average in the Texas League the next year, despite an ankle injury, led to his promotion to the Cardinals in September. Although he was able to play both infield and outfield, Eddie got into only nine games with St. Louis, all as a pinch-runner, scoring four times. Phillips started 1954 with Houston before being promoted to Columbus in the American Association. He would spend the next five seasons in Class AAA on six different teams. He also played in Panama for three winters, helping Carta Vieja to the pennant in the 1954–55 season. In March 1959, he married Joyce Ann Easley. After 1960, his playing career came to an end. He worked for the American Cyanamid Chemical Company for twenty-five years. He still lives in Hannibal, Missouri.

The bonus rules of 1946–50 and 1953–57 led to a lot of young players sitting on major-league benches rather than developing in the minors. Since they weren't ready to do anything else at that level, many were used extensively as pinch-runners. Some, like Al Kaline, went on to have great careers. Others, like **Tommy Carroll**, never achieved much else in baseball. Born September 17, 1936, in New York City, Tommy starred both athletically and scholastically at Bishop Loughlin Memorial High School. He then went to Notre Dame. After compiling a .550 batting average as a freshman and playing semipro ball in the summer, he was highly sought by professional teams. The Yankees beat out a dozen others, signing Carroll to a bonus estimated at anywhere from $35,000 to $60,000. Due to his bonus, he had to remain on the Yankees' roster for two years. In those seasons, he got into 50 games, pinch-running in 33 of them. He also pinch-ran twice in the 1955 World Series, which he called the greatest thrill of his career. At 6-foot-3, he was quite tall for a shortstop, and the Yankees tried him at third base in 1956. Following his bonus stint, the Yankees optioned him to Richmond for 1957, where he hit with some power but managed only a .213 batting average. He raised that to .283 in 1958, splitting the season between New Orleans and Denver. After that season, he did a six-month stretch in the army. For 1959, the Yankees sent him to Kansas City, but the now 22-year-old saw little action there and was sent down to the minors. Although he tried playing winter ball in Venezuela that year to help his chances of progressing, Tommy never returned to the majors. After playing a few more years, he left baseball and launched a long career in the State Department, serving as a diplomat in several countries in South America.

Mack Edwin Burk was born April 21, 1935, in Nacogdoches, Texas. Like Tommy Carroll, he was a bonus player, condemned to sit on a bench for two years. In Stephen Austin High School in Houston, he was an infielder. He got a basketball scholarship to the University of Texas in Austin, where he also caught for the baseball team. In his first start for the basketball team, he suffered a broken collarbone, which sidelined him the rest of the school year. He got back into action in the summer, playing for the Mechanics' Uniform Supply team in the American Baseball Congress and helping them win the national championship with a .420 batting average. Several major-league teams recruited him after that, and he signed with the Phillies for an estimated $40,000 in August 1955. Burk reported to the club in 1956. Philadelphia signed him as a catcher, but he got into only one game in the field; he also got to the plate just once, rifling a single off

Joe Nuxhall. His other 13 appearances were as a pinch-runner. Early in the 1957 season, Burk was drafted into the army, serving a six-month tour of duty. Following his release, he played ball in Panama. The bonus rule was revoked after the 1957 season, so Philadelphia was able to option Burk to the minors. He spent most of the 1958 season with Williamsport in the Eastern League. The Phillies did recall him briefly during the summer and used him once as a pinch-hitter. In 1959, he started out in the Eastern League, but after going 11 for 14 with three home runs over the Memorial Day weekend he earned a promotion to Buffalo in the International League. But the next year Mack was in the Sally League and then called it a career. After baseball, he worked in electrical-supplies sales. He still lives in Houston.

Don Eaddy escaped the bonus-rule trap but couldn't escape the long arm of Uncle Sam. Born February 16, 1934, in Grand Rapids, Michigan, Eaddy was a three-sport star at the University of Michigan. Playing under former major-leaguer Ray Fisher, he found baseball to be his best game; he was all-conference four times, making the All-America team as a senior third baseman. He led the Big Ten in stolen bases his senior year. After graduating with a bachelor-of-science degree, Eaddy was recruited by several teams. Not wanting to sit on a bench for two years as a bonus player but also hoping to get a shot in the big leagues quickly, Eaddy accepted an offer from the Chicago Cubs for a major-league contract at less than the bonus limit. He began his professional career as a shortstop with Des Moines in the Western League; in his first game he started a triple play. After a few games, he was sent to the Three-I League, where he finished the season with a .304 batting average. After getting a look in center field in spring training with the Cubs, Eaddy was back with Des Moines to start 1956. Don was carrying a .390 batting average after 11 games when he was called up by the air force for active duty. He spent the balance of 1956 and the next two years in the service. When he returned to baseball in 1959, Chicago was able to keep him on the roster as a twenty-sixth man, due to his status as a veteran. However, not long after cutdown day, the Cubs sent him down to the Eastern League. He soon earned a promotion to Fort Worth and in late July returned to Chicago for the balance of the season. Unfortunately, he didn't get to play much in either stint with the Cubs. Eaddy was used in just 15 games, 14 of them as a pinch-runner. Out of options, he was outrighted to Fort Worth after the season. He also went to Cuba in the winter, leading the league in walks and helping Cienfuegos win the Caribbean Series. Eaddy continued to play in the Cubs organization for five more years; he never stole more than nine bases in a season. In the winter of 1963–64, he helped Cinco Estrellas win the International Series. His .347 batting average in Nicaragua helped convince the Cubs to give him another look in 1964. They listed him as a candidate for the second-base job left vacant by Ken Hubbs's death, although he had played very little there, being mainly a third baseman. Ultimately, he didn't play there much in spring training either, mainly working at shortstop. He went back to the minors, where he closed out his career as a utility player for Salt Lake City. Following baseball, Don owned several Burger King franchises. In 1996, he was elected to the Grand Rapids Sports Hall of Fame. He died of cancer on July 8, 2008. One of four children, Don Eaddy was survived by his wife, Christine.

Roy Gleason was another player whose career was interrupted by military service. The only person to serve in Vietnam after playing Major League Baseball, he suffered serious battle wounds and never made it back to the big leagues. Roy William Gleason was born April 9, 1943, in Melrose Park, Illinois. A star outfielder and pitcher at Garden Grove High School in California, he signed with the Dodgers in June 1961 for an amount reported as being anywhere from $55,000 to $108,000. They envisioned him, at 6-foot-5½ inches and 227 pounds, as another Frank Howard but with speed. (He ran the 100-yard dash in 9.7 seconds.) A right-handed hitter in high school, he was taught by the Dodgers to switch-hit in the Arizona Instructional League. After looking him over in spring training in 1962, Pete Reiser said he "has the size, desire, speed, and arm to become a great player." As it turned out, the one thing he lacked was the ability to make contact. In the California League that year, he struck out 214 times in 448 at-bats. For his career, he would strike out an average of .48 times per at-bat. He did cut down his strikeouts some in the Northwest League in 1963, and in September he was called up to Los Angeles. Gleason appeared in seven games as a pinch-runner and one as a pinch-hitter, smacking a double. Roy never achieved the greatness predicted for him; those eight games were the extent of his major-league career. By 1965 the Dodgers were losing patience with him; he had been removed from the 40-man roster and, after a horrible start in the Northwest League, some consideration was given to converting him into a pitcher. He made a few appearances on the mound, but his arm proved to be as wild as his swing. In 19 career innings he walked 37 batters. He moved around a lot in the Dodgers organization. Gleason joked that "they don't even send me a contract anymore, they just mail me a new road map." In 1966 he did manage to lead the Northwest League in homers, as well as in strikeouts. Roy got his draft notice in April 1967 and soon shipped out to Vietnam. In his eight months there he served with distinction, winning a Bronze Star for pulling three injured soldiers to safety. Promoted to the rank of sergeant, he led search-and-destroy missions. On one such assignment, an explosion sent shrapnel through his leg and left wrist. That was the end of his military service. Roy went back to baseball, although his grip was weak due to his wrist injury. After one more year in the Dodgers' chain, he was drafted by the California Angels, who had him play in the Mexican League in 1970. Once again, he hit for power but struck out inordinately often. In January 1971 he was involved in a truck crash and suffered a broken collarbone. Trying to come back too soon, he reinjured it, bringing his playing career to an end.

Charlie Finley had many innovative ideas as owner of the Athletics. One of these was to include on the roster a player just to pinch-run. While Herb Washington was the most notorious of these players, the first to embody Finley's concept was **Allan Lewis**, the "Panamanian Express." Born December 12, 1941, in Colon, Panama, Lewis attended Felix Olivares High School. Signing with the Kansas City Athletics in 1961, he spent his first season in Albuquerque in the Sophomore League. Lewis did well enough to earn a promotion to the Florida State League in 1962, which would be his home for most of the next five seasons. Although he maintained a good batting average there (.298), he rarely walked and hit for very little power. During the winters, he would return home to Panama and play in the winter league there. In 1965 he made the Florida State League all-star team, stealing 76 bases. That still wasn't enough to earn him a further promotion, but he did finally grab Charlie Finley's attention in 1966 by leading the league in runs and hits while stealing a league record 116 bases. The A's purchased his contract and made him the subject of Finley's great experiment. Earlier pinch-runners rarely stole bases but that was what Lewis was there for. In 28 pinch-running appearances in 1967, he stole 14 bases in 19 attempts. (In his minor-league career his success rate was greater than 80 percent.) Lewis spent part of the season with the Athletics' Southern League team in Birmingham; he helped them to a pennant and hit .381 in the Dixie Series victory over Albuquerque of the Texas League. The A's cut him from their roster after the season, but he wasn't discouraged. In Panama that winter, he led the league with a .374 batting average as Balboa won the league championship. Lewis started the 1968 season in Birmingham and was promoted to the A's, now in Oakland, in August. The next few years were more of the same; he split his time between playing full-time in the minors and pinch-running for the A's. While Lewis could hit and field, he rarely got a chance to do so with the A's; he had only 31 plate appearances in 156 games during his six seasons with them. Allan never really won the acceptance of his Oakland teammates; many thought his roster spot should have gone to a more complete player. Management didn't always agree; when Reggie Jackson was hurt in the 1972 League Championship Series, they got permission to add Lewis to the World Series roster, and he pinch-ran in six of the seven games. Although he was caught stealing both times that he tried running on Johnny Bench, he did score the tying run in Game 4 and the final run in their 3–2 win in Game 7. Lewis's last year in the major leagues was 1973; he suffered a dislocated shoulder just before spring training ended, and at 31 he seemed to have lost some speed; he stole only 7 bases in 11 attempts in 35 games, although he did score a career-high 16 runs. He also scored a big run in the League Championship Series. His teammates voted him only a one-tenth share of their World Series money; meanwhile, he was voted the most popular player on Birmingham by their fans. After his playing career, he worked as a coach in the Panama League and as a scout for the Cleveland Indians and the Phillies, becoming the Phillies' Latin American scouting supervisor in 2003.

Donald Allen Wallace beat the odds to make the major leagues but couldn't stick around for long. Born August 25, 1940, in Sapulpa, Oklahoma, where his father owned a service station. Don attended Oklahoma State University, where he played shortstop on the baseball team, which made it to the NCAA finals in 1961. As a junior and again as a senior, he was third-team All-American. Following his graduation in 1962, he signed a contract with the Baltimore Orioles organization and played for Aberdeen in the Northern League. Wallace led the league with a .325 batting average and drew 76 walks in 89 games. Following the season, he was claimed by the St. Louis Cardinals in the first-year player draft. Failing to make the Cardinals, he was sold back to the Orioles, who sent him to Elmira in the Eastern League. Playing mostly second base, he was named to the league all-star team and that fall was drafted again, this time by the New York Yankees. The Yankees played him in AAA for the next two years, the first in the International League, where he was voted Richmond's most popular player and second fastest runner in the league. He also finished as runner-up for the Silver Glove award at shortstop for the second straight year. Then in 1966 he was optioned to Seattle, where as team MVP he helped the Angels to their first pennant in 11 years. That offseason saw him drafted for the third time, with Wallace becoming a member of the California Angels. Staying with the Angels for the first two months of the 1967 season, he saw action in 23 games, in 14 of them as a pinch-runner. He had some success in that role; in the April 21 game, he broke up a double play by avoiding the second baseman's tag, and Jim Fregosi followed with a two-run game-winning home run. However, he failed a couple of times. The previous day he was caught stealing home for the last out of the game, and on May 30 he failed to tag up in time to score the tying run in the eighth inning. Wallace wasn't a good enough hitter to win more playing time; his biggest weakness was an almost complete lack of power. On June 5, the Angels returned him to the minor leagues. Late that season, the Angels sent him to the Mets to complete an earlier deal for Hawk Taylor. Wallace had obtained a master's degree in education and by 1965 had taken an offseason teaching job at a high school in Kansas City. Having advanced to the position of assistant principal by 1967, in 1968 he was unable to return to playing until June, after the school year ended. Barely a month later, he retired from baseball, turning full-time to his career in education.

Herman Hill spent parts of two seasons with the Minnesota Twins, mainly as a pinch-runner. Just as he seemed on the verge of breaking out of that role, tragedy struck. Born in Tuskegee, Alabama, on October 12, 1945, one of 13 children, Herman Alexander Hill signed with the Twins as an undrafted free agent in 1966. After struggling his first year in the Gulf Coast League, Hill made the necessary adjustments and in 1967 became a Florida State League all-star. Stealing 58 bases in 68 attempts, Herman led the league in on-base average. He started the next season in the Carolina League and quickly earned a promotion to the Southern League. A .300 batting average and 31 steals for Denver in 1969 (after stealing 36 bases for Charlotte the year before) encouraged the Twins to call Herman up in September. He got into 16 games for them, 13 as a pinch-runner, scoring four runs. Hill, a left-handed-hitting outfielder, was once timed at 9.5 seconds in the 100-yard dash and could get down to first base in 3.4 seconds. In the winter, he played for Caguas in Puerto Rico. He went back to AAA to start 1970 but was recalled by the Twins in June. He spent three weeks with Minnesota, getting into 14 games, playing center field and pinch-hitting as well as pinch-running, but a .105 on-base percentage sent him back to Evansville. In September he was back with the Twins and this time was used mainly as a pinch-runner. After the season, the Twins, looking to bolster their bullpen, traded Hill and a minor-leaguer to the St. Louis Cardinals in exchange for Sal Campisi and Jim Kennedy. Once again, Hill played winter ball, this time for Magallanes in Venezuela. On a day off there, Herman went swimming with his wife and some of his teammates. A powerful wave pulled him out to sea and, although the others tried to rescue him, one nearly dying in the attempt, Hill drowned. He was the third career pinch-runner to meet that fate.

John Robert Gamble Jr. was born February 10, 1948, in Reno, Nevada, to John Sr. and Muriel (Westergard) Gamble. A shortstop at Carson City High School, he was drafted in the second round of the June 1966 amateur draft by the Los Angeles Dodgers. Gamble played that summer and the next in the Pioneer League. He stole only 8 bases in those two seasons, but for Daytona Beach in the Florida State League in 1968 he swiped 38 in 46 tries. His hitting and fielding didn't progress as quickly; he made 76 errors that year. After a brief stint in the California League in 1969, he spent the balance of that season and all of the next back with Daytona Beach, where he started playing third base. Although he had only a .298 slugging average in 1970, his 60 steals in 75 attempts were enough to get him drafted by the Detroit Tigers' organization. With the Tigers, he advanced up to AA in 1971 and to AAA Toledo in 1972, splitting time between short and third. In September 1972 he was called up by the Tigers and got into six games with them, four as a pinch-runner. In 1973 he was back in Toledo but was recalled by the Tigers in mid-May. Gamble scored the winning run in his first game back as a pinch-runner with Detroit. The Tigers used him six more times, always as a pinch-runner, before returning him to the minor leagues. In 1974 the Tigers moved their AAA affiliation to Evansville in the American Association, and Gamble finished his career there in 1976.

Perhaps the greatest pinch-runner in history, **Matt Alexander** pinch-ran 271 times, stealing 91 bases and scoring 89 runs, all records. He was born Matthew Alexander Jr. on January 30, 1947, in Shreveport, Louisiana. At

NATIONAL BASEBALL HALL OF FAME LIBRARY, COOPERSTOWN, N.Y.

Matt Alexander holds pinch-running records in three categories—appearances as a pinch-runner (271), stolen bases (91), and runs scored (89). In 1975, with Herb Washington now gone, Alexander and Don Hopkins became the Oakland A's "designated runners."

Bethune High School, he was an all-city basketball player and also pitched on the baseball team. His senior year, 1965, he helped them to the Louisiana State AAA Championship, getting two pitching wins in the playoffs, including one against Vida Blue. Matt played baseball at Grambling State University, making the all-conference team twice, and was later named to the Southwest Athletic Conference Hall of Fame. Chosen by the Chicago Cubs in the second round of the June 1968 amateur draft after his junior year, Matt started his professional career in the Pioneer League. Alexander made the all-star team as a second baseman there, although he stole only two bases. An .825 OPS and 23 steals in 71 games in the Midwest League the next year earned him a midseason promotion to the Texas League. At this point, he served two years in the navy. On returning to civilian life, he went back to the Texas League, where he stole 38 bases in 41 attempts. Alexander was promoted to AAA in 1973 and got his first taste of the major leagues in August, seeing action in 12 games for the Cubs, mostly as a pinch-runner. The following season he was with the Cubs most of the year, getting a chance to play third base when Bill Madlock was hurt, but eventually a pulled leg muscle slowed him down. Since he was out of options, the Cubs sent him outright to Wichita after the season. And then, a week into the 1975 season, the Oakland A's acquired him to be their newest "designated runner." His new teammates, who were unhappy with the Herb Washington experiment and less than thrilled with having a second roster spot filled by runner Don Hopkins, soon took a liking to Alexander. Matt, who replaced Washington on the Oakland roster, was a switch-hitter who could play both infield and outfield and was a smart runner as well. Gene Tenace called him "100 percent better than Hopkins or [Washington]." Alexander wasn't used in any League Championship Series games that year, however. With the club weakened by free agency, the A's gave up on Alexander after the 1977 season. Out of baseball, he started attending barber college back home in Shreveport. When rosters expanded in September 1978, though, the Pittsburgh Pirates signed him, and he would be with them on and off through the 1981 season. Although once again used mainly as a pinch-runner, Matt came through when asked to hit, going 12 for 27 with the Bucs. In 1979, when Pittsburgh won the NL East, Alexander finally got to participate in the postseason, scoring a run in his only LCS game and being caught stealing in Game 2 of the World Series. When the Pirates released him, he continued his playing career in the Mexican League. In 1983, at the age of 36, Matt proved he could still run, stealing a league-record 73 bases. He played a few more years in Mexico and then retired.

The Oakland A's, happy enough with their "designated runner" experiment in 1974, decided to add a second such speedster in 1975, although this one would be a real baseball player, **Don Hopkins**. Hopkins was born January 9, 1952, in West Point, Mississippi. He starred in four sports at Benton Harbor High School. Hopkins helped the baseball team to the Michigan state championship; he also ran a 9.5 second 100-yard dash for the track team. After high school, he signed as an undrafted free agent with the Montreal Expos. After a brief stint in the Gulf Coast League in 1970, he advanced to the Class A Northern League in 1971. Here he first showed his ability as a base stealer. Despite garnering only 39 hits in 191 at-bats, he stole a league-leading 39 bases. An .843 fielding average as an outfielder showed his weakness with the bat was matched by his glove. The following year, he set a New York–Pennsylvania League record with 63 stolen bases. Hopkins was thrown out only 9 times in 70 games. He split 1973 between the Florida State and Eastern Leagues, stealing an additional 58 bases, including 5 in one game for Quebec City. A .232 slugging average in the Eastern League, though, overshadowed his running. In 1974 he finally showed some promise with the bat, managing a .366 on-base average in the Carolina League. He also saw time in AA and AAA that year. Near the end of spring training in 1975, his contract was purchased by the Oakland A's. The idea was to have another runner who, like Allan Lewis, could be used in the field and could hit when needed. However, the reality was that Hopkins rarely did either, playing only 10 innings in the outfield and getting only 8 plate appearances in his 82 games in 1975. His 74 games as a pinch-runner is second only to Herb Washington's 92 in 1974. In addition, Hopkins in the major leagues wasn't as successful on the bases as he had been in the minors. He carried a career 84 percent success rate in the minors but had stolen only 15 bases in 24 attempts when the A's sent him back to AAA in early August. He did better when recalled in September, stealing 6 bases in as many tries, but in 1976 the A's decided they could get along without his services, bringing him back in September for just three more pinch-running appearances. After one more year in AAA, his playing career came to an end.

After Matt Alexander's release in 1977, the Oakland A's waited less than a year to add another pinch-runner to their roster. **Darrell Lee Woodard** was born December 10, 1956, in Wilmar, Arkansas, to Eardee and Arthalene (Sanders) Woodard. At Bell High School in Los Angeles, California, he earned letters in four sports. After high school he signed with the A's as an undrafted free agent. A shortstop, he spent his first two years in professional ball in the short-season Northwest League. In 1975, he led the league in fielding average as the league's all-star shortstop and had a fine .408 on-base average. However, he had only seven extra base hits in 246 at-bats. He spent the next two seasons in the California League, reaching base at a good rate but showing almost no power. Woodard shifted to second base during the 1976 season. In 1977, teamed with Rickey Henderson on Modesto, Woodard stole a remarkable 90 bases in 97 attempts, while Henderson added a league-leading 95 steals. The following year saw him playing in the AA Eastern League; in August he was brought up to the A's. In his first game, on August 6, he scored the winning run as a pinch-runner. Darrell got into 33 games with Oakland, 22 as a pinch-runner. He also saw action at second base and even once at third but failed to get a hit in nine at-bats. As a pinch-runner, his success was mixed, being thrown out stealing four times in seven attempts but also scoring nine times. The following year he was involved in an unusual transaction as the A's sent him and another player to the Miami team in the new Inter-American League in exchange for George Mitterwald, who was to serve as Oakland's bullpen coach. Miami won both halves of the abbreviated season; when the league ceased play on June 30, Woodard joined Midland in the Texas League before finishing the year with Wichita in the American Association. Darrell started in the South Atlantic League in 1980 and worked his way back to AA, playing for Birmingham in the Southern League in 1981 and 1982, but Woodard's playing career ended there.

Alberto Lois was once called "a young Roberto Clemente." Like Clemente, he was sometimes accused of malingering, and his career ended prematurely. Unlike Clemente, however, he never became a star. Alberto Lois was born May 6, 1956, in Hato Mayor, Dominican Republic, to Eligio and Lucio (Feliciano) Lois. He was signed for the Pittsburgh Pirates by legendary scout Howie Haak in 1974. That year he played 119 games in the Western Carolinas League, stealing 37 bases in 49 attempts. However, he would never play as many as 100 games in any subsequent season. Repeated injuries, some of which the Pirates suspected were not serious enough to keep him out of the lineup, limited his playing time. Lois also reported late to spring training each year, causing the Pirates to question his desire. Nelson Norman, former Pirates shortstop, who played ball with Lois when they were youngsters, said Lois was undisciplined and yet so talented that he would come to a game drunk and still get two or three hits. Still, he advanced rapidly through their farm system. In 1976, 12 triples and 24 stolen bases in 65 games in the Texas League led to his promotion to AAA. He closed the season in Charleston of the International League with a .300 batting average. In 1977, he got off to a fast start at Columbus but the injury bug struck again, and Lois played only 42 games that year. He was hurt again in 1978, and he spent time down in the Carolina League getting some playing time. Come September, though, the Pirates called him up, although he would see limited action. It was pretty much the same story in 1979. This time, however, he was recalled in mid-August for a week and then again in September, doing nothing but pinch-running in 11 games, scoring six times. During the winter, Alberto returned home and played in the Dominican Winter League. Then a tragedy brought his playing career to a screeching halt. On his way home from a game, driving a truckload of friends, he tried to beat a train to a crossing and failed. The resulting collision cost the lives of six of his passengers.

Lois's right eye was injured in the wreck, and his impaired vision left him unable to play again.

Thaddeaus Inglehart (Ted) Wilborn was born December 16, 1958, in Waco, Texas, to Charles and Yvonne (Inglehart) Wilborn. His brother Chuck played several years in the San Diego Padres' organization. Ted was drafted in the fourth round of the June 1976 amateur draft by the Yankees and was assigned to Oneonta of the New York–Pennsylvania League, where he struggled. His second season in pro ball was spent in the Florida State League, where he also had trouble hitting, although he did draw 45 walks in 262 plate appearances. It was his third season that was his breakthrough year, 1978. Formerly a left-handed hitter, he starting switch-hitting. Sent back to the NYP, Wilborn stole 57 bases in just 65 games for Oneonta. Combined with a .428 on-base percentage, that was enough to induce the Toronto Blue Jays to make him a Rule 5 draftee. Required by the rules to keep him on their active roster for three months or risk losing him, the Blue Jays used Wilborn in 22 games, 15 as a pinch-runner, before optioning him to the International League. Following the season, the Yankees reobtained Wilborn in a multiplayer trade. They sent the switch-hitting outfielder to their Nashville farm team, recalling him in September. Ted got into eight games with New York, pinch-running in four of them. That was the end of his major-league career. He spent 1981 back in Nashville, leading the Southern League in runs scored and for the first time playing some at second base. After the season, Wilborn was traded to the San Francisco Giants along with Andy McGaffigan for Doyle Alexander. Ted spent several more years playing minor-league ball. His playing career came to an end after just one game in the International League in 1987. ■

A version of this article appeared originally online at http://members.dslextreme.com/users/brak2.0/legmen.htm.

Sources

Baseball Magazine, Binghamton Press, Boston Herald, Chicago Tribune, Hartford Courant, Los Angeles Times, New York Times, Portsmouth Times, Scioto Voice, Tacoma News Tribune, Tennessean, The Sporting News, Washington Post

Ancestry.com. http://www.ancestry.com/.

Arkush, Michael. "Five-Star Ball Player: Roy Gleason." *The VVA Veteran*, May/June 2004.

Baseball Almanac. "Grambling State University Baseball Players Who Made It to the Major Leagues." www.baseball-almanac.com/college/grambling_state_university_baseball_players.shtml.

Baseball Reference. www.baseball-reference.com/.

Tony Grullón. "Beisbol y Salud." http://espanol.geocities.com/saludybeisbol/archivos/desde_panama.htm.

Biographical Register of the Department of State, 1974.

College Football Data Warehouse. "John R. 'Dinny' McNamara Records by Year." http://cfbdatawarehouse.com/data/coaching/alltime_coach_year_by_year.php?coachid=1576.

Figuerdo, Jorge S. *Cuban Baseball: A Statistical History, 1878–1961.* Jefferson, N.C.: McFarland, 2003.

Heritage Quest. www.heritagequestonline.com/hqoweb/library/do/index.

Johnson, Lloyd, and Miles Wolff, eds. *The Encyclopedia of Minor League Baseball.* Durham, N.C.: Baseball America, 1997.

Lee, Bill. *The Baseball Necrology.* Jefferson, N.C.: McFarland, 2003.

Marazzi, Richard. *Aaron to Zipfel*, New York: Avon Books, 1985.

Marazzi, Richard, and Len Fiorito. *Baseball Players of the 1950s: A Biographical Dictionary of All 1,560 Major Leaguers.* Jefferson, N.C.: McFarland, 2004.

Moffi, Larry, and Jonathan Kronstadt. *Crossing the Line: Black Major Leaguers, 1947–1959.* Jefferson, N.C.: McFarland, 1994.

National Baseball Hall of Fame Library. http://abner.baseballhalloffame.org/search.

New York Public Library. www.nypl.org/.

Pioneer League. www.pioneerleague.com/.

Ruck, Robert. *The Tropic of Baseball: Baseball in the Dominican Republic.* Westport, Conn.: Meckler Publishing, 1990.

Rutgers University Athletics. www.scarletknights.com/.

Society for American Baseball Research Collegiate Committee database. www.ncaa-baseball.com/sabr/database/?m=5&s=174.

Society for American Baseball Research Encyclopedia. http://members.sabr.org/members.cfm?a=rtl&rtl=enc.

Society for American Baseball Research Scouts Committee.

Society for American Baseball Research. *Minor League Baseball Stars*, revised edition. Cleveland: SABR, 1984.

The Sporting News. Official Baseball Register. Charlotte, N.C.. The Sporting News.

The VVA Veteran. www.vva.org/veteran.html.

Wright, Marshall. *The International League Year-by-Year Statistics, 1884–1953.* Jefferson, N.C.: McFarland, 1998.

Herb Washington's Value to the 1974 A's

Scott Schleifstein

TWO WEEKS before the start of the 1974 season, Oakland Athletics owner Charles O. Finley signed Herb Washington as a "designated runner"—in the long, storied history of Major League Baseball, the first and only player whose sole responsibility was to run the bases. Baseball historians and fans have not treated "Hurricane Herb" Washington kindly over the years. Washington is often cited as a sideshow à la Bill Veeck's midget Eddie Gaedel—as an example of Finley's flamboyant if not downright bizarre ownership style or as just some kind of strange joke. One pundit dubbed Washington "the most superfluous (hence greatest) hood ornament on the biggest, baddest Blue Moon Odomest Cadillac in the league."[1]

On learning that he had collected 29 stolen bases in his only full season in the majors, I had as my original intention in writing this article to recall and honor Washington's achievement. I saw Washington as vaguely heroic, the star of a reality-TV drama, "So You Want to Be a Major League Baseball Player?" The establishment, save Finley, expected Washington to fall on his face (figuratively, if not literally), making him the ultimate underdog. Surely, I thought, my research would prove that the critics were wrong in their hasty, probably mean-spirited dismissal of Washington. I knew in my heart that those 29 stolen bases had to mean something, especially since the A's were world champions in 1974.

ALLAN LEWIS, "THE PANAMANIAN EXPRESS"

Perhaps the best place to start is with the man to whom the A's previously assigned their pinch-running duties: Allan Lewis. Lewis began his career with the Kansas City Athletics in 1967. During his career (which ended with his release after the 1973 season), Lewis stole 44 bases in 61 attempts for a 72.1 percent success rate. Lewis's highest yearly stolen-base total was 14 in 1967.

Although theoretically Lewis could hit and field, he did neither with much proficiency. A's manager Dick Williams commented that "he was strictly a runner. I don't know if Lewis even owned a glove."[2] If anything, Lewis was an "emergency" fielder. In *Baseball's Last Dynasty: Charlie Finley's Oakland A's*, Bruce Markusen recounts a 15-inning loss to Chicago on September 19, 1972, when Lewis, "who almost never played a defensive position," pinch-ran for first baseman Mike Epstein in the eighth inning and played right field, where he remained until the fourteenth inning.[3]

It is therefore something of a misrepresentation to say that Washington deprived a "real" ballplayer of his roster spot.[4] If Washington replaced anybody, it was Lewis. In signing Washington, Finley decisively (and perhaps misguidedly) embraced the notion of the designated pinch-runner. In switching from a player whose *major* function was pinch-running to another for whom that was his *sole* function, Finley merely refined a tactic he had already developed with Lewis. In other words, perhaps the real innovation can be found with the use of Lewis in 1973. Finley's signing of Washington merely built on that precedent.

THE DH REVOLUTION

The institution of the designated-hitter rule also provides some important perspective for evaluating Herb Washington's 1974 performance. For many (including me) who as baseball fans came of age after the American League had adopted the "designated pinch-hitter" for the 1973 season, the DH is a given, but it should be remembered that the introduction of the DH represented a drastic rules change.[5] Other ideas proposed by Finley to spice up the game for the modern era were interleague play, the three-ball walk, and the designated pinch-runner.[6] In the version of the DH rule proposed by Finley, a pinch-runner would be used *without* the replaced player (i.e., the batter) being removed from the game. The designated runner would apparently complement the designated hitter, taking over the baserunning chores if and when the DH reached base. When the final ballot among American League owners featured the DH but not Finley's "DR," Finley voted against this diluted version of his original designated-hitter rule.[7]

As reported in the *Philadelphia Inquirer* in October 1974, A's manager Alvin Dark, speaking of Washington's contribution to the team, advocated use of the designated pinch-runner. "What I'd like to see baseball try next is using a designated runner for the designated hitter. How much longer would a Mickey Mantle have been around with somebody to run for him?"[8] In spring

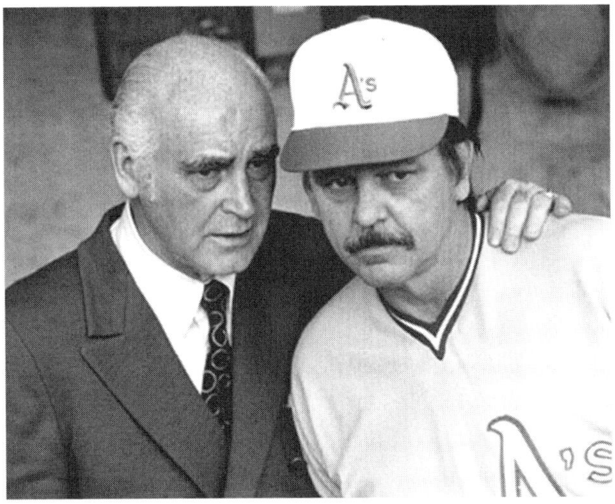
COURTESY OF THE OAKLAND ATHLETICS

A's owner Charlie Finley and manager Dick Williams (1971–73). Williams managed Allan Lewis, Herb Washington's predecessor as the A's "designated runner," a position Finley wanted the American League to formalize.

training 1975, the year *after* Washington's turn as a pinch-running specialist, the American League granted Finley's request to use Washington as a pinch-runner up to four or five times per exhibition game.[9]

Against this backdrop, the idea of a designated pinch-runner does not sound so crazy anymore. Now that MLB had already taken the radical step of allowing a position player to bat for a pitcher throughout the course of a game, having a player "do the running" for a hitter can be seen to represent a natural extension of that thinking. As with the DH, the objective is the same—to inject more offense into the game. It is logically inconsistent to accept the DH on the one hand and, on the other, to reject the designated pinch-runner as absurd or silly. The two differ only in *degree*, not *kind*. If anything, the designated runner is a less extreme modification, as only one *aspect* of the offensive player's responsibilities has been transferred to another player. Compare this to the designated-hitter rule, which completely eliminated the pitcher as an offensive player, thereby altering the very rhythm of the game.

WHY HERB WASHINGTON?

At first glance, at least, one can readily understand why Finley chose Washington to be his designated pinch-runner. He was fast. Washington was a four-time All-American at Michigan State University, lettering in track and football. Among his other accomplishments, he set records for both the 50- and 60-yard dash as well as capturing the Big Ten Conference championship for the 100-yard dash in 1970, 1971, and 1972. After seeing Washington compete in an indoor track meet on television, Dark recommended that Finley sign him.[10] Such was Washington's ability that a live tryout on a baseball diamond was deemed unnecessary by Dark; apparently neither Dark nor Finley was concerned that Washington's only previous baseball experience was in high school. Dark and Finley weren't the only ones who saw in Washington's foot speed the potential to excel at the highest levels of professional sports. The NFL's Baltimore Colts and the World Football League's Toronto Northmen both wanted to sign Washington as a wide receiver.[11]

THE STATISTICS

In the 1974 campaign, Washington stole 29 bases in 45 attempts, for a success rate of 64.4 percent. Here's how Washington's performance stacks up against those of the other top ten AL base stealers in 1974:

Table 1.

Player	Rank	Steals	Attempts	Percentage
Billy North	1	54	80	67.5
Rod Carew	2	38	54	70.3
John Lowenstein	3	36	53	67.9
Bert Campaneris	4	34	49	71.4
Freddie Patek	5	33	48	68.8
Mickey Rivers	6	30	43	69.8
Don Baylor	7	29	41	70.7
Herb Washington	**7**	**29**	**45**	**64.4**
Tommy Harper	9	28	40	70.0
Paul Blair	10	27	36	75.0

Table 1 shows that, to some extent, Washington's performance was weaker than those of the other top American League basestealers in 1974. Table 2 corroborates this initial conclusion as it provides a look at Washington's statistics in the context of the sabermetric of net stolen bases, which gives a more refined and realistic assessment of Washington's value.[12]

Table 2.

Player	Rank	Net Stolen Bases
Paul Blair	1	+9
Rod Carew	2	+6
Don Baylor	3	+5
Bert Campaneris	4	+4
Mickey Rivers	4	+4
Tommy Harper	4	+4
Freddie Patek	7	+3
Billy North	8	+2
John Lowenstein	9	+2
Herb Washington	**10**	**-3**

COURTESY OF THE OAKLAND ATHLETICS

Alvin Dark, A's manager (1966–67, 1974–75), saw Washington run in an indoor track meet and recommended that Finley sign him. Dark commented to a reporter that Washington "won eight games for us by himself" in the second half of the 1974 season, although scrutiny of the record suggests that the manager overestimated the value of his designated pinch-runner.

By this measure, Washington's baserunning actually did more harm than good, *hurting* the A's chances of scoring (and winning). The lost scoring opportunities of the caught-stealing outcomes overshadowed the positive effect of his 29 total stolen bases. It also bears noting that the other top AL basestealers all landed on the plus side of the ledger, representing a net gain to their teams.

Another sabermetric, run-expectancy matrix, confirms what tables 1 and 2 tell us. Using run-expectancy matrix, one can gauge the impact of the attempted stolen base (be it successful or not) on a team's potential to score runs. Data from Baseball-Prospectus.com show the likelihood of a team scoring during the 1974 season. For example, with a runner on first base and no outs, a team scored, on average, .826833 times in 1974; in contrast, with no runners on base with one out, teams scored only .24098 times.[13] When we follow this reasoning, a failed stolen-base attempt decreases a team's likelihood of scoring by resulting in an out and removing a baserunner; it is the cost of a caught-stealing. In my example, that cost is .585853 runs.[14]

To apply run-expectancy matrix to Washington's 1974 season, I reviewed play-by-play accounts of all A's games in which Washington attempted a stolen base (available via Retrosheet.org) to determine how his performance affected the A's opportunities to score runs. The result: Washington cost the A's 1.11054 runs over the course of the season. Even more egregiously, during the stretch drive to the end of the regular season in September and October, the cost balloons to 1.79352 runs. Against divisional foes, Washington's cost is even higher, topping out at 2.18809 runs.[15] These numbers become all the more decisive in that, unlike the case of Allan Lewis, Washington's baserunning was the only way he could contribute to the A's success.[16]

The data support the notion that there is an art to a basestealing—something more than raw speed alone is needed for success. If anything, it is this skill as practiced by an experienced player that makes the stolen base attempt an informed risk (notwithstanding the gospel of sabermetrics) as opposed to a "Hail Mary" desperation tactic. It seems safe to assume that Washington's performance suffered because he failed to augment his natural abilities with baseball knowledge.[17] As some of his critics sardonically commented at the time, Washington was operating at a distinct disadvantage as there was no starter's gun and/or runners blocks on the infield.[18] More specifically, even with the tutelage of Los Angeles Dodgers' basestealing legend Maury Wills[19] and teammate Billy North[20] (among others), Washington lacked the ability to effectively read pitchers' pick-off moves and get a good lead or jump.[21]

THROUGH AN (ALVIN) DARK LENS

With the foregoing in mind, it is interesting to consider Athletics' manager Alvin Dark's take on Washington's season. As noted above, Dark commented to Bill Lyon of the *Philadelphia Inquirer* that "Herb has won eight games for us by himself since July 1." Dark then cited two games as proof of his point: "In Minnesota we put him in and they pitched out three straight times. We went on to a four-run inning. In Anaheim they were so worried about him that they kept pitching out and we got three runs and won 7–5."[22]

Let's look at each game individually. The second game was the A's 7–5 win over the California Angels on July 2, 1974. Washington was inserted into the game as a pinch-runner for Joe Rudi with one out in the eighth inning. At the time, Oakland led California 5–3. On the strength of a home run and double by Angel Mangual, the A's had already knocked starter Frank Tanana from the game. Oakland's starting pitcher, Ken Holtzman, had been touched up for seven hits through the first five innings but none in the sixth or seventh. As Washington entered the game, the game was close and the outcome still in doubt.

As Dark suggested, the Angels' worrying about Washington may have resulted in pitcher Skip Lockwood walking Gene Tenace. But, maybe not. Dark's thesis is at least somewhat suspect, as Tenace led the American League with 110 bases on balls—many pitchers gave Tenace a free pass without the "distraction" posed by Washington. More tellingly, Tenace fared well against Lockwood over the course of his career, hitting .318 (7 for 22) with two home runs, four RBI, and six walks in total. Given that former A's manager Dick Williams was at the helm of the Angels and obviously knew the opposition well, it is improbable that Lockwood or California took Washington too seriously. Moreover, Lockwood must have found his groove quickly, as he struck out the next batter, the "hot" Angel Mangual, who had driven in four runs off Tanana. The decisive blow was a single, by pinch-hitter Pat Bourque, that scored Washington and Tenace. (Dark incorrectly recalled that the A's scored three runs in the inning—they actually scored two). From the play-by-play summary at Retrosheet, it appears that Pat Bourque's clutch hitting proved decisive and that Washington had precious little to do with the favorable result. So far, Dark is 0–1.

The Minnesota game mentioned by Dark is tougher to pinpoint. A review of Oakland's 1974 contests against the Twins in Minnesota suggests that Dark was referring to a game on May 21.

In that game, Washington pinch-ran for pinch-hitter Sal Bando in the seventh inning. At the beginning of the inning, the score was tied at 1–1. Oakland scored six times in the inning, with four of these runs coming after Washington had entered the game; thus, when Washington made his appearance, the score was 3–1 in Oakland's favor. According to Dark's account, Minnesota focused their attention on Washington, yielding a walk to Billy North. This put runners on first and second with none out. In this instance, given North's relatively pedestrian career numbers against relief pitcher Tom Burgmeier (who had relieved starter Joe Decker after the A's scored on a Gene Tenace home run to start the inning)—0 for 2 up to this point, 3 for 12 (all singles) in his career—Dark's case for Washington's effect on the pitcher is at least somewhat stronger. Bert Campaneris then laid down a sacrifice bunt, moving Washington to third and North to second. Burgmeier served up a sacrifice fly to Joe Rudi, scoring Washington, followed by a two-run homer to Reggie Jackson. For the final run of the inning, Pat Bourque doubled home Angel Mangual, who had singled. Again, it is tough to see how Washington affected the outcome beyond possibly contributing to the walk to North. Still, it is worth noting that Burgmeier previously had Joe Rudi's number. Rudi was 0 for 5 against Burgmeier up to this point, and in his career he had a paltry two hits off him in 16 at-bats, for a .125 average.

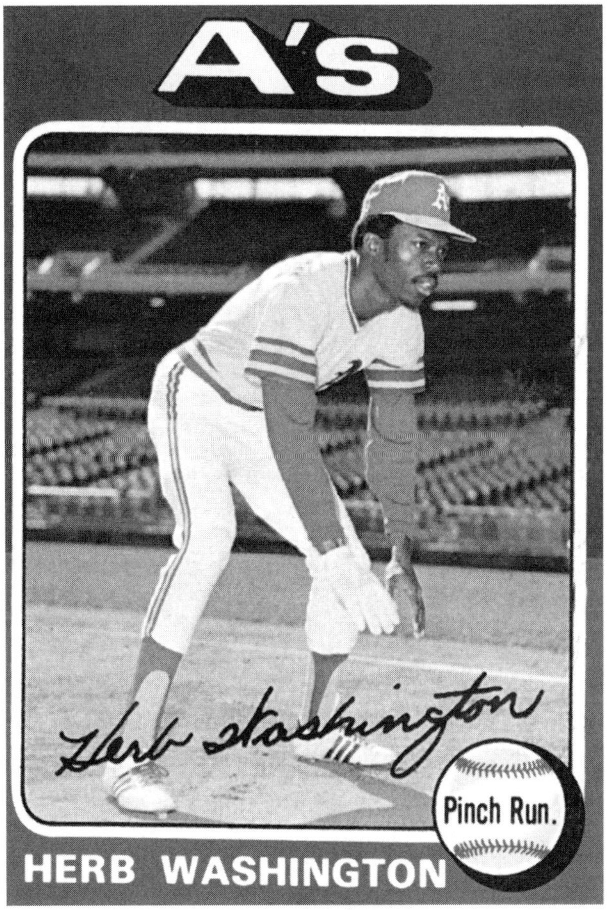

HERB WASHINGTON, 1975, NO. 407, COURTESY OF THE TOPPS COMPANY, INC.

In two seasons (1974–75) for the Oakland A's, Herb Washington scored 33 runs, stole 31 bases, and was caught stealing 17 times. Run-expectancy matrix applied to his 1974 season indicates that his performance cost his team more runs than it gained.

On the other hand, one of those two hits would be a home run. In any event, the real muscle in the inning was provided *before* and *after* Washington was on the field. While this is a somewhat closer call than the Angels game, Dark is 0–2.

Puzzlingly, Dark in his comments about Washington omitted several appearances in which Washington did demonstrate value to the team. In the eighth inning of the August 2 game at Chicago, with two outs, Billy North singled off Wilbur Wood and stole second. Sal Bando knocked in North with a single, tying the game at 2–2, prompting White Sox manager Chuck Tanner to summon relief pitcher Terry Forster to stop the bleeding. Washington came in to pinch-run for Bando, stealing second. Reggie Jackson then drove home Washington with a single, giving the A's a lead they would not relinquish.

On August 13 against the Yankees, the A's led 3–1 going into the bottom of the seventh. Replacing Dal Maxvill (who had drawn a walk), Washington stole second off Doc Medich and Thurman Munson and took third on Munson's throwing error, one of three errors for Munson on the day. Now, rather than having a man on first with none out, the A's had a runner on third base. Billy North singled Washington home, giving the A's a three-run cushion and ending Medich's day. The A's scored twice more that inning en route to a 6–1 triumph.

More stunning still is Dark's claim that Washington "can't lose us a game" because "he can't strike out with the bases loaded" or "drop a fly ball."[23] Overall, I counted eleven different situations during the 1974 regular season where Washington's performance directly hurt the A's chances of winning a ballgame.[24] By way of illustration:

- On May 4 against Cleveland, Washington pinch-ran for Pat Bourque in the seventh inning. Gaylord Perry picked Washington off first, but Washington took second on an error by first baseman John Ellis. Undeterred, Perry picked Washington off second base, ending the inning in a game Cleveland won 8–2.

- On May 7 against Baltimore, Washington pinch-ran for Gene Tenace with one out in the ninth inning and the A's trailing by six runs. Angel Mangual lined out to second baseman Bobby Grich, who threw to first baseman Enos Cabell to complete the double play and end the ballgame. Where was Washington going? He should have been anchored to first base, as the play was in front of him.

- On August 19 against Milwaukee, Bert Campaneris led off the eighth inning with a single. Washington was inserted as a pinch-runner and was promptly caught stealing second. The Brewers would prevail 1–0.

- On September 25 against Minnesota, Washington replaced Jesus Alou in the sixth inning and stole second base. (So far, so good.) Billy North sacrificed Washington to third. Then Twins catcher Phil Roof picked Washington off third, ending the rally and preserving the Twins' 1–0 lead. The Twins would go on to win the game by that count.

In the Lyon article, Herb Washington takes up his own *pro se* defense of his baseball credibility, noting that, in a game against Cleveland's Gaylord Perry, he scored from third base "on a short fly to left." With a little sleuthing, we know that Washington is speaking of the A's–Indians game on July 8. With one out in the top of the ninth inning and Cleveland holding a one-run lead, Joe Rudi tripled off Perry. Washington ran for Rudi. A Gene Tenace sacrifice fly scored Washington with the tying run. The A's went on to win the game in the tenth inning. Washington exacted revenge on Gaylord Perry for his rough treatment about two months earlier.

Here, Washington may have a point. A ball hit to left is tougher to score on than a ball hit to center or right: The throw from left to the third-base side of the plate is shorter. Also relevant is that the left fielder, John Lowenstein, had only an average arm.[25] Washington's speed very well *could have* made the difference, enabling him to score when someone else might not have.

In sum, however, the statistical evidence clearly suggests that Washington's stint as a "designated runner" was pure folly. If anything, the A's succeeded in capturing their third consecutive championship in spite of (not because of) him. Rather than being a "hood ornament"—a thing of aesthetic appeal, which does not affect a vehicle's performance—Washington *impaired* the functioning of the "biggest, baddest Blue Odomest Cadillac in the league." ■

NOTES

1. See Josh Wilker, "Herb Washington" (7 December 2006), http://cardboardgods.baseballtoaster.com/archives/609836.html (accessed 30 April 2009).
2. Glenn Dickey, *Champions: The Story of the First Two Oakland A's Dynasties—and the Building of the Third* (Chicago: Triumph Books, 2002), 35.
3. Bruce Markusen, *Baseball's Last Dynasty—Charlie Finley's Oakland A's* (Indianapolis: Master's Press, a division of Howard W. Sams, 1998), 128.
4. Among others, A's catcher and first baseman Gene Tenace expressed this view. See Markusen, 287.
5. The *Baseball Digest* (April 1973) devoted nine pages to "The Designated Pinch-Hitter Rule," including "Pro" and "Con" columns by Shirley

Povich (of the *Washington Post*) and Harold Kaese (of the *Boston Globe*), respectively.

6. Markusen, 17; see also Dickey, 11–12.
7. Markusen, 183–84.
8. Bill Lyon, "They Scoffed but Dark Says Washington Has Won 8 for A's," *Philadelphia Inquirer*, 13 October 1974.
9. "A's Runner on Spot This Time," UPI, 20 March 1975 (from National Baseball Hall of Fame, player file for Herb Washington).
10. Dickey, 77.
11. If anything, Washington had more recent experience as a football player than as a baseball player. According to the article "Herb Washington" (November 2003), at Simply Baseball Notebook: Forgotten in Time, http://z.lee28.tripod.com/sbnsforgottenintime/id24.html (accessed 30 April 2009), Washington was a wide receiver on the Michigan State football team in 1971 and 1972, catching one pass for 41 yards
12. For an explanation of "net stolen bases," see, for instance, Rich Lederer's article "Net Stolen Bases: Leaders and Laggards" (25 October 2006), Baseball Analysts, http://baseballanalysts.com/archives/2006/10/net_stolen_base.php (accessed 30 April 2009). In general, the underlying concept is that "caught stealing" must reflect not only that an out was recorded but also that a runner has been removed from the basepaths and a scoring opportunity eliminated. As Retrosheet categorizes being picked off as a form of caught stealing, I used the following formula to derive net stolen bases: Net stolen bases = Stolen bases – (2 x caught stealing).
13. See Baseball Prospectus, www.baseballprospectus.com/statistics/sortable/index.php?cid=148993 (accessed 30 April 2009).
    For an introduction to run expectancy matrix (as well as a more general application of sabrmetrics to stolen base attempts), see "Thou Shalt Not Steal" (14 January 2009), Backell's Big Blog of Bodacious Brewing Brainstorms, www.sportingnews.com/blog/backell/130093 (accessed 4 May 2009).
14. When considered in the context of run-expectancy matrix, the stolen-base attempt can be fairly characterized as something of a gamble. The cost of failure (an out and the loss of a baserunner) outstrips the potential benefits (moving a base runner into scoring position without sacrificing an out). To illustrate using the above example: If the runner had stolen second base with no outs, a team's likelihood of scoring would rise only to 1.07689. This represents a "gain" of .25006 runs, as compared to the possible cost of .585853 runs.
15. Still, this figure is something of a restatement of the immediately preceding calculation, as from September 2 through the end of the 1974 season the A's played against only teams in the AL West.
16. As Sal Bando pointedly commented, although Lewis's talent may have been negligible, he "could play a position here or there if you needed somebody." See Markusen, 209.
17. Markusen recounts an early regular-season game where Washington asked his manager whether he should steal second base—even though the base was occupied at the time. Markusen, 294.
18. See article "Finley Worships Speedsters," 13 April 1974 (from National Baseball Hall of Fame, player file for Herb Washington).
19. Markusen, 286–87.
20. See article "A's Washington Is Gaining Respect of His Teammates," 18 August 1974 (from National Baseball Hall of Fame, player file for Herb Washington).
21. As Washington was a true neophyte, the issue of the comparative merit of *jump* versus *lead* is moot here.
22. See n. 8.
23. See n. 7. For absolute irony, the date of the Lyon article coincided with that of Washington's ignominious performance in the ninth inning of Game 2 of the 1974 World Series, when he was picked off first base by Los Angeles Dodgers reliever Mike Marshall. The Dodgers won Game 2 and evened the series at one game apiece.
24. I admit to a significant amount of subjectivity here, especially as I relied on the play-by-play feature of Retrosheet. In most instances, Washington's successes and failures on the basepaths did not affect the outcome of the game, and his mistakes were "harmless errors." For example, in the July 30 game against Texas, Washington pinch-ran for Pat Bourque and stole second base in the sixth inning. As the A's held an 8–2 lead at the time and would eventually win 11–3, it is clear that Washington's stolen base had no effect on the outcome of the game.
25. In 1974, Lowenstein had 5 assists as a left fielder, compared to 13 for Lou Piniella and 11 for Carlos May.

He May Be Fast, but Is He Quick?

Former Players Talk About Baserunning

Jim Reisler

During the 2007 baseball season, Jim Reisler interviewed nine former major-league players about baserunning. Following are transcripts of his interviews with three of them—Tim Raines, one of the game's leading basestealers; Tommy John, a pitcher; and Butch Wynegar, a catcher.

TIM RAINES

With 808 career stolen bases, Tim Raines is one of the top basestealers in the history of the game. A native of Sanford, Florida, Raines spent 23 big-league seasons compiling a lifetime batting average of .294 while playing for the Expos, White Sox, Yankees, and three other teams.

After appearing briefly for Montreal in 1979 and 1980, the switch-hitting Raines established himself as one of baseball's premier leadoff men by batting .304, stealing a league-leading 71 bases, and scoring 61 runs in the 88 games of the strike-shortened 1981 season, after which he was named National League Rookie of the Year.

Raines then led the league for the next three years in a row in stolen bases, achieving his career high of 90 in 1983. A seven-time All-Star, he is the only player in major-league history to steal 70 or more bases in six straight seasons.

Raines's .334 batting average in 1986 led the league. In 1990 he was traded to the White Sox, where he spent five years. He then signed with the Yankees, where he played three years and was a part of World Series championships in 1996 and 1998. Early in 1999 Raines signed as a free agent with Oakland, but halfway through the season he was diagnosed with lupus.

Raines recovered, however, and was back in the big leagues in 2001 with the Orioles, where he joined his son, Tim Raines Jr. With Tim Sr. in left field and Tim Jr. in center field, the the two of them became the second father-son combination, after the Griffeys, to play on the same team. After finishing his career with the Florida Marlins in 2002, Raines became a coach and a minor-league manager. When interviewed in 2007, he was coaching the Harrisburg Senators. He is currently manager of the Newark Bears.

NATIONAL BASEBALL HALL OF FAME LIBRARY, COOPERSTOWN, N.Y.

Tim Raines's 808 career stolen bases rank fifth on the all-time list. "Speed is part of the overall package," he says, "but reaction time is still more important."

I never really kept track of the number of stolen bases I had at any one time—at least not the way people today keep track. If I had, I'd have probably stolen a lot more bases—probably more than a thousand. For me, stealing bases meant helping the team win games; it wasn't about stats.

I stole bases because that was the way our team won games. In Montreal we utilized speed, so I utilized mine. I wasn't a home-run hitter; my game was getting on base and trying to make something happen. I don't really remember any significant stolen bases—number 100 or number 300, for instance. The one exception is number 500, which came when I was with the Yankees and we were playing against the Expos in Montreal. Doing it where I'd spent a lot of years made it special.

In hindsight, what might have helped me steal more bases and get me into the Hall of Fame was stealing more when games were out of hand. Normally, when you're up or down eight runs, the other team won't hold you on base. But I didn't run in those situations, because doing so would be seen as showing up the opponent. I was afraid the other team would retaliate by throwing at one of my teammates or me. Rickey Henderson would usually go in that situation, and so would Vince Coleman and a lot of guys, regardless of the score. They've since changed the rules; today, if the game is out of hand and they're not holding you on, you can steal a base but not get credit for it. But I still wouldn't run, even if it meant a thousand stolen bases would get me to the Hall; I didn't play the game that way and wasn't concerned with stats. I just played to win.

When I started in the big leagues, I used sheer speed to steal bases. Back then, the pitchers weren't as concerned about baserunners as they are today. If you stole a base, they'd resolve to strike out the next two batters, so it didn't really matter to them if you were on base or not: They didn't have the slide step or quick release to the plate. Those things alone can reduce a pitcher's time to the plate to 1.1 seconds, from 1.4 seconds or 1.5 seconds, making it a lot harder for the runner.

Nowadays, pitchers—even the power pitchers—go to instructional leagues, where they're taught how to develop a slide step. And speed has even changed catching; today, teams hire catching instructors who go around and work with catchers on their timing. They try to get catchers to work on their throws to second—getting them to reach the bag more quickly, usually in 1.8 or 1.9 seconds. Doing that gives the team in the field more of a chance.

The changes have meant that speed isn't so big a part of the game today. In my day, there were usually three or four guys who stole a lot of bases—myself, Rickey [Henderson], Vince [Coleman], Ozzie Smith, and Lonnie Smith. Vince, Ozzie, and Lonnie were part of those Cardinal teams; they ran all the time, and were pretty much the only team that relied, big-time, on the stolen base. Most teams had one or two guys with a chance to steal 50 or more bases a year.

At the same time, teams probably have more green-light guys today. If you demonstrate that you can steal bases, a lot of managers today will just let you run—though the minute you're not successful, you'll be shut down. When I got to the big leagues, Ron LeFlore had been with Montreal, so the team was certainly used to speed. Ron had the green light, and I was similar. So they took a chance with letting me run, and it worked out.

My method of stealing wasn't to crouch low like Rickey, but to take more of a standing lead—an athletic position. It was my way, which made stealing bases more of a reaction move. I had to work on it; my thing was to maintain my flexibility and speed by running a lot and doing a lot of stretching. In the offseason I always played basketball to maintain my fitness. And I picked up knowledge about the opposing pitchers pretty fast; I learned, because I figured when I got older, I wasn't going to have the same speed, so I could use that knowledge to my advantage. We'd go through every pitcher and his times to the plate, what kind of motion and pitches he'd tend to throw with men on base, and the catchers' times. So when I got on base, I already knew what the pitcher was likely to do.

Take Pedro Martinez. Every time with a guy on base, he takes a big windup on the first pitch to the next batter and delivers it in 1.4 or 1.5 seconds. Then on every pitch after that, he speeds up and delivers the ball in 1.1 seconds or thereabouts. With Pedro, I knew his tendencies, so, if I got on base and he was on the mound, I knew to go on his first pitch.

When you're taking about speed, Rickey was fast, but there were a lot of guys who were faster. What Rickey had was quickness; his first step was as quick as anyone's. There's a difference between reaction to what you see and how quick you react to it—and the best basestealers know that. The key is having instinct, which you can't teach, no matter how much speed you have. Lou Brock had that instinct.

Also, to be a good basestealer, you need to have the mentality that "I'm going to get a bag every time I'm on base, I don't care who's catching and who's pitching." Even when you're thrown out stealing, you have to keep that confidence. For the most part you're stealing off the pitcher, but you have to let the catcher know that "it's me and you." Even if it's usually the pitcher you're victimizing, keep in mind that the catcher is probably going to call for fastballs, or three or four fastballs and then a pitchout, or a fastball up and away—a good pitch for throwing to second—to do what he can to catch you out.

Stealing bases is a cat-and-mouse game. A lot of times, a baserunner at first can look in and tell if it's going to be a pitchout. I'm trying to get the signs, especially as the game goes on. It's all part of that other dimension, that running, like an ability to hit home runs, brings to a team. The other team always knew when Raines came to town, "We're going to have to keep him off the bases." And they knew if they did that, they'd have a chance to win the game. But the other team also knew that unlike a home-run hitter, they couldn't walk me, or even groove it down the middle, because I could hit, too.

Somebody who can steal disrupts everything. The middle infielders are moving around. The catcher is fidgety. The pitcher is all screwed up. And everybody

NATIONAL BASEBALL HALL OF FAME LIBRARY, COOPERSTOWN, N.Y.

With 752 career stolen bases, Vince Coleman ranks sixth on the all-time list, one place behind Raines, whose career was ten years longer. In 1983, Coleman stole 145 bases with Macon in the South Atlantic League, setting an Organized Baseball record.

else on the other team is saying, "Well, if he goes, I got to back the play up." Everybody is moving. And not only does the team have to worry about the guy on base, but they still need to concentrate on the guy at the plate. Meantime, the guy at bat loves it because he's looking for something they're bound to groove right over the plate so the catcher has a good ball to throw. So the team at bat tries putting a batter behind the guy on base, someone who can take pitches and handle the bat. With a home-run hitter, all you do is move back to the wall, or hope your pitcher strikes him out. Stolen bases change the whole game.

I developed my speed from playing football. In high school [Seminole High School in Sanford, Florida] I played four sports—football, basketball, and baseball, and ran track. In the spring I played baseball, and on days when we didn't have a game, I did track. I never really practiced track, but just went out and did the meets—running the 100, the relays and the 330-yard intermediate hurdles, and long jumping. The first time I ran the 100, I broke the school and conference record. And though I never really practiced the long jump, I set the school record, which lasted for a good 20 years, until it was broken by a guy who became an Olympic triple jumper.

Being a running back in football helped me develop quick feet. It's a pretty basic exercise: When guys come after you, you just run faster. So to me, a guy trying to tackle me is a lot like stealing a base—you need quickness and a good first step. Playing basketball helped me maintain my quickness as well—and so did playing sports with my family, starting with my dad, who played baseball, and my brothers, who played football, basketball, and baseball.

All my brothers were older, which meant growing up, I always had to play with older guys if I wanted to play at all. So when I was five I was playing baseball—and catching—in a league against eight-year-olds, when I should have been playing tee-ball. I remember one time when a guy ran me over at the plate, and I cried. But I loved it; I was playing with my brothers in a league where I wasn't supposed to be playing, but they let me play. At a young age, it helped me feel the competition against bigger and supposedly better kids. I learned to rise to the talent level, so by the time I got to competing against people my own age, it was like a man playing against boys.

Once I reached the major leagues, it was a lot like being a kid again and playing against my brothers. I told myself that I shouldn't feel like a rookie, because I'd been competing against older, bigger athletes my whole life. That helped, because you have to have that

NATIONAL BASEBALL HALL OF FAME LIBRARY, COOPERSTOWN, N.Y.

With 1,406 career stolen bases, Rickey Henderson easily tops the list, Lou Brock at 938 coming in a distant second. Like Coleman, Rickey would run "when games were out of hand," according to Raines, whereas Raines was concerned not to show up the opposition.

confidence going into the big leagues; otherwise, you're not going to be around long. You have to feel like you fit in. Montreal called me up briefly in 1979, and then again in 1980, when I went 1 for 20. But I always thought that I could compete against these guys; all I needed was a chance. So in '80, I went down to Triple A, to Denver, and told myself that, when I go back up, I'm going to be ready. I won the Minor League Player of the Year Award and a batting title and set the league record for stolen bases.[1] So then I said to myself, "Okay, now that I proved to the minor leagues that I'm beyond their level . . . I'm ready for the big leagues."

In 1981 I went up for good, and it didn't feel like such a big deal, because I was ready for the transition. The best thing to happen early on came in my first game of my first full season: I walked my first time up,[2] stole second, and scored when the ball got away. That was the biggest thing for my confidence; I was able to do something that most guys just don't do. People said, "Wow!" And I said to myself, "Okay, I'm here."

In my day, Rickey and I were the two guys people would talk about when it came to stolen bases. But we could run and were both good hitters. People don't always talk about Rickey's ability at the plate—but he had 3,055 career hits, and has more career home runs leading off a game than anyone in history [81], and had power [297 lifetime home runs]. The ability to steal bases is what kept me in the major leagues early in my career, but, as my career extended, it was my ability at the plate that distinguished me, I think. I won the batting title in 1986, hit .300 or more eight times, and could hit home runs [170 homers, lifetime]. Yet people don't look at it that way, in part because I played in Montreal (and out of the spotlight) for so long. They never put two and two—the ability to run *and* hit—together. Either you were a runner, a hitter, or a power hitter; Rickey and I were all three, and even as leadoff guys, we drove in runs.

At the same time, basestealers don't really seek one another out. We don't have to; Rickey had his way of doing things, I had mine, and Vince Coleman had his way. The only major difference between myself and them was the way I stood up or bent down when taking a lead or my first step. But I paid attention to what Rickey and the others were doing, so, when it comes to coaching and teaching, I can draw on what they did. I tell young players the way Rickey did it, Coleman did it, and I did it; that way, we can try 'em all and see which works best.

Though I played a lot of years in Montreal, what helped me get some exposure was playing in the All-Star Game (seven in all). My first couple of years, we had a bunch of guys make the All-Star team: Andre Dawson, Gary Carter, Steve Rogers, and myself, so people knew about us. In 1981 we won the NL East and lost to the Dodgers in the championship series, but I swear we had a better team than they did. We had some good teams and had a great minor-league system, but didn't have those one or two players who could have put us over the hump. The Expos didn't have the money, and a lot of people didn't want to play in Montreal.

In rating ballplayers today, speed is part of the overall package, but reaction time is still more important, to my mind. You can have the fastest guy in the world, but if he doesn't know how to read the pitcher, or if his reaction time is a step slow, he doesn't do a team much good. When I was 30 I wasn't as fast as I was at 22, but I had learned how to pick and choose my attempts. If there was a breaking-ball pitcher, even though he was a slide stepper, I'd pick a certain count and go. For pitchers I knew well, I'd try to anticipate when he might throw over. Having speed changes the dynamic of the game; with speed on the bases, you can expect catchers to call a lot of fastballs; they like throwing guys out and don't want to be the guys who give up the stolen bases. And pitchers don't want to get guys into scoring position.

On this team [the Harrisburg Senators], we have one green-light guy, and even he's shut down by the manager occasionally. We also don't know the pitchers in the minor leagues; sometimes, all we know about the opposing pitcher is that he's a left-hander or a right-hander. We take it game by game; we time the opposing pitchers and work on timing. The difference in the big leagues is that they have stats on everything.

Steve Boros, my first-base coach in Montreal, was the first guy who got me into stats. He'd give me and all the guys our times to first base and tell us the pitcher's times to the plate. I learned that any pitcher who would deliver the ball at 1.3 seconds and above, I figured I had a chance. But most pitchers didn't have the slide step back then, so I figured I had a chance to steal on pretty much anyone.

When I played, most of the power pitchers had big kicks, and they weren't that concerned with trying to speed up their deliveries. They figured that by changing their mechanics, they would add several miles per hour on their fastballs. It's not that they weren't concerned; they'd throw over and try to pick you off, and you had catchers who called more fastballs in case you ran.

Today, you still have guys who go through the wind-up, but they take a peek at the runner at first; back then they weren't really concerned. And for the team at bat, they seldom want to take a chance at a stolen base in front of their three, four, or five hitters. They want to give those guys a chance to drive runners home. Look at Boston, who haven't had much speed since Johnny Damon went to the Yankees. They have Coco Crisp,[3] who can run but is not a blazer, and is often shut down. That team is built on power. ■

Notes

1. In 1980, Tim Raines, with Denver, hit .354 and stole 77 bases. He stole 71 bases for the Expos in 1981 and reached a career high of 90, again for the Expos, in 1983.
2. Several at-bats are combined in Raines's memory of this game. In his first regular-season appearance at the plate, on April 9, 1982, he flew out to left. He walked on his fourth plate appearance.
3. Crisp played for the Boston Red Sox through 2008. In November 2008 he was traded to the Kansas City Royals.

TOMMY JOHN

Tommy John is noted for his big-game mastery in 26 big-league seasons—and for undergoing the pioneering ligament-repair operation that would eventually become known as Tommy John surgery—an operation most thought would end his major-league career.

John, a left-hander, made his big-league debut in 1963 with the Cleveland Indians and earned a reputation as one of the American League's premier control pitchers. Traded to Los Angeles in the winter of 1971, John in 1974 permanently damaged the ulnar collateral ligament in his pitching arm, prompting a revolutionary surgical operation. The surgery, performed by Dr. Frank Jobe in 1974, involved replacement of the ligament in the elbow of John's pitching arm with a tendon from his right forearm. After a year's recovery, John was back in the Dodgers' rotation in 1976.

John went on to pitch until 1989 and earned 164 of his 288 victories after his surgery. In 1976, John received the Hutch Award for displaying honor, courage, and dedication to baseball both on and off the field. Following the 1981 season, he was named winner of the Lou Gehrig Memorial Award, which is given to the player who best exemplifies the character of Lou Gehrig. John had three seasons of 20 or more wins, he was selected to four All-Star Games, and he played in four World Series.

NATIONAL BASEBALL HALL OF FAME LIBRARY, COOPERSTOWN, N.Y.

Tommy John had difficulty holding runners on base when he joined the National League in 1972, but Maury Wills coached him to speed up his motion, and he learned from watching tape of Jim Kaat's quick release.

Today, John serves as manager of the independent Bridgeport Bluefish. The once revolutionary and experimental operation that bears his name has now become standard, and many well-known pitchers, including Kerry Wood and John Smoltz, have benefited from Tommy John surgery.

The best basestealers? When I started out, one was Luis Aparicio. He was tough. If he played in this era, he may have 100 stolen bases. Back then, you would steal a base only when it was appropriate. Today, players just steal at any time.

The first time I ever saw Luis was in 1959 when he was with the "Go-Go" White Sox. He was like a rocket. But for the most part, American League players just didn't steal a lot of bases back then, nor did they into the late '60s. After Luis, the White Sox didn't have any basestealers, and neither did the Tigers or the Red Sox. Why? It was the way the game was played and the mentality back then. American League players would sit back and hit the long ball.

There were some exceptions. Rod Carew of the Twins was a great basestealer, and in 1969, he stole home seven times. He tried it on me once with Bob Allison at the plate, but I saw him start to break out of the corner of my eye, and just threw home in a quick motion. I got him, and the Twins claimed I had balked. But the umpire's decision stood. I got him.

But when I went to the National League in 1972 with the Dodgers, the mentality about stolen bases was different. In the NL, the idea was to create runs. When I got there, Lou Brock and Joe Morgan were the premier basestealers. In my first year with the Dodgers, I played with Maury Wills, one of the best. Then the Dodgers brought up Davey Lopes from the minors, and he became one of the very best as well.

Joining the National League, I had the hardest time in holding runners on base. I had pitching coaches work with me, but they couldn't get through to me, and my problem continued. But then at spring training at Vero Beach with the Dodgers a year or so later, Maury, who was coaching, took me out to one of the half-fields and we had a session. I went to the mound, and every time I'd go home, he would take off from first; I couldn't go to first. I asked, Could he tell when I committed to the plate? Maury was "reading" me—picking up my gestures. He told me that he could steal off me any time he chose—and that the only way I could ever get anyone to hold at first was if I sped up my motion and went to home more quickly.

At the time, Jim Kaat was a member of the White Sox, and had developed a quick release with runners on base. So when the Dodgers were in Chicago to play the Cubs, I called the White Sox and asked them to set up a tape of Kaat pitching. They agreed, and when we were playing at Wrigley Field, the Dodgers gave me permission to go to Comiskey Park, where I watched a 30-minute tape of Kaat pitching. Based on what I saw, I started working on a motion like Kaat's. It was quicker—and all of a sudden, I was getting to the plate fast enough so runners on base couldn't steal off me. I got to the point where I was getting the ball to home in 1.1 seconds, which is phenomenally fast.

Most big-league catchers can get the ball to second base in about 1.9 seconds. So between my pitching and their throwing to second, it would take only three seconds. That was fast—and fast enough to catch runners. They couldn't steal. My new motion got guys to stop stealing off me.

From that point, only certain guys were going to run on me. Contrary to the book *Moneyball* and the thinking of Billy Beane, stolen bases may not mean a lot over the long haul, but baserunners can use them to create havoc in a game. Baserunners make a team in the field do things they don't want to do, all to keep them from running—starting with pitchers making a bad pitch home. If you're a pitcher, you can't put the focus on home *and* on a runner at first base. It has to be one or the other.

A good baserunner gets into a pitcher's mind. If a pitcher gives 50-50—that is, he focuses on both home and on the runner in an equal amount—then he can't make a quality pitch. Pitchers *have* to pay more attention to the batter than they do a runner. It's got to be that way.

In my case, though, I'd had enough experience when I got to the National League that I "quick" pitched and didn't worry about the baserunner. I would just come set and throw home—and even if a runner had a walking lead, he still couldn't steal off me. I could get the ball to the plate faster than he could steal.

When I came up, prospects weren't evaluated much on their speed. But today, you hear a lot about "five-tool players"—those who excel at hitting for average, hitting for power, baserunning and speed, throwing ability, and fielding abilities. Those tools are teachable, all but speed, which is an exception. Speed and a 95-mile-an-hour fastball are things you're born with; you either have it or you don't.

You *can*, however, teach good baserunning. Bernie Williams was fast, but not a good basestealer. He could go from second to home or first to third well, but he never developed any skill in stealing bases. On the other hand, Maury Wills wasn't especially fast, but he was quick, and became the premier basestealer of his day. Later in my career, Don Baylor and Jose Canseco were both good basestealers—not people you thought of as exceptionally fast, but able to run the bases well and able to take advantage of a situation.

Good basestealers need to read the pitchers. They need to anticipate situations in which to run and know when to run. And they have to be able to do what Maury could do, which is to reach top speed after their first step. There were a bunch of guys who could probably beat Maury going first to third base, but in his prime, no one was better than Maury in getting from first to second.

Maury told me once that, contrary to the common thought, it was easier for him to steal on a left-handed pitcher than a right-hander. Left-handers face first base but give it away easier, he said. Maury could take a good lead and draw a throw two and three times in a row, and be able to read that pitcher and know exactly what he could do. Maury was a very savvy ballplayer.

If the count is 0–1, it's generally a good time to run, because the pitcher is liable to follow with a breaking ball. If it's a 1–0 or a 1–1 count, it probably isn't a good time to run, because the opposing manager may think he can afford a pitchout. But if you're going to steal with a hitter's count of 2–0, 2–1, or 3–1, you're taking a risk and kind of taking the bat out of the batter's hands. In most situations, if the batter sees you running, he's going to take the pitch. If you're running later in the count, you had better make it.

Good baserunners can also steal signs by taking a good lead and peeking in at the catcher's signs. Rickey Henderson could do that. On the other hand, Rickey couldn't steal off Bob Boone if his life depended on it. The reason was that Boone had a particular thumb signal for the pitcher to "throw over" to first base. Boone would open his legs just a little as he was giving the sign and let Rickey see that he was telling the pitcher to throw over. But in reality, the sign was for the pitcher to throw a fastball, which he'd then do with Rickey crossed up and staying at first base.

For pitchouts, Boone had another sign—a series of signs, actually—in which he would pump his fingers four consecutive times. In Rickey's case, it worked again—and kept him close to the bag.

A good baserunner adds a dimension to your offense. They get in the head of the pitcher. And they make the infielders play up and stay closer to the bag. Baserunners get the second basemen, for instance, to "cheat in," as we call it, by keeping a step closer to the plate in case of a bunt. That means you can't cover as much of an area if the hitter sends the ball by you.

There's a lot that goes into basestealing and baserunning. As a manager, I don't think enough thought goes into it.

In the majors, players get to know the pitchers. But in the minor leagues, we don't know many of the opposing pitchers—and so we give our players the green light. If they get a good jump, they can run. If they feel they can steal a base, they can run. That goes for about five of our players, who have the green light.

In this league, we have a watch on the opposing pitchers. If they deliver to the plate in 1.4 or 1.5 seconds, which isn't fast, we usually tell our baserunners that they can go. We don't look for speed necessarily, but if they have it, well, that's gravy.

To my mind, basestealing has very little to do with the ballgame, except in the last three innings. You can steal four, five, or six bases early in the game, and a home run gets you right back in the game. But if you're down a run in the late innings and it's a close game, stolen bases can mean a lot. You can steal second and get to third on a bunt, you can score on a sacrifice fly—and it's a new game.

Today's premier basestealer? Probably José Reyes of the Mets. There are some good baserunners out there, but basestealing has gotten more challenging with the smaller ballparks. When they get smaller, it's not necessary to steal bases to score runs. You can wait for the fat pitch and it's gone. ■

BUTCH WYNEGAR

Described on a Minnesota Twins blogsite as "Joe Mauer before there was a Joe Mauer," Butch Wynegar was a switch-hitting high-school catcher from York, Pennsylvania, when he was selected by the Twins in the second round of the 1974 draft. After winning the Appalachian League batting title (.346) in his first pro season, Wynegar reached the major leagues in 1976 at the age of 20, and that season he became the youngest position player to play in the All-Star Game.

An outstanding defensive catcher, Wynegar was named The Sporting News*'s American League Rookie of the Year that season, after hitting .260 with 10 home runs and 69 RBIs. He would be an All-Star again in 1977 and would play 13 big-league seasons, mostly with the Twins, and later with the Yankees and Angels. In his best season, with the 1983 Yankees, Wynegar hit .296 and caught Dave Righetti's no-hitter.*

After his playing career ended, Wynegar was a minor-league manager and coach in the Baltimore Orioles' and Texas Rangers' farm systems before he joined the Milwaukee Brewers as batting coach in 2003. He now coaches the Scranton–Wilkes-Barre Yankees.

NATIONAL BASEBALL HALL OF FAME LIBRARY, COOPERSTOWN, N.Y.

Butch Wynegar's first manager in the majors was Gene Mauch, who directed his pitches to cut their delivery time from 1.5 or 1.6 seconds down to 1.2 or 1.3. As a coach, Wynegar tells his catchers to aim for the standard 1.9 seconds on the throw to second.

In my day, there were a bunch of guys who could steal bases. Mickey Rivers of the Yankees was one. And the Oakland A's had a number of basestealers, guys like Rickey Henderson; Herb Washington, the designated runner; Billy North; and Miguel Diloné, who could fly. Kansas City had a bunch of great runners as well, like Willie Wilson, Frank White, and Amos Otis.

I'd say that 90 percent of stolen bases are swiped off the pitcher. Today, there are statistics—basically [there's] a stat on the Internet for anything you want to find—for the combined time a pitcher throws to plate (1.3 seconds is typical) and a catcher then throws to second base (in, say, 2.0 seconds). That's a total of 3.3 seconds from the time a pitcher releases the ball to the time a catcher gets it to second—which is too slow for a fast runner, who can usually get from first to second in about 3.1 seconds. Today you can keep track of all these things.

It's almost funny to compare all these statistics to the lack of stats when I got to the big leagues in 1976. I had just turned 20, and though I knew how to catch, I still had a lot to learn, namely about basestealers. I remember being so wrapped up during my first season about when a guy was going to run that I had about 18 passed balls. Sure, we practiced our throws to second and to third, but I never knew what my times were until later in my career. I didn't think about it; I just tried to be as quick and accurate as I could in my throws.

A team's tendency to run is really up to the manager. Billy Martin was very aggressive, and he would run in any situation with anyone and at any time. When he was managing Oakland, Billy used an old play on me, shortly after I'd come up: With runners at first and third base and two strikes on the batter, the guy at first would take a secondary lead and trip and fall. So of course, I'd get the ball, cock my arm, and throw to first—with the guy at third coming to the plate the second I commit to first. He scores, and we retire the guy at first in a rundown. It was a preset play that required the runners to leave their bases at the right time and some pretty good acting on the part of the first-base runner, who had to fall down. If only I'd cocked my arm and stopped and looked at third, we'd have had the guy coming from third. But being a young catcher, I fell for it.

Gene Mauch was my first big-league manager, as well as my mentor and father figure when I was away from home. He was the one who taught me pretty much everything about the game—helping me refine what I learned as a kid from my dad. I remember Gene taking all the pitchers aside at spring training and telling them they simply had to cut down the time delivering the ball to the plate—from 1.5 or 1.6 seconds down to 1.2 or 1.3—all to give the catcher a chance to catch basestealers.

Gene recognized when a pitcher was slow and tried to deal with it. As a catcher, I got sick and tired, early in my career, with pitchers taking their time delivering the ball to the plate, and then having to make up for it. I began hurrying my throws and bouncing them in the dirt, or throwing the ball into center field because my footwork got out of whack. We were playing the A's one day when Rickey Henderson stole second, and I looked at the scoreboard and saw "E-2," and I said to myself: "F— this! Give me a chance to catch Rickey Henderson. All I want is a chance to throw in 1.9 seconds down to second and make an accurate throw." That was the turning point in my career behind the plate; I vowed to myself to set myself and make a good throw, regardless of a runner's jump. Because of that mentality, I became a better thrower, and the monkey was off my back.

Being 20 at the time and catching experienced and successful pitchers like Bert Blyleven and Davey Goltz, who were both about ten years old than me, I couldn't very well go out to the mound and say, "Give me a pitch I can throw on, will you?" So I vowed to myself to make more accurate throws, and knew that Gene would deal with getting the pitchers to deliver the ball more quickly. I had to take care of myself and do my job as best I could.

As a catcher, dealing with baserunners was still a matter of not trying to be so quick. I tell our catchers here all the time that if you can throw to second in 1.9 seconds, stick with that speed and you'll be okay. Don't come out and try to be Ivan Rodriguez and throw the ball to second in 1.7 seconds. You'll get airballs if you try to throw too fast.

Gene taught me something else about how to be a better catcher: He told me to get to know the pitching staff. "Every one of them has a different personality," Gene said. "I want you to know your staff inside and out—what they throw, when they want to throw it, what they eat for lunch, and what they eat for breakfast." He wanted me to really know my pitchers, know their strengths, weaknesses, and tendencies, and how to talk to them. If nothing else, I had to become a psychologist; if I knew Jimmy Hughes had a big leg-kick, which made him slow to the plate, I had to find some way to get him to deliver the ball a little faster, so I'd have a chance to catch a baserunner. No wonder so many catchers become managers and coaches; we're experts at dealing with so many different personalities. We're dealing with the manager and in scouting meetings. Yup, we're the psychologists of baseball.

Even when you get a good runner at first and he doesn't want to go, the catcher doesn't know that. That was my problem catching during my first couple of years in the big leagues: I always had one eye on the pitcher and my other eye down at first, if a good runner was on base. The pitcher gets concerned, too, and throws over to first a bunch of times. His rhythm is disrupted. The whole game changes.

There was a time when catchers didn't have to hit, when the three basics were receiving, throwing, and blocking. If you could do those things at a high standard, then you had a good chance to make the big leagues. But today's game has become so oriented to offense that catchers have to hit. The same thing goes for shortstops: In contrast to the old days, when a lot of them were Punch-and-Judy hitters who could field and had rocket arms, today's shortstops are guys like Derek Jeter and Miguel Tejada, who can hit the ball out of the ballpark.

The focus on offense has made the stolen base a lot less prevalent than in my day. Those old Oakland and Kansas City teams oriented their whole teams around speed. The Royals had [Willie] Wilson, [Frank] White, [Amos] Otis, Al Cowens, and George Brett. Their whole lineup could run, and playing them was like a track meet. Oakland could [do that] too, and there were days when they just ran rampant and I was helpless, I had no chance in throwing their guys out.

Brett was a good example of a guy who wasn't a speed demon, but knew how to run and steal bases. He was smart on the base paths, a guy who knew he couldn't outrun the ball, so he had to be heads-up when running. You seldom see a basestealer get on first and then just run. The good ones are looking for a good count to run on, a breaking ball or a changeup.

When we played the Red Sox at Fenway Park, my arm got out of shape, because they ran so often that it was almost not worth even trying to throw people out. It was just rat-a-tat, all the time. Between the designated hitter and the small ballpark, their attitude was just to bombard your opponent. Though I never played in the National League, I spent four years there as a coach in Milwaukee, and I've got to admit I like the NL style of play: There's more running—though it doesn't take much to outrun the American League—and there's no DH. That means there's more strategy, too: Do we pinch-hit for the pitcher? Do we bunt the runner over? Do we run in this pitch? There's a lot of thinking going on.

The orientation on offense today isn't because players are quicker. I'll admit that they're bigger and stronger. But from a catcher's standpoint, the first thing scouts will tell you is they can't find catchers these days. It was at the suggestion of a White Sox scout that I became a catcher in my junior year of high school; he came up to me after a game and said, "Butch, have you ever thought about catching?" I was a third baseman and pitched a little at the time, but I had good hands, a good arm and switch-hit—though I lacked range at third. The scout's thought was [that] a switch-hitting catcher with a good arm could reach the big leagues pretty quickly. Fortunately, I had a high-school coach who agreed, and so I became a catcher, which I'd played some in Little League. By the time I reached the big leagues, I had three years of catching under my belt.

The good basestealers, just like good baserunners, learn to be good by working at it. We encourage everyone, even runners who aren't that fast, to work on baserunning. I knew I wasn't speedy, but to score on a base hit from second, I knew that I had to learn how to take a good lead. So, I'd work on baserunning during batting practice and focus on trying to read the ball off the bat, and try to get a good jump. You'll see that a lot of good baserunners aren't necessarily the fastest. Being a good runner comes down to instinct and focusing on getting a good lead and learning the pitchers.

Here at the Triple-A level, where we don't always know much about the opposing pitcher, we'll give a watch to the first-base coach who will time the pitcher's delivery, and then talk about it with the runners. If the pitcher takes 1.5 seconds to the plate, our runners are usually free to go. Do it right, and someone who isn't speedy can learn his way around the bases. John Wathan, who set the catcher's record for most stolen bases in a season (36 for the 1982 Royals), was a good example; he had a knack for taking a good walking lead and being able to steal a base. Carlos Lee, who I coached in Milwaukee, is another; he's a big guy and not a burner, but he can run the bases.

We try to get our players to be aggressive on the bases. We want to find out who likes to run and who can run, so except for the catcher, everyone is encouraged to run; [they] have the green light here to run, unless we specifically take the "run" sign off. As for the New York Yankees, there's only a handful of guys who run; with all those great batters and power, they don't have to run. That goes for most of the American League; a lot of teams don't have to run.

It pays to study the pitchers. Sometimes they'll tip off when they're going to the plate and not realize it. Some pitchers will tip off their pitches by setting themselves with their hands away from their body and follow with a fastball, or set themselves with their hands closer to the body, which means an off-speed pitch. Throwing an off-speed pitch means they need to get a better grip on the ball, which means that sometimes they'll keep their hands closer to their body. Knowing what pitch is on the way can affect a lot, from the hitters to the baserunners.

There's a lot that goes into the game that the average fan doesn't realize. They think we come to the park at 4:00 P.M., take batting practice, and then play the game and go home. But a lot of these players are here at noon or 2:00 P.M. and taking batting practice, spending time in the indoor cage, or stretching. And you have guys watching video. A lot is going on.

There's a lot going on during the game as well. We watch the pitchers and watch the opposing coaches and try to pick up the signs. All of a sudden we'll know they're about to hit and run, or steal. And then they'll know we have their signs, and they'll change 'em.

Sign stealing is a big part of baserunning. I talk to our catchers all the time about keeping their arms in enough when giving the signs so the runner and the first-base coach can't see. The only guys who should be able to see your signs are the pitcher, shortstop, and second baseman. Catchers can get lazy and keep their legs apart, and boom, the other team knows their signs. I even remember a time when I was coaching a college team, and we picked up the sign because the opposing catcher was keeping his elbow close to his body when he wanted a fastball, and away from his body for a breaking ball. We pummeled the poor kid on the mound, and he had no clue what was happening. His catcher was giving the signs away. But picking up these things is the fun part of the game. ■

Estimating the Dollar Value of Players

Vince Gennaro

AS FANS we often question the offseason free-agent signings by baseball GMs, wondering how the value of some mega-contracts could possibly be justified. Why does Barry Zito command $126 million over seven years from the Giants, or is CC Sabathia "worth" $161 million over seven years to the New York Yankees? Is this rational decision-making at its finest, ego-driven mania, or something in between? While there may be no definitive answers and certainly no "final word" on player value, there is an analytical path we can follow to at least shed some light on the rationale of the spending decisions of MLB GM.

There are several approaches to the question "How much is a player worth?" One way to measure "value" is to estimate the market value of a player as reflected by his price (i.e., the value of his contract) in the free-agent market. A second approach is to assess a player's economic value to his team—how much additional revenue (and asset appreciation) he could be expected to generate for his prospective employer. This article focuses on the latter approach, assessing the economic value of a player to his team, called his marginal revenue product—the amount of incremental revenue a team can be expected to generate owing to the win-contribution of a player's performance on the field. By estimating the amount of revenue a team would generate with and without a "3-win" or "4-win" player, we can estimate the dollar value of the player to the team. The concept of marginal revenue product as applied to a player's value refers to the marginal *quality* of the player and its impact on revenues versus some predetermined baseline, usually a replacement-level player.[1]

The process to estimate a player's dollar value follows two key steps: Convert a player's performance into a win-contribution to the team and translate changes in the team's on-field performance into its impact on team revenues and the value of its assets. Fortunately, numerous statistical analysts have translated a player's performance into his win contribution to his team. Wins above replacement player (WARP) from analysts at Baseball Prospectus, win shares above bench (WSAB) from Dave Studenmund at the Hardball Times, and value sins (VW) from Fangraphs.com, derived from Tom Tango's wins above replacement (WAR) metric, are examples of this effort. However, in order to convert a player's win contribution into dollar value, we need to delve deeply into the team's economics and financials to better understand how revenues fluctuate with the team's on-field performance. By applying regression analysis to individual team attendance, broadcast revenues, and other revenue streams, we can estimate how a team's annual wins impact each of these revenues, while adjusting for such factors as new stadium openings, past work stoppages, and previous postseason appearances. (See the sidebar for a comparison to other research in this area and for some additional detail regarding my methodology.) Furthermore, by analyzing the relationship between attendance revenues and an MLB team's other revenue categories, we are able to gain a more complete picture of the impact that winning has on team revenues. (An in-depth analysis of the win–revenue analysis of all MLB teams is one of the subjects of my book *Diamond Dollars: The Economics of Winning in Baseball*.)[2] Having taken this approach in some instances with team-specific proprietary data and, in other cases, with team-specific publicly available data, I've reached four important conclusions that generally apply to the win–revenue relationhip for all MLB teams:

Winning and revenues are highly correlated and behave in a predictable and measurable way, influenced by the strength of the team's brand, the loyalty of its fans, and the size of its market. Each team's win–revenue relationship is unique, which means that a player's value is best defined in the context of a team.

Winning affects revenues over a range—generally, from 70 to 100 wins for a season—but, at the low and high extremes (< 70 and > 100), winning has little impact on revenues. For example, if the San Diego Padres should improve on their 63-win season of 2008 by winning 68 games in 2009, the effect on revenues is expected to be negligible.

The fan response to winning is somewhat lagged. Statistically speaking, the strongest relationships between wins and attendance occur when wins are defined as a combination of the previous and current year's annual win totals. This makes intuitive sense since a team's season-ticket renewals and advance sales are influenced by the team's just-completed season as well as by fans' perceptions of offseason trades and player signings. If a team gets out of the gate strong with a winning April and May, it bodes well for second-half ticket revenues. If the team sustains their performance for the balance of the season, that is likely to benefit advance sales for the following season.

A significant revenue windfall occurs when a team reaches the postseason. This is due to a pattern of fan behavior that is commonplace across all of baseball but is most pronounced when a team reaches the playoffs after having missed qualifying for several years or more. The implication of this finding is that not all wins between 70 and 100 are equally valued. Those wins that heighten the chance of a postseason appearance are clearly valued at a premium.

THE POSTSEASON EFFECT

When a team reaches the postseason, particularly after a prolonged absence, a predictable pattern of fan behavior occurs, which translates into a revenue windfall. Two recent examples of this impact were triggered by the 2005 White Sox and the 2006 Tigers. Once a team qualifies for October baseball, fans invariably scramble for playoff tickets, only to find the seating selection or price in the secondary market disappointing. With their newfound optimism about the future prospects of their favorite team, some fans decide to purchase full- or partial-season tickets for the next season. They view these as "options" on future playoff seats. In addition, the newly validated playoff team experiences strong advance single-game sales for the coming season as well as improved broadcast ratings, which can lead to more advertising revenue.[3] Corporate sponsors jockey for position to secure their team affiliation, and even luxury-suite demand increases as the team's games become a more desirable customer entertainment option. Furthermore, teams show greater resolve to raise ticket prices—and fans show a greater willingness to absorb them—for a playoff team. From the inception of the wild card in 1995 through 2008, teams that reached the postseason raised ticket prices for the following year, on average, 4.5 percent more than teams that did not reach the postseason.[4]

An important conclusion about the playoff windfall is its *multiyear* benefit. Even if the team fails to reach the postseason for the next several years, not all of the newfound supporters disappear immediately. My analysis of attrition rates of playoff teams suggests that, while the revenue effect declines each year, it may take up to five years before the last *new* season ticket-holder gives up hope and fails to renew. When added to the game revenue from the playoff games (including concessions, etc.), the estimated flow of revenues from a postseason appearance is shown in figure 1. The net result of summing all of these revenue effects can be a future revenue stream with a net present value (NPV) equal to 20 to 30 percent of a team's local revenues, beginning in the season following a team's playoff appearance. (The White Sox received an added financial "kicker" from the team's increased popularity after winning a world championship.)

Figure 1. Postseason Effect—% of Revenues by Year

(100% = total impact of Reaching the Postseason)

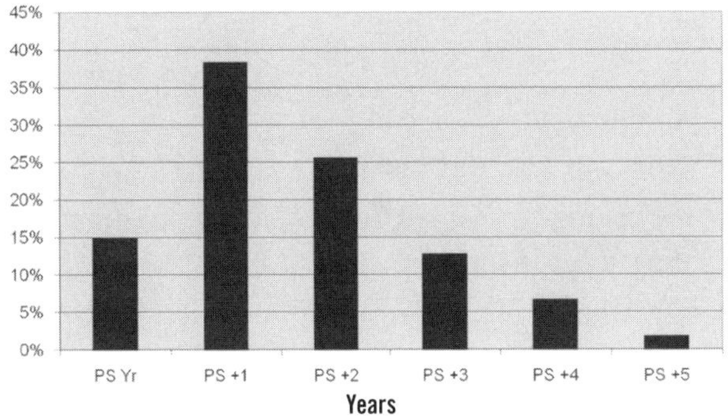

For a team, such as Philadelphia or Seattle, whose revenue base is in the second or third quartile for MLB teams, reaching the postseason could mean anywhere from $30 million to $40 million (NPV), while winning a world championship could double that amount. For teams in the top quartile, such as the Los Angeles Dodgers and New York Mets, the postseason value could be more than $50 million.[5]

How do we integrate the value of the postseason into the win-revenue relationship? One way is through a two-step process that allows us to create an *expected value* of the postseason that corresponds to each win total. The first step involves analyzing the historical probabilities of recent divisional and wild-card races. By applying a logistic regression we can estimate the probability of reaching the postseason at each win total. Given the quality disparity in recent years between the two leagues, it is not surprising the results yield a different probability for an AL versus NL team. (See figure 2.) To complete the process, we take the probability of reaching the postseason at each win total and multiply that by the total value of the postseason. The net result is an estimate of a team's win-revenue relationship, including the expected value of the postseason—a team's *win-curve.*

Figure 2. Probability of Reaching the Postseason 2002–2008 Data

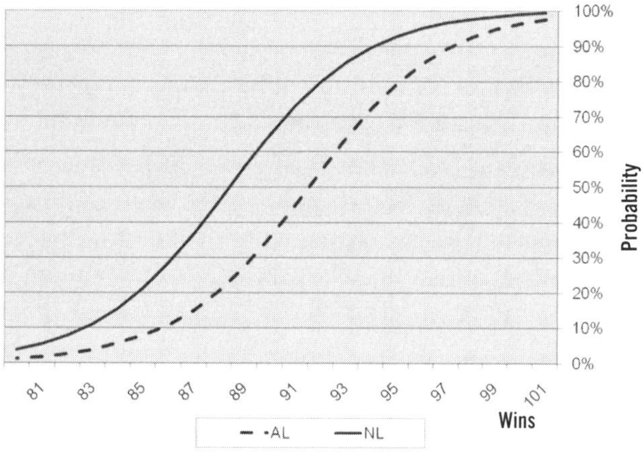

COURTESY OF THE NEW YORK YANKEES

Is CC Sabathia worth $161 million over seven years to the New York Yankees? The answer involves recognition that the monetary value of a win in a big market like New York is greater than that of a win in a small market like Kansas City.

A PLAYER'S VALUE IS SITUATIONAL

A team's win-curve is the culmination of all revenue sources and their relationship to a team's on-field performance. The example in figure 3 shows an estimated win-curve for the 2008 New York Mets, with the postseason effect overlaid on the in-season win–revenues. (Note: The win-curve begins at 70 wins, the point from which the incremental revenue from winning is measured.) The postseason effect causes the win-curve to be nonlinear. When a team is in contention, it is operating along the steepest portion of the win-curve, meaning that a few more wins (or a few less wins) carry the highest financial value. Consequently, a player's dollar value—his marginal revenue product—is greatly influenced by where his team is on the win-curve. For example, if the Mets add a 4-win player to an otherwise 88-win team, the player is expected to generate $20.5 million in revenue. The same player added to an 80-win team would generate only $10.5 million. In the first example, our player elevates the Mets to a 92-win team, thereby improving the Mets' probabilities of reaching the postseason by 34 percentage points. In the latter example the Mets are only 9 percent more likely to make the postseason due to the roster addition. (See figure 3.) The marginal value of the last piece of the puzzle can be much higher than the value of the same player added to an 80-win team.

Figure 3. New York Mets' Estimated 2008 Win-Curve

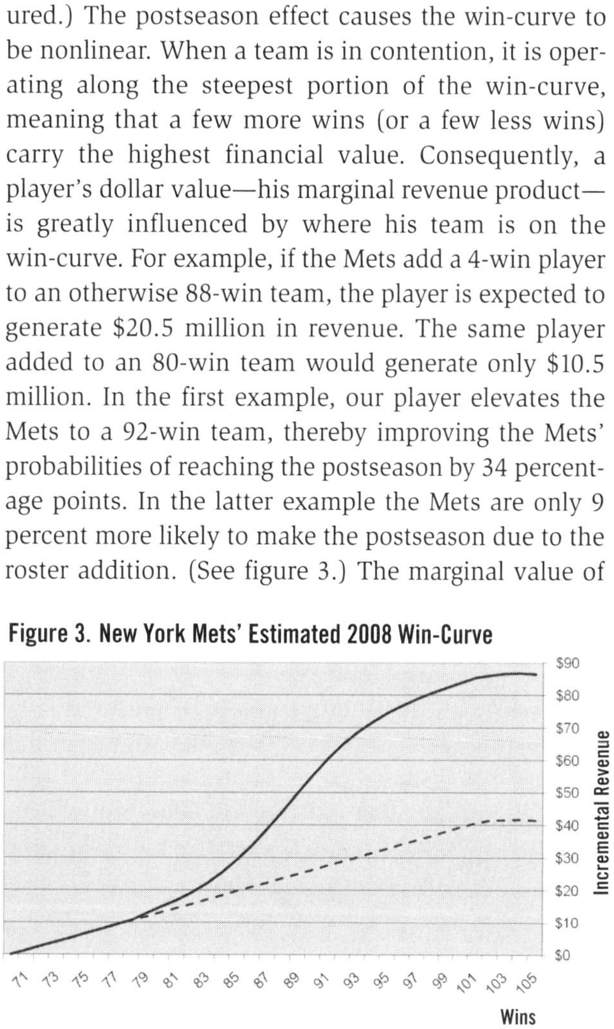

Let's apply this approach to prospectively valuing the Mets' Carlos Beltran for the 2009 season.[6] In our example, we will examine how Beltran's value is impacted by both his performance *and* the team's performance. According to fangraphs.com, Beltran has averaged approximately 5.5 value wins over the past six years. Before the 2009 season, the Mets are once again filled with optimism. The team narrowly missed the postseason in 2007 and 2008 and they hope to contend once again in 2009. Let's begin with the scenario that defines Beltran as a 5-win player added to an 85-win-baseline Mets team—meaning a team that would be expected to win 85 games with a replacement player, instead of Beltran, in center field. Under this scenario, Beltran raises the probability of the Mets reaching the postseason by 44 percentage points—from 21 percent to 65 percent—and, in doing so, a 5-win Beltran has an expected value of $26.2 million. The $26.2 million consists of $19.8 in expected value of achieving the postseason revenue stream and $6.4 million in the value of 5 wins, independent of achieving a playoff spot. Figure 4 shows various scenarios of Beltran performance, in the context of various team performance scenarios and the resulting expected dollar value of Beltran.

It is interesting to note that, at *both* the low end and the high end of the team-performance scale, Beltran's value drops. At the low end it conjures the image of the famous Branch Rickey quote to Ralph Kiner, "We could have finished last without you," while the high end of the team performance scale implies they likely would have advanced to the postseason without Beltran. According to the estimates in figure 4, Beltran would not "earn" enough revenue to cover his salary as a 3-win player. As a 4-win player, he would justify his salary only if the Mets were an 84-to-89-win team without him. If Beltran turns in a 5-win performance, he is expected to generate the revenue to cover his salary as long as the Mets ultimately win 87 to 95 games. Our win-curve analysis demonstrates that a player's value is *situational*, dependent not only on a player's performance but also on *team performance—its location along the win-curve.*

An interesting implication of this analysis is the "accountability" for delivering value. If Carlos Beltran performs at a 5-win level but the team is an 81-win-baseline team prior to his performance, the estimate

Figure 4. Carlos Beltran — What If?
Incremental Revenue from Various Performance Scenarios

Baseline Wins w/o Beltran	3-win season	4-win season	5-win season
89	$ 14.9	$ 18.7	$ 21.8
88	$ 16.1	$ 20.5	$ 24.3
87	$ 16.6	$ 21.6	$ 26.0
86	$ 16.2	$ 21.7	$ 26.7
85	$ 15.1	$ 20.7	$ 26.2
84	$ 13.5	$ 19.0	$ 24.7
83	$ 11.7	$ 16.8	$ 22.3
82	$ 10.0	$ 14.5	$ 19.6
81	$ 8.4	$ 12.4	$ 16.9

Other Research on Player Value and Further Discussion on Methodology

Shortly after free agency became a reality three decades ago, as a graduate student at the University of Chicago, I embarked on a project to estimate the marginal revenue product for major-league players. (The results of the project became the topic of an article in *The Sporting News* in the spring of 1979.) The resurrection of this project several years ago led to my series of team-specific models to estimate the relationship between a team's on-field performance and its resulting revenues.

The process combines statistical analysis—primarily multiple regression—and detailed financial analysis of the key factors that drive a team's profit-and-loss statement. In these instances I am using publicly available data. I divide a team's revenue into three categories: attendance, broadcast, and all other. The process begins with a team-specific regression model, with average annual per-game attendance as the dependent variable. (The reason team-specific is important is that the differing local economics of teams mean that the value of a win to the Yankees may be 4 times the value of the same win to the Kansas City Royals, rendering useless an analysis that pools all teams and deals in MLB averages.) The independent variables include those that reflect a team's wins—last year's and the current year's wins—and dummy variables to adjust for the impact of new stadium openings, work stoppages, and other nonrecurring events. This model creates the foundation of a team's win-curve by quantifying the win-attendance relationship. By multiplying the estimated attendance values by the average ticket-price data compiled and published by Team Marketing Report, we can translate this estimate into attendance revenues. The next step is to impute the impact of wins on all other revenues, using a team's historical ratio of attendance to all other revenues published in financial data released as part of the Blue Ribbon Panel Report. (For teams that have provided proprietary data, the process of developing the win-curve is considerably more involved, as it enables me to analyze each separate revenue stream.)

The final revenue category, broadcast, requires different approaches depending on whether the team has ownership in a regional sports network (e.g., Yankees and Red Sox, with YES Network and NESN, respectively) versus a more "traditional" broadcast arrangement with a Fox Sports–type local affiliate. In the former scenario I analyze the networks' household penetration, distribution fees from cable/satellite operators, and advertising revenues and rates. In an attempt to create "transparency" between the broadcast entity and the team, I "credit" the team with the relevant broadcast revenues that are attributable to winning. In the latter case I use a fixed fee plus a small performance bonus for reaching the postseason.

A key to estimation of the win-curve is a detailed analysis of the postseason and its impact on all of a team's revenue streams. This analysis is aided by teams that have shared their proprietary data. The additional level of detail provided by proprietary data has enabled me to make inferences about how various revenue streams respond to postseason appearances for teams in comparably sized markets.

In "Is Alex Rodriguez Overpaid?" his chapter in *Baseball Between the Numbers*, Nate Silver, a driving force behind the success of Baseball Prospectus, detailed his work in the area of player value. One significant difference in Silver's approach is his MLB-wide model of team wins and revenues, in which he stops short of creating team-specific models that differentiate the value of a win in New York versus one in Kansas City. My team-specific models not only differentiate between the value of a win in New York and the value of a win in Kansas City, but I further differentiate the win-curves of teams within a city, such as the Yankees and Mets, the Cubs and White Sox. One similarity in our two approaches is the way in which we incorporate the value of the postseason into the value of a win—by taking the probability of reaching the postseason at each win level and multiplying that by the estimated dollar value of the postseason.

COURTESY OF THE NEW YORK METS

Carlos Beltran has averaged about 5.5 value wins over the past six seasons. His value to the Mets drops at the low as well as at the high end of the team-performance scale. "We could have finished last without you," as Branch Rickey told Ralph Kiner.

of $16.9 million in incremental revenue suggests that Beltran will fail to "earn" his $18 million salary for 2009. However, in this example, the accountability for Beltran's shortfall in value may fall on team management for failing to provide Beltran with a sufficient supporting cast, since he would have earned his salary if the team were a bit more competitive. (See figure 4.) In other words, when signing a player of Beltran's stature (and compensation), it is implicit that, for the player to deliver value comparable to his salary, the team will likely need to be competitive. This reality often makes the free-agent market a cost-prohibitive option for teams that are noncompetitive.

As MLB grows as an industry, more teams are managing their business with the analytical tools necessary to make $100-million decisions. For the most astute teams, gone are the days of pure instinct and gut feel as the basis for signing a free agent. More teams are relying on statistical analysis of game situations to influence their in-game tactics and on statistical analysis of players to influence their roster choices. The disciplined, more objective analytical approach is now spilling over into the boardroom, as teams evaluate commitments of mega dollars to key players. Intuitive judgment will always be a critical factor in successfully running a MLB team—it's just no longer the only factor. ■

Notes

1. An analogy in a non-sports business environment would be to compare a top-quartile salesman in a firm to the "replacement level" salesman that could be hired off the unemployment rolls. (In times of high unemployment, replacement level can rise significantly.) Suppose your top-quartile salesman is expected to sell $500,000 worth of products annually, with a net margin of $125,000 (net of all product costs and associated expenses, except his compensation), and a replacement salesman is expected to deliver $60,000 in net margin dollars; then the marginal revenue product of the top-quartile salesman is $65,000 over replacement level.
2. Vince Gennaro, *Diamond Dollars: The Economics of Winning in Baseball* (Hingham. Mass.: Maple Street Press, 2007).
3. Most teams have multiyear agreements for their broadcast rights, which means team broadcast revenues may be fixed for any given year. On the other hand, teams that own a share of a regional sports network (Red Sox and NESN, Yankees and YES, etc.) share in both the annual fluctuation—in ad rates and the change in the asset value of the network—resulting from on-field performance.
4. The level of success a team has during its postseason run has an impact on the size of the postseason effect. When the 2005 San Diego Padres qualified for the postseason with only 82 wins and then were ousted with three straight playoff losses to the St. Louis Cardinals, much of the potential benefit of reaching the postseason was negated by the Padres' poor performance. The combination of their modest win total and their poor showing failed to provide a motivating fan experience, nor did it validate the Padres as a bona fide future postseason contender.
5. Given evidence of the "postseason effect," simply analyzing a team's revenues as a function of wins is likely to miss the impact of the postseason and lead to an erroneous conclusion as to the impact of on-field performance. Approximately 10 to 15 percent of the postseason revenue stream will likely occur during the year the team reaches the postseason, about 40 percent will occur the following year, and the remaining 45 to 50 percent will occur in years 2 through 5 following the postseason appearance.
6. For the purpose of this analysis, I am operating with the assumption that the Mets' win-curve did not change from my 2008 estimates. In reality, once some of the financial parameters of the new Citi Field become available, I would expect to conclude the win-curve will shift considerably, yielding additional revenue at each win level.

Low Risk—Any Reward?

Eric Seidman

WHILE it makes big headlines when a team signs a free-agent superstar, there are at least as many cases of a team signing an average—or below-average—player in hopes that his performance will exceed his modest salary requirements. Here, I investigate "low-risk" pitcher signings of this type, to see if and when they work out.

Without fail, each offseason brings with it a multitude of personnel concerns for each team. Players lost to free agency need to be replaced; those no longer effective require upgrades; and it seems that every team has the worst bullpen in the league. While the big-name, big-money acquisitions hog the headlines, the majority of transactions involve less money given to average, slightly above-average, or risky players.

These moves have come to be known as "low-risk, high-reward." If little money is being committed, it seems to be a worthwhile investment to take a flyer on a formerly successful veteran; he may be able to regain past form. If not, the club will not suffer much because their commitment was not great in the first place. With these signings becoming more prominent each year I decided to investigate, with respect to pitchers, whether or not teams are actually rewarded highly for their low-risk signings.

DEFINING LOW RISK, HIGH REWARD

The first aspect of these signings refers to contract length. "Low risk" implies a lack of commitment to the duration of a contract. When discussing the contract duration I am going to consider the following situations to be of low risk:

- minor-league deal
- waiver claim
- 1-year deal
- 1-year deal with option

The second part of low-risk signings involves offering the pitcher a lesser contract in exchange for his getting another shot at playing in the major leagues. When we determine monetary criteria, the major factor to take into account is the differential in team payrolls. It would not be fair to set a maximum dollar value at, say, $4 million, because for different teams that would account for a different percentage of total payroll.

Four million dollars would equate to 3.96 percent of the payroll of the 2007 Chicago White Sox. It would account for as much as 10.71 percent of the payroll of the 2004 Washington Nationals. Clearly the figure was more significant to the Nationals, because it represented a higher percentage of their payroll. Then you've got instances of 2008 Alex Rodriguez making as much as the 2007 Florida Marlins!

And so to use percentages of team salary makes more sense than to use raw figures. In order to qualify as a low-risk, high-reward pitcher signing, one must meet the aforementioned duration criteria as well as account for no more than 5.25 percent of the team payroll. On a team of 25 players, each will average 4.0 percent; I allowed an extra 1.25 percent to give some leeway to small-market teams in rebuilding phases. For consistency's sake, though, I evaluated all of these signings on a case-by-case basis in order to determine if any truly should not merit inclusion. For the most part the moves I logged consisted of salaries below 4.0 percent.

LOGGING TRANSACTIONS

Using the ESPN.com transaction archive, I logged all of the moves from October 2002 through August 2007 that met the contract-duration criteria. Through the USA Today Salary Database, I determined individual and team salaries. After entering all of the data, I removed any signing in excess of the 5.25 percent. This left me with 352 pitcher signings to examine.

It is interesting to see the frequency, or lack thereof, per team. For instance, the Cleveland Indians made 22 such moves in this span,whereas the San Francisco Giants made only two: Al Levine in 2005 and Russ Ortiz in 2007. I expected to have five pages consisting solely of Athletics transactions but found only eight qualifying moves. It then dawned on me that Billy Beane has an undying love of young arms, and his low-risk signings were more on the offensive front.

As for individual players, a fair number had been low-risk signings as many as three times. However, only three pitchers achieved the feat four or more times: Terry Mulholland (5), Pedro Astacio (4), and James Baldwin (4). For the record, of the thirteen total seasons between these three pitchers, only Astacio's

2005 with the Padres and Mulholland's 2004 with the Twins actually produced significantly positive results.

Table 1 shows the number of low-risk pitcher signings per team.

DETERMINING THE AMOUNT OF REWARD

With everything logged, I decided to use Keith Woolner's VORP (value over replacement player) statistic to gauge the actual reward levels of these signings. VORP made the most sense to me since the statistic acknowledges the contributions made by league-average players; though these players are not superstars, it would not be fair to deem them ineffectual in a zero-sum game like baseball. Other statistics will use average players as the 0.0 baseline, but VORP uses a below-average player.

In its simplest definition VORP measures the amount of runs contributed above what a replacement-level player would produce in the same percentage of team plate appearances. With respect to pitchers, it refers to the amount of runs saved above what a slightly below-average pitcher would give up if given the same amount of opportunities.

It does not account for defense in the way that Win Shares does but, because we are measuring pitchers, the amount of runs saved vastly outweighs this. I am not sure any general manager has ever signed a pitcher primarily for his defensive ability.

In terms of logging statistics, only the VORP total(s) for the duration of the low-risk contract qualified. For instance, if a player signed a low-risk deal in 2003 and then went on to have productive seasons with the same team in 2004 and 2005, only the 2003 VORP was recorded. The 2004 and 2005 seasons were under different contracts unlikely to meet the 5.25 percent maximum. Additionally, due to the productivity of the initial low-risk season, the risk no longer exists; the team understands what type of production the pitcher could provide. Signing him to a deal still 5.25 percent or less of the team's salary would not necessarily qualify as low-risk but rather as a reasonable upgrade over the low-risk contract.

ANALYZING VORP

In order to determine if these signings worked out, the question of what constitutes reward must be answered. Clearly, anything 0.0 or below would be detrimental, as 0.0 would imply no reward to the team, and a value less than that would imply that the pitcher's effect on the team was actually negative. Additionally, players never called up to the big leagues after signing a low-risk deal provided no reward, as they were never given a shot. While this would not necessarily be negative on the scale of Jose Lima's 2005 season, it would still suggest that no reward was earned. The question then becomes: How do we analyze positive VORPs?

After some careful thought it was determined that, while anything above 0.0 is technically positive, there are different levels of positive rewards. A pitcher could provide low reward, medium reward, or high reward. Here is the reward criteria in terms of VORP totals:

Negative Reward: VORP < 0.0
No Reward: VORP = 0.0 or N/A
Low Reward: VORP = 0.1 to 9.99
Medium Reward: VORP = 10.0 to 19.99
High Reward: VORP = 20.0 +

Table 1. "Low-Risk" Pitcher Signings, 2002–2007

Arizona, 12	Milwaukee, 13
Atlanta, 10	Minnesota, 8
Baltimore, 9	NY Mets, 20
Boston, 14	NY Yankees, 10
Chicago (AL), 6	Oakland, 8
Chicago (NL), 8	Philadelphia, 9
Cincinnati, 20	Pittsburgh, 11
Cleveland, 22	San Diego, 13
Colorado, 19	San Francisco, 2
Detroit, 8	Seattle, 9
Florida, 10	St. Louis, 19
Houston, 17	Tampa Bay, 15
Kansas City, 15	Texas, 9
LA Angels 5	Toronto, 12
LA Dodgers, 10	Washington, 9

LOW-RISK BREAKDOWN

Of the 352 low-risk pitcher signings in this five-year span:

16 were high-reward
47 were medium-reward
101 were low-reward
96 were no-reward (0.0 VORP or never called up)
92 were negative-reward

By combining the five subjects into two—medium-reward or higher-reward, and then everything else—we are left with 63 significant rewards and 289 instances of little, no, or negative rewards. Essentially, from September 2002 to August 2007, these low-risk pitcher signings have truly worked out approximately one-sixth of the time (17.8 percent).

The highest reward belonged to Chris Carpenter, who recovered from Tommy John surgery and had a then career year in 2004 with the Cardinals. Jaret Wright had the second-best reward, during his 2004 season with the Atlanta Braves. (Incidentally, Wright also had

COURTESY OF THE BALTIMORE ORIOLES

In 2007, Jeremy Guthrie of the Orioles had a WAR (wins above replacement) of 3.82, third-highest in the period 2002–7 for pitchers who had been either signed to low-risk contracts or claimed off waivers. Guthrie's one-year deal in 2007 was for $380,000.

the second-worst VORP of low-risk pitcher signings, during his 2003 season with the Padres. Wright's 2003 VORP was –15.7, a distant second-to-last from Jose Lima's –31.6 in 2005.)

VORP TO WAR

Using the rule of thumb that 10 VORP runs equates to one win above replacement (WAR) allows us to quantify the results in a form more suitable in determining team contribution. Carpenter's 40.5 VORP equates to 4.05 wins; his production in saving runs relative to the amount a replacement-level pitcher would surrender resulted in a contribution of about four wins. The numbers essentially stay the same as they are merely being scaled down, but converting saved runs to wins helps in determining whether or not these moves are worth the risk.

Here are the low-risk pitchers accounting for two or more wins above replacement:

Pitcher	WAR
Chris Carpenter (2004)	4.05
Jaret Wright (2004)	3.99
Jeremy Guthrie (2007)	3.82
Paul Byrd (2005)	3.54
Takashi Saito (2006)	3.36
Jeff Suppan (2003)	3.25
David Bush (2006)	3.09
David Riske (2007)	2.77
Kenny Rogers (2003)	2.54
Russ Springer (2007)	2.51
John Thomson (2003)	2.51
Todd Jones (2004)	2.49
Tom Gordon (2003)	2.11
Darren Oliver (2006)	2.10
Mike Timlin (2003)	2.04
Steve Trachsel (2007)	2.03

WORTH THE LOW RISK?

Now that the results are there, we can use them to determine whether the low-risk signing is a sound strategy. By simply looking at the breakdown of reward types shown earlier, we can deduce that, in this span of five years, only a small percentage of low-risk pitcher signings have provided a significant reward. This does not necessarily undermine the strategy, however, as it is important to analyze the results with the mindset of a prospective general manager unable to know whether his low-risk pitcher will work out.

When we try to determine whether the strategy is worth continuing, the ideas of betting and probability come into play. The Cardinals gambled on Chris Carpenter and their strategy paid off immensely. However, the success of the strategy depends on how often it pays off overall, not on how well certain select moves pay off. If you make five low-risk pitcher signings and only one of them works out, no matter how much that pitcher produced, the strategy does not look very sound—80 percent of those signings were not worth it.

The key here is to find the sum total of salaries and wins above replacement among these pitchers and then calculate how much each win costs. With this group of 352, the salaries add up to $214.2 million, and they combine for 110.4 WAR. This results in a salary of approximately $1.94 million per win. Generally speaking, the more reliable free agents will cost somewhere between $4 million and $7 million per win above replacement. Signing low-risk pitchers appears to be a sound strategy because a general manager is paying significantly less money per win. If the low-risk pitchers had cost somewhere near the aforementioned range or even more, then the strategy would not make sense. If you are going to end up paying a similar amount per win, then it is a much safer investment to sign a pitcher who brings with him less of a question mark.

When it comes to these signings, though, it is important to remember that for every Chris Carpenter there are four Bruce Chens. It might make sense to take a flyer on a pitcher to fill out a rotation, but to build the majority of a rotation with these pitchers would not be a good use of payroll. ■

The Little Corporation

Professional Baseball in San Francisco, 1953–1955

Charles D. Johnson

OF THE MANY minor leagues that existed in professional baseball at the end of World War II, the Pacific Coast League (PCL) was at the pinnacle, the one with the best players, several fine stadiums, and robust attendance. In 1946, total attendance for the league was 4,068,372, a PCL record, dwarfing that of any other minor league.[1]

Things were so good, in fact, that Paul I. Fagan, who owned the San Francisco Seals of the PCL, had for many years been leading the charge to get the PCL recognized as a third major league. The idea made a lot of sense. Spurred by the manufacturing boom created by the war, the West was already one of the fastest-growing areas of the country, and every sign suggested that postwar growth would accelerate.[2] Fagan won the support of his fellow owners in the PCL in his efforts to upgrade the league. But, as with other sensible ideas in baseball, this one was doomed, because it threatened the interests of the major-league owners.

At Organized Baseball's 1945 winter meetings, PCL president Clarence H. "Pants" Rowland petitioned his fellow minor-league executives to approve the PCL request to become a major league. After winning their support, he went to the majors with a bold proposal to make the first radical change in the major-league organization since the turn of the century.

Complicating the PCL issue for the majors was Rowland's demand that all eight teams of the PCL be elevated to the majors. To the major-league owners, the Los Angeles Angels and the San Francisco Seals were obvious possibilities for inclusion in the major leagues, but the other PCL clubs were less attractive. The San Diego Padres were surrounded by Mexico, the desert, the Pacific Ocean, and Los Angeles. The Hollywood Stars had transferred from San Francisco (where they'd been the Missions) only in 1938, and, although they would win pennants in 1952 and 1953, they usually drew fewer fans than their crosstown rivals, the Angels. The Oakland Oaks were successful after the war under the management of Casey Stengel, but whether the Bay Area could adequately support two major-league franchises remains unclear even today. The Sacramento Solons, Portland Beavers, and Seattle Rainiers completed the eight-team league, and none of those communities appeared ripe for a major-league franchise.

At the 1945 meetings, the major-league owners rebuffed the PCL petition. The same request was reintroduced the following year, and, though the request itself was denied, the PCL did make some gains. The majors agreed that, if one of its teams were to relocate to a PCL city, the club would have to pay indemnities to the local team and to the rest of the PCL. In 1947, the PCL petition was turned down once again, with baseball commissioner Happy Chandler replying with a proposal that the major leagues expand to ten teams in each league, with the four additional teams located in Los Angeles and San Francisco.[3]

Chandler's position was consistent with the history of the major leagues' treatment of the minors. After cultivating the Western market for fifty years, the PCL was to be brushed aside and its most lucrative cities grabbed by the reigning powers of the East and Midwest.[4] In addition, Chandler's proposal managed to split the PCL owners into factions. While it was obvious that Los Angeles and San Francisco might achieve major-league status, it was much less certain that the others would. Why should the PCL owners see their league gutted and their franchises' values decreased, only to bring major-league baseball to the circuit's two largest markets?

At the outset of the 1950 season, Paul Fagan suggested that the PCL might withdraw from Organized Baseball and operate independently if its concerns were not satisfactorily addressed by the major leagues.[5] His warning led to meetings with the commissioner, who at the end of the 1950 season announced that the major leagues might confer "Four A" status on the PCL, elevating it to a unique position in the game's structure.[6]

This ploy succeeded for a year. In August 1951, the PCL again called for a means for its becoming a major league but added that, if such action were not taken by the end of the year, the league would indeed withdraw from Organized Baseball.[7] The threat assumed significant credibility because it came at the same time the Monopoly Subcommittee of the House Judiciary Committee was holding hearings on baseball's exemption from antitrust law, focusing specifically on the PCL's status. Subcommittee members were curious to know why, in spite of the tremendous demographic changes in the twentieth century, major-league ball continued to be limited to a few Northern and Midwestern cities.[8]

The major-league owners, under their new commissioner, Ford Frick, were ready to cut their losses rather than risk any legislative tampering with the antitrust exemption. During the 1951 winter meetings, Frick announced a scheme to upgrade minor leagues to major-league status. A new classification above Triple A was established for leagues or groups of at least eight teams whose aggregate markets included at least 10 million people, whose ballparks had an aggregate capacity of 120,000, and who had an average paid attendance of over 2.25 million for the preceding five years.[9]

The only Triple A league to qualify for this "open" classification was the PCL. Not surprisingly, PCL officials reacted enthusiastically. PCL President Rowland termed Frick's proposal "encouraging," and congratulated him on his "insight" into the Coast League's "unusual and special problems." Likewise, members of the Monopoly Subcommittee lauded the commissioner for his swift and decisive action.[10]

With the heat on the major-league owners thus turned down, Frick two weeks later announced the specific requirements for those "open" classification leagues seeking to make the final step up to major-league status: an aggregate market of 15 million, ballpark capacity of more than 25,000 for each franchise, and paid attendance in excess of 3.5 million for each of the previous three years. Two of the requirements showed that the majors were not intent on expanding their own ranks: no PCL franchise played in a park seating 25,000, and PCL attendance had declined by almost half since 1947.[11]

And the fans, by and large, understood what was going on. James Crusinberry reflected in *Baseball Magazine* in June 1951 that fans in Los Angeles and San Francisco were becoming indifferent to their teams because they had fallen under the spell of a "major league voodoo."[12] With every new hearing of the House Subcommittee on Monopoly, or every rumor of franchises moving or league executives meeting, fans in the principal PCL markets wanted to know when major-league baseball would arrive.

Crusinberry wrote that the press in California, like the fans, often ignored the local teams to report on major-league games thousands of miles away. Having achieved the peak of its success, the PCL was divided between cities that relished the game as it was and those that were distracted by the future.[13]

Frustrated in his aspirations to elevate the Pacific Coast League to major-league status, reeling from falling attendance and financial losses said by some to be as large as $200,000 in each of the past two years, distrusted by many of his fellow owners, and lambasted by most of the press for his "autocratic" ways and lack of the common touch, Paul Fagan offered in May 1953 to sell his troubled San Francisco Seals baseball club for $250,000. But under the terms of Fagan's proposal, the $250,000 would buy only the Seals franchise and its players. Fagan would keep the real estate and Seals Stadium, leasing it to the new Seals owner for $30,000 per year, with the lessee maintaining the property and assuming the property tax obligations on the stadium.[14]

The press speculated that potential buyers included former Seals stars Joe DiMaggio and Lefty O'Doul in partnership with former Seals general manager Joseph Orengo; singer Bing Crosby; San Francisco real estate baron Louis Lurie; and the Philadelphia Phillies of the National League, who were intent on building up their farm system.[15] But immediate reaction among baseball people was that Fagan's "demands" were "preposterous." Clarence "Brick" Laws, owner of the Oakland Oaks, when asked if he considered the sale price and the rental a fair investment for such a baseball operation, said bluntly, "I certainly wouldn't do it." In Sacramento, Charles Graham Jr., who had previously owned an interest in the Seals, said he had no desire to return, "especially at that price."[16]

Laws and Graham proved to have assessed the situation accurately. Although there were some nibbles, no buyers were found in the next few months. Meanwhile, the Seals continued their mediocre on-field performance, and attendance was down, making the franchise even less desirable for an investor interested in the bottom line. The Seals would finish the 1953 season fifth in the eight-team PCL, with total attendance of 175,459, down 12 percent from that of the poor 1952 season, and a fraction of the 640,643 total attendance in 1947.[17]

Finally, in September 1953, under continuing pressure from his fellow owners, Fagan reached an agreement to sell the Seals franchise and players to the PCL itself for $100,000, much less than the $250,000 he had wanted in May. Retaining ownership of Seals Stadium, Fagan agreed to lease the park to the league for a period of five years. The lease provided that the league pay Fagan ten cents for each admission, guarantee the upkeep of the park (estimated to cost between $43,000 and $75,000 annually), and assume responsibility for property taxes on the real estate (estimated to be $36,000 annually). The sale contract also stipulated that all present employees of the Seals,

DAVID ESKENAZI COLLECTION

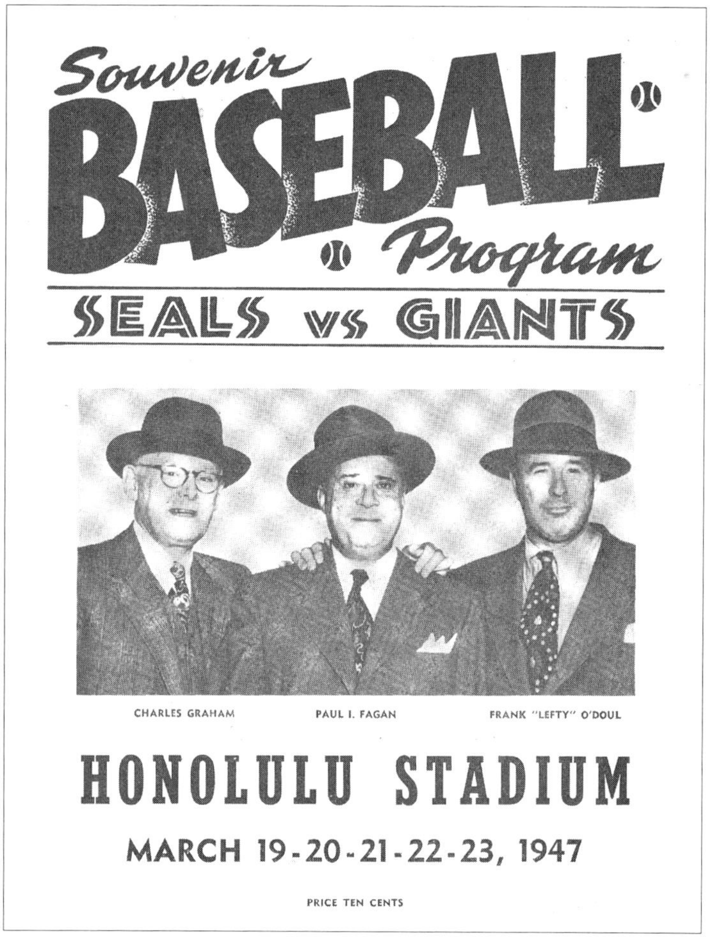

Paul I. Fagan, center, *owner of the San Francisco Seals. In 1953 he sold the franchise to the Pacific Coast League for $100,000 but retained ownership of Seals Stadium, which he leased to the PCL, and stipulated terms that were advantageous to him.*

including field manager Tommy Heath, be kept on the payroll. Office equipment, seat cushions, and the club's baseball gear—baseballs, bats, uniforms—were relinquished free of charge by Fagan.

Fagan was able to protect his interests in more ways than just the advantageous lease provisions. In recognition for Fagan's "sacrificing the club for such a small sum," the sale agreement also provided that, if during the term of the stadium lease the major leagues desired to place a franchise of their own in the San Francisco market, Fagan could repurchase the Seals franchise for $100,000. He also had the right to buy back the franchise within thirty days after the close of any season, also for $100,000. Furthermore, the PCL could not resell the club without Fagan's approval of the purchaser.[18]

Fagan, who had made his fortune in shipping and then branched out into Bay Area real estate and sugar plantations in Hawaii, had done well with this agreement. Knowing that the major leagues had agreed to compensate the owner of any PCL franchise in a city where they might move a team, Fagan was determined to preserve that potential windfall for himself. He also held onto Seals Stadium, keenly aware that the property at 16th and Bryant Streets was ultimately more valuable serving a purpose other than as a site for minor-league baseball games.

Despite the advantageous terms of the sale agreement, Fagan made it clear that he did not sell of his own volition. "The league wanted me to, so I complied with their desires," he said, almost tearfully, at the press conference announcing the sale.[19]

Under its bylaws, the PCL could not operate the Seals itself, so the owners immediately appointed Damon Miller, who had served as Fagan's general manager and secretary, as custodian, and authorized him to form a corporation that would operate the franchise. Miller had the option of looking for new owners to bankroll the club or to try and buy the club himself. In a surprise announcement, Miller said he had no intention of looking for new buyers. While he admitted he "[didn't] know all the answers yet," Miller did have a hazy plan of sorts.

> "We shall form a little corporation, probably to be made up of old employees of the Seals, but I think I can handle this thing myself. . . . I may require a little help [in the form of loans from the PCL], but baseball doesn't have to be a losing proposition here. It can be made to pay and show a profit."[20]

Damon Miller was an unlikely baseball magnate. An accountant, he had joined the Seals' staff in 1933 for the purpose of keeping track of soda and peanut sales. When Paul Fagan assumed sole ownership of the club in 1950, he elevated Miller to the position of club secretary, from which Miller oversaw the team's travel and certain business matters. In 1952, Fagan made Miller general manager, nominally in charge of all baseball operations, but most sportswriters considered this a "glorification," since Fagan was an owner who did his own general managing. *San Francisco Examiner* writer Prescott Sullivan, for one, had a pessimistic view of the Seals' prospects under Miller.[21]

But Miller was determined. As he had promised, he approached the Seals' few remaining employees about buying into the franchise. Eight employees, including Miller, paid a total of $20,000 for shares of voting stock. Miller bought $10,000 of the stock. Accountant Gladys Ferguson, office secretaries Ruth Merrill and Lila Wulff, box office manager John Craig, concession manager Bob Hirsch, radio announcer Don Klein, and field manager Tommy Heath together owned the rest. Miller, Hirsch, Heath, Craig, and Merrill were elected directors of the corporation, officially named San Francisco Seals, Inc., but known by sportswriters and fans simply as "the Little Corporation."

At an all-day meeting at Los Angeles's Biltmore Hotel on October 29, the PCL owners voted unanimously to accept the bid of the Little Corporation to take over the Seals franchise. The Little Corporation paid the PCL $10,000, and the PCL set no time limit under which the Little Corporation had to pay the remaining $90,000 the PCL had paid Fagan. Miller informed the press that this detail was to be decided in the future "by mutual consent." The Little Corporation also made a $10,000 deposit on the stadium lease, and used the $15,000 advance paid for radio broadcast rights by Emil Sick's Seattle Brewing Company to pay initial operating expenses.[22]

Shortly after their October league meeting, though, the PCL owners started to reconsider the award of the Seals franchise to the Little Corporation. Unsure that Miller yet had enough capital to operate a team, and fearing that the league would be liable for any debts incurred by the new group, on December 2 the PCL owners revoked the franchise. Speaking on behalf of the PCL, league president Clarence Rowland stated that the immediate reason for revoking the franchise was the Little Corporation's failure to lease Seals Stadium directly from Paul Fagan so that the league would be released from all liability under the lease agreement it had with Fagan, as well as the Little Corporation's failure to provide sufficient financing to justify the league's assumption of any risk.[23]

Miller, who was not even aware that the league owners were meeting, was enraged both at the secrecy and at the action taken. "My first information was from a writer I met on the elevator," he said. "I am just sick about the whole affair. I thought I was dealing with friends and found out they were back stabbers."[24]

Miller immediately took action on two fronts. First, he contacted his attorney and publicly threatened the league owners with an injunction suit. Then he contacted San Francisco civic leaders and had them flood Rowland with telegrams of protest. With these weapons, Miller extracted Rowland's promise that, if Miller did not file suit against the PCL, the league would take no action regarding sale of the franchise until the December 11 PCL owners' meeting.

A statement Miller issued to the press pointed out that, contrary to what the PCL demanded, the Little Corporation could not lease Seals Stadium directly from Paul Fagan. Miller had already contacted Fagan about just such an arrangement and been rebuffed. Fagan told Miller that he already had a lease agreement with the PCL, and that that was the agreement he meant to be binding. Miller also explained that the PCL's action was null and void, since as a unanimously elected league director, Miller was entitled to be notified of the owners' meeting and to vote on any resolutions put before the owners at such a meeting.[25]

It is possible that reasons unrelated to the financial standing of the Little Corporation prompted the PCL owners to try to strip Miller's group of the franchise. Bill Veeck, the former owner of the Cleveland Indians and then the St. Louis Browns of the American League, admitted that he had informed the PCL owners of his interest in bidding for the Seals franchise if Miller could not qualify for lack of money, and that the league had "invited [him] to put in a bid for the Seals." An application on behalf of Rudie Schaffer, a former employee of Veeck's, and a check for $25,000 had been submitted, with the promise that the franchise would be purchased outright with substantial backing. Schaffer also offered to provide Fagan with $50,000 if he would eliminate the clause under which Fagan could buy back the Seals franchise within thirty days of the end of any season. Veeck frankly admitted that he would "go in" with Schaffer if Schaffer's bid were accepted by the PCL.[26]

Brick Laws was the PCL owner who said he wanted to see Miller make good on his efforts to control the Seals franchise. Laws, who had lost a small fortune backing the Oakland Oaks, blamed the collapse of support for the Seals during the Fagan regime in part for the attendance troubles his own franchise was having. He thought Miller's group, especially in its adopted role of David against Goliath, could rekindle a fire amongst San Francisco's baseball fans that would benefit all the teams of the league. But, he cautioned, "[i]t can't be done on $20,000. Damon needs to throw $100,000 into the kitty" before the December 11 owners' meeting.[27]

On December 3, the Little Corporation opened its fight to regain the Seals franchise. An advertising campaign was launched to promote sales of discounted tickets (a book of ten $1.25 tickets for only $10.00). In a public statement, the Little Corporation asked that fans flood Seals offices with wires and letters of protest "against the action of PCL President Clarence Rowland

and the league directors who are attempting to rob Miller of the franchise."[28]

Meanwhile, San Francisco civic leaders and fans, strongly resenting the league's action, rallied to support the Little Corporation. Members of the Chamber of Commerce asked to attend the December 11 owners' meeting so they could place their pledges of support for the Miller group before the league directors. Walter Brown, president of the Chamber, said the organization would do whatever it could to "help Miller over this hurdle." Thomas Brooks, chief administrative officer of the City of San Francisco, and Harry Ross, the city's controller, fired off wires to Rowland and began organizing a campaign of support by city employees.[29]

Perhaps most important for the Little Corporation's future, John Drenth, a San Francisco branch manager of a national insurance company, made out a personal check for $1,000, offering to buy stock in the Little Corporation. Drenth explained his plan to sports writer Art Rosenbaum. "There must be ninety San Francisco business executives ready, willing and able to invest $1,000 each in the Seals. If Miller had $100,000 cash to hand Rowland on December 11, I do not think the offer would be rejected, particularly when it was shown San Francisco businessmen were behind the Seals, financially."[30]

Miller, with the prodding of the San Francisco press, took Drenth up on his offer. On December 7, the Seals president announced that the Little Corporation was amending its articles of incorporation and would place on the open market $100,000 of nonvoting preferred stock, available for $10 per share. There was to be no limit on the number of shares any one person could buy. "The Seals' fate is now in the hands of the people," Miller stated.[31]

By issuing non-voting preferred stock to any new stockholders, Miller and his original shareholders, who held voting common stock, would be able to retain control of the Little Corporation. The bylaws of the corporation were amended to provide for payment from any profit of a five-percent dividend to owners of preferred stock; thereafter, profit would be divided on a proportional basis among common and preferred stockholders if the board of directors decided to declare a dividend. In the event of the corporation's dissolution, preferred stock would be redeemed at $10.50 a share, and then common stockholders' stock would be redeemed in proportion to the amount of liquid funds the corporation had.[32]

In Los Angeles, President Rowland said that the $100,000 would help, but not necessarily win the battle. "As of now, Miller and his group are just like any other bidder for the franchise. If they can raise enough money, or get big money behind them, then they're in."[33]

The baseball fans of San Francisco responded enthusiastically. *Chronicle* sportswriter Will Connolly wrote that he could not remember when baseball was talked about more in San Francisco than during the three weeks preceding Christmas in 1953. By noon on December 9, $20,000 in checks and cash had arrived by mail or been personally delivered at Seals Stadium. Contributors included Victor Grecan, "representing my pals on the waterfront," who walked in with $1,500, and Claire Smith, daughter of former Seals owner Charles Graham Sr., who appeared at Seals offices with a check for $1,000. Even Seals pitcher Al Lien, after obtaining permission from the minor-league president's office, invested $1,000.[34]

Hundreds of investors had provided a total of $44,080 by the morning of December 11, and Miller took those checks, along with thousands of wires and letters of support, with him to the PCL owners' meeting that day at the Alexander Hamilton Hotel in San Francisco. He also had other inducements for the owners. On the basis of the strong public support shown over the previous three days, two corporations had stepped in to help Miller. The Golden Gate Broadcasting Company, whose KSAN-TV would be broadcasting Seals night home games, had agreed to back an indemnity bond to relieve the PCL directors of any liability under the stadium lease. (Sherwood and Norwood Patterson, the father-and-son owners of the Golden Gate Broadcasting Company, also obtained a first-refusal option to buy the Seals in the event the Little Corporation sold the franchise.) In addition, the Pacific National Bank had loaned the Little Corporation $50,000, asking for no collateral. The cash was to be turned over to Paul Fagan in exchange for wiping out the controversial "recapture clause" that allowed Fagan to take back the Seals on thirty days' notice. With this new backing, the Little Corporation won the unanimous approval of the PCL owners, and was re-awarded the Seals franchise.[35]

The Little Corporation had won, and Miller knew just who was responsible. He issued a statement to the press thanking "most of all the people of San Francisco for the wonderful support they have given us."[36]

Over the following weeks, the Little Corporation sold more stock, until a total of $91,000 had been invested in the club by 1,800 fans throughout California. Miller also negotiated a deal by which KSAN-TV paid the Little Corporation $75,000 for the rights to broadcast Seals home night games, and hammered out an installment plan by which the Little Corporation would pay the PCL the balance of the $90,000 it still owed the league for the Seals franchise. Miller considered paying the common stockholders some of their back salaries (they hadn't gotten a paycheck since October 1) but considered the fact that neither he nor his fellow investors had been paid in quite some time was a fine marketing tool with which to solicit more purchasers of preferred stock.

On opening day, April 6, 1954, the Seals played before 10,783 at Seals Stadium. (Predicted attendance had been as high as 20,000.) The Seals and their ace pitcher, Tony Ponce, were beaten by the Seattle Rainiers, 8–5. The Seals played poorly in subsequent games, losing 21 of their first 28 contests. Attendance reflected the team's poor performance. The Seals drew 9,534 on April 11, but on most days, attendance hovered between 1,200 and 3,000. By the end of the month, fans seemed to have disappeared. Only 737 attended the April 28 game against the Hollywood Stars, and only 942 came out for the game the next day. On the highly promoted "Family Night," Friday, April 30, when a paying adult could bring his or her kids (and probably the neighbors') for free, attendance was a disappointing 2,695.

Crowds had been particularly small at night, with San Francisco's typically cool summer evenings being the main complaint. Two weeks into the season, the Little Corporation announced that henceforth all night games scheduled for Wednesdays and Thursdays would instead be played at 1:30 P.M. Night games would only be played on Tuesdays and Fridays. In addition, women would be admitted to the park on Tuesdays, Wednesdays, Thursdays, and Saturdays for only seventy-five cents, fifty cents less than the regular admission price.[37]

The common stockholders of the Little Corporation saved money on salaries by doing two and three jobs. Ruth Merrill, the corporation's secretary, routinely worked the ticket window at night games. Gladys Ferguson, accountant, did office work from 9 to 5, then worked as a cashier for night games, and when that work was well in hand, took charge of ushers during the games.[38]

As the season played itself out, the Seals proved more exciting than good. They won only ten of their first 35 games, and manager Tommy Heath decided that if veteran players were that poor, why not let the kids see what they could do? Heath cut some of the older players, and a core of younger talent, including catcher Nini Tornay, Jim Westlake at first base, Mike Baxes and Reno Cheso platooning at third, and Bob DiPietro in the outfield, rose to the occasion. The team played better ball, and at the end of May, the Seals started on a tear, winning 10 straight, and 24 of 31.

The rejuvenated Seals made up those early losses and finished at 84–84, in fourth place right behind the Oaks, thus qualifying for the PCL playoffs. The Little Corporation's travails, exciting play, and an unusual number of native San Franciscans on the team all led to renewed fan interest. The Seals led the league in attendance with 298,908, and exceeded their break-even goal when a single Governor's Cup playoff game was included.[39]

For the year, the Little Corporation netted $464. While there was real pleasure at the Little Corporation's success in its first season, more realistic observers were concerned. Total league attendance had only increased by a little over 13,000. Miller's group had not been able to defray any of its major obligations, and even the salaries they had declared for themselves had not been paid in full.[40]

The Little Corporation made little changes to its marketing strategies in the off-season, and they no longer had the luxury of thousands of new investors sending in their small checks. Tommy Heath was signed to a two-year contract through the end of the 1956 season, and essentially it would be the same Seals taking the field in 1955.

The 1955 season proved to be a disappointment. The inability of Clarence Maddern to provide batting punch, the retirement of pitcher Bob Muncrief, and the fade-out of pitcher Adrian Zabala crippled the Seals. By mid-season, the club, paced by the brilliant hitting of DiPietro, began making noises, but then DiPietro broke his leg. After wasting a good start and then languishing in the depths of the second division for most of the 1955 season, the Seals claimed sixth place, 15 games out at 80–92. League attendance increased slightly, but Bay Area figures spelled impending doom. Seals attendance dropped more than 140,000 to 161,570, seventh in the league. Only Oakland's 141,397 was worse. As the Seals limped to the finish line, the officials of the Little Corporation knew they had lost their battle. They were broke. The *Chronicle*'s headline for the last day of the season was "'Little Corp' Is Now the 'Little Corpse.'"[41]

The PCL owners felt they had to find a more flush owner to take over the Seals franchise. Purchase of the Seals would entail an immediate outlay of considerable cash just to keep howling creditors away from bare and accessible heels. It would take $20,000 to buy 100 percent of the common stock then outstanding. A debt of $30,000 was still owed the PCL, and the $50,000 bank loan floated in the winter of 1953 was overdue.

Recognizing these problems, the PCL owners gave Miller until the annual league meeting, scheduled in Seattle on September 12, 1955, to find a buyer. Otherwise, the PCL would reclaim the Seals franchise from the Little Corporation.[42]

Sherwood and Norwood Patterson, the owners of KSAN radio and television, stepped forward to discuss with Damon Miller the prospect of exercising their option to purchase the financially distressed club. Sherwood Patterson was a former evangelist from Denver who wore a cowboy hat, carried a bible, and wanted to "save our Seals as part of my fight for [*sic*] juvenile delinquency." In a September 2, 1955, meeting with directors Miller, Heath, and Klein, the Pattersons asked the Little Corporation members to waive back salaries, amounting to $30,000. (Tommy Heath, for example, had not been paid for his services as manager since the end of June.)[43]

Despite the Little Corporation's outstanding debt, the Pattersons came to an agreement with Miller and his group on September 3. The media tycoons agreed to pay $20,000 for the common stock of the Little Corporation, a small portion of back salaries, $50,000 on the bank loan, plus $30,000 owed to the PCL, approximately $30,000 in other outstanding debts, and to assume the obligations of approximately $97,000 in preferred stock sold to the public in 1953. Some observers estimated the total debt of the Seals to be as high as $284,000. The deal was contingent on the PCL owners accepting the Pattersons as new owners of the Seals.[44]

But no sooner had the Pattersons exercised their option than rumors circulated that they would not be approved by the PCL owners at their Seattle meeting. There was speculation that the league owners had already lined up a buyer of their own. Others wondered whether the Pattersons genuinely had the resources to pull off the deal. If the Pattersons backed off, Los Angeles furniture dealer Tony Longo, a friend of Tommy Heath, said he was ready to buy out the Little Corporation for cash.

Once Longo showed interest in the franchise, Damon Miller showed an interest in sabotaging the Pattersons' chances with the PCL owners. Miller, who had a rocky relationship with the Pattersons dating from the Seals' 1954 decision to play fewer night games after KSAN had planned its television schedule and advertising around those night games, told the press, "We think that Longo should have the franchise in the interest of the Seals and all concerned."[45]

Miller claimed that his preference for Longo resulted from his desire to save the money of the non-voting, preferred stockholders by getting the PCL's permission to allow the Little Corporation's ownership to change hands while retaining its corporate identity. He feared the league's directors would merely declare the Little Corporation bankrupt, take back the Seals franchise, and sell it to the highest bidder, thus voiding the non-voting stock.[46]

The main stumbling block to finding a buyer was not the back pay for the Little Corporation employees, nor the debts of the corporation. Paul Fagan, who spent most of his time in Hawaii and was no longer involved with baseball, was the shadow that scared off potential buyers. Fagan still owned Seals Stadium, and the Seals' lease on the ballpark had only three more years to run. Fagan had made no secret of the fact that once the lease expired he wanted to tear down the stadium and use the land for some more profitable enterprise. In addition, should a major league locate a club in San Francisco, Fagan had a right to buy back the Seals for $100,000 and claim the windfall fee the majors were obligated to pay the owner of any PCL franchise in San Francisco.

At the much-anticipated meeting of the PCL owners in Seattle on September 12, the Pattersons suddenly decided they did not want the Herculean role of rescuing the Seals. The league owners then gave the poverty-stricken Little Corporation ten more days in which to come up with a qualified buyer. Miller promptly handed that role to Tony Longo, who was named temporary general manager of the Seals, a job he would forfeit unless he came up with the money necessary to purchase the club.[47]

Longo started negotiating with various major-league teams for the sale of some Seals players. On September 21, the Kansas City Athletics bought shortstop Mike Baxes, outfielder Dave Melton, and pitcher Bill Bradford for cash, a player to be named later, and options on the services of any of the three sold players in case they did not make the big club's roster. Longo claimed the deal realized the equivalent of $85,000 to the Seals in cash and services.[48]

But when it came time for the PCL owners' meeting in San Diego on September 25, Longo was nowhere in sight. Longo had promised Miller he would be in San Diego with a certified check to purchase the team, and his absence "perturbed" Miller, who announced that Longo's stint as general manager was at an end. The owners decided the sale of the players to the Athletics justified setting up a committee to help the Little Corporation find "a suitable purchaser or investor." On the committee with Miller were the new league president, Claire Goodwin, and club presidents Bob Cobb of

Hollywood, John Holland of Los Angeles, and Brick Laws of Oakland.[49]

October 1955 proved to be a month full of speculation, as the Little Corporation wooed any big-league club that showed an interest in investing in or buying outright the Seals franchise. Lou Perini, owner of the Milwaukee Braves, spoke of interest in moving his Toledo Sox of the minor-league American Association to San Francisco, and sent his vice president, Joseph Cairnes, to San Francisco for discussions with civic leaders and PCL president Goodwin. Hank Greenberg, general manager of the Cleveland Indians, came out to San Francisco for discussions with Miller about purchase of the franchise and with Paul Fagan about revisions to the lease at Seals Stadium. Fagan wasn't much for changing the terms of the lease, but did offer to go in with Greenberg if Greenberg wanted to buy the Seals and move the franchise to a ball park they would construct on the peninsula, where, Fagan emphasized, "the population is going and the weather will always be better than in San Francisco." Neither the Braves' nor the Indians' interest came to anything, though.[50]

DAVID ESKENAZI COLLECTION

Clarence H. "Pants" Rowland, president of the Pacific Coast League. In December 1953 he announced that the league was revoking sale of the Seals to Damon Miller and the Little Corporation, whose principals persisted in their effort to buy the club.

In the midst of this uncertainty, Tommy Heath, on October 27, resigned as manager and as a director of the Seals. Heath split his stock and gave equal shares to Damon Miller and Bob Hirsch. He said he was still owed more than $8,000 in back pay. "It doesn't look as though we [the Little Corporation] will be in business very long," Heath told the press. "It is reasonable to assume that if the club is sold the new owners will probably want to bring their own manager with them."[51]

Finally, in a November 10 owners' meeting in Vancouver, British Columbia (where the struggling Oakland Oaks franchise would now move), the PCL voted to reclaim the San Francisco Seals franchise by forfeiture. The Little Corporation still owed the league $30,000 of the original $100,000 franchise price tag. The PCL owners put a price of $200,000 on the franchise, a figure the Milwaukee Braves, who were then still in the running to purchase the club, were unwilling to pay.[52]

Miller was, again, "very much perturbed" by what he considered the PCL's "early" forfeiture of the franchise. "What did they have to do that for, at this time? After all, they didn't have a buyer yet. We're as anxious as anybody to sell to the proper person. . . . [I]nstead of giving me an opportunity to try for new capital, to operate legally, they have left me here in confusion."[53]

Later in November, the annual major-minor–league meetings were held in Columbus, Ohio. PCL president Claire Goodwin was there, discussing purchase of the Seals by the vast Sheraton hotel chain, which was represented at the meeting by Bill Rosensohn. At the same time, California League president Jerry Donovan was busy in Columbus trying to broker a deal by which any prospective major-league team could buy the Seals. Donovan, a native San Franciscan, had for two weeks been carrying on discussions with another native San Franciscan, Joe Cronin, general manager of the Boston Red Sox. After nine hours of deliberation on the evening of November 28, the PCL owners voted, 6–1, to award the Seals franchise to the Red Sox.[54]

That evening, at a joint press conference in Columbus, Donovan and Cronin announced that the Red Sox had bought the Seals franchise from the PCL for $150,000. The money was to be paid in two installments, on December 15, 1955, and February 1, 1956. Fifty thousand dollars of the purchase price would go to the PCL, $6,750 would go to former Seals manager Tommy Heath as partial back pay, and the rest to the Little Corporation.

Damon Miller was in the same hotel in Columbus where the deal was made, but he hadn't heard of it until the press phoned him. "I don't know where that $50,000 figure owed the league comes from," he said. "We owe the league $30,000 on a promissory note, we have a bank note for $50,000, and we owe $10,000 to Brick Laws for Billy Serena, whom we bought last summer. Tommy Heath has some back salary coming, but not $6,750. The rest of the money, about $60,000, I guess, goes to the preferred stock holders." As to the investment of the common stockholders, "we just lose that money."[55]

The Little Corporation was probably doomed to fail. A top minor-league franchise could not run on an initial $100,000 investment, especially with the extra obligations the Little Corporation was expected to carry. While it was not unusual for a ball team to rent the stadium in which it played, the terms of the lease with Fagan were particularly hard. The rental, upkeep of the stadium, and property taxes the Little Corporation was expected to pay amounted to a frightening $95,000 per year, more than the major-league Indians paid for their use of Municipal Stadium in Cleveland.[56] Seals Stadium was getting old, and the Little Corporation quickly fell behind on necessary maintenance, making a day or night out at the stadium less attractive to a potential customer.

With inadequate capitalization, the Little Corporation could not overcome the economic and social forces moving against minor-league baseball in the late 1940s and the 1950s. In the economics of baseball before World War II, competition for the fans' entertainment dollar came principally from the movies. The growth of television and the automobile changed that.

The whole country was moving in those days, and San Francisco was no exception. Postwar prosperity and government policies such as the G.I. Bill of Rights and the interstate highway programs shifted populations out of the city. Installment-buying made cars more affordable, and cars in turn permitted independence and mobility. Families that for generations had crowded into the apartments and attached houses of San Francisco fled en masse to the suburbs. As fans were freed from the cities by their cars, they found new diversions, and baseball had to become more competitive.

Television changed things, too. By 1952, the major leagues broadcast on NBC to the West Coast a Saturday game of the week. (In addition, a major-league game was broadcast nightly on San Francisco's KYA radio.) Fans could now, in their own home, watch or listen to a better product than minor-league ball, and fan loyalties began to change. The Yankees, Giants, and Dodgers now had loyal fans not just in New York City, but throughout the United States, and even in San Francisco.

Finally, the rampant speculation about major-league expansion or movement of established franchises to the West Coast obviously hurt attendance at Seals games. Three major-league teams had moved to new cities since March 1953, and major-league owners such as Phil Wrigley of the Chicago Cubs, Clark Griffith of the Washington Senators, and Bill Veeck of the St. Louis Browns had spoken about the inevitability of major-league baseball moving to the West Coast.

Such speculation had become so vocal that baseball commissioner Ford Frick issued a directive forbidding such "major-league talk" around minor-league cities because it hurt the minor-league product. But Ford's

DAVID ESKENAZI COLLECTION

Seals Stadium, home of the San Francisco Seals from 1931 until the team relocated to Phoenix in 1957. It was demolished in 1959. Rental, upkeep, and property taxes cost the Little Corporation $95,000 a year, more than the major-league Indians paid for their use of Municipal Stadium in Cleveland.

stricture was too little, too late. San Franciscans wanted the major-league product, not the Seals. A *San Francisco Chronicle* poll of baseball fans conducted at the end of the 1955 season found that almost 50 percent of respondents followed major-league baseball more closely than they did PCL baseball.[57]

December 1955 marked the end of the line for the bookkeeper, the broadcaster, the secretary, the concessionaire, the usherette, and the box office chief, the little people who took over a ball club a millionaire could not afford and that, ultimately, they could not maintain. Damon Miller and his Little Corporation strove gallantly against impossible odds, and though victory eluded them, they managed to keep professional baseball alive, if barely, in San Francisco. For that, they won the city's admiration and gratitude. ■

Bibliographical Note

These bibliographical comments are intended to exhaust neither the available literature on the subjects nor the materials I have consulted. They do include, however, my sources of factual information and the writings that have directly influenced my interpretations. Four works on the history of the Pacific Coast League have been published. Ken Stadler, a Los Angeles newspaperman, wrote *The Pacific Coast League: One Man's Memories, 1938–57* (Los Angeles: Marbek Publications, 1985), which has information and stories about the teams (especially the Los Angeles Angels and Hollywood Stars) and players, but little on the business of the PCL. Bill O'Neil's *The Pacific Coast League, 1903–1988* (Austin, Tex.: Eakin Press, 1989) and Dick Dobbins and Jon Twichell's *Nuggets on the Diamond: Professional Baseball in the Bay Area from the Gold Rush to the Present* (San Francisco: Woodford Press, 1994) deal almost exclusively with the game on the field and not the workings of the front offices, although Dobbins and Twichell do devote a couple of pages to the colorful Paul Fagan and a couple to the Little Corporation. The lone scholarly work, Paul J. Zingg and Mark D. Medeiros's *Runs, Hits and an Era: The Pacific Coast League, 1903–1958* (Urbana: University of Illinois Press, 1994) is indispensable and does contain considerable material on the PCL as a business, although unfortunately it does not mention the Little Corporation or its travails at all.

Two books by Neil J. Sullivan, neither dealing specifically with the PCL, proved useful and influenced my conclusions about the reasons for declining fan interest in the PCL and the Seals. *The Minors: The Struggles and Triumph of Baseball's Poor Relations from 1876 to the Present* (New York: St. Martin's Press, 1991) provided a thoughtful discussion on the impact of television on the minors and the PCL, and also provided useful information on the PCL from articles in *Baseball Magazine and Baseball Digest*, two periodicals unavailable in library collections in the Bay Area. *The Dodgers Move West* (New York: Oxford University Press, 1987) is an excellent work, containing much information on the economics of professional baseball, including the impact of television, the automobile, and a changing society on the business of the game in the 1940s and 1950s, and on the majors' exploitation of the PCL during that period.

For information about player performance, statistics, and attendance, I relied on Dennis Snelling, *The Pacific Coast League: A Statistical History, 1903–1957* (Jefferson, N.C.: McFarland, 1995), although its records are not nearly complete, and *The Encyclopedia of Minor League Baseball* (Durham, N.C.: Baseball America, 1993), edited by Lloyd Johnson and Miles Wolff.

Most of the facts and quotations in my paper come from newspaper articles in three San Francisco dailies: the *San Francisco Call-Bulletin*, the *San Francisco Chronicle*, and the *San Francisco Examiner*. Of the three papers, the *Call-Bulletin* was the only defender of Fagan and his regime, and all three responded enthusiastically to Miller's efforts to form a corporation and attract fan-investors, to the extent of providing what amounted to free publicity and uncritical articles in the early days of the Little Corporation. The columns of the *Examiner*'s Prescott Sullivan were a notable exception to this "rah-rah" coverage. Throughout the life of the Little Corporation, Bob Stevens of the *Chronicle* provided the most insightful, and readable, writing on the Seals, both those on the field and those in the front office.

Notes

1. Paul J. Zingg and Mark D. Medeiros, *Runs, Hits, and an Era: The Pacific Coast League, 1903–58* (Urbana: University of Illinois Press, 1994), 111–12.
2. Indeed, between 1940 and 1950, California saw a 53 percent increase in population and became the second-largest state in the nation; Zingg and Medeiros, *Runs, Hits, and an Era*, 107–8.
3. Neil J. Sullivan, *The Minors: The Struggles and the Triumph of Baseball's Poor Relations from 1876 to the Present* (New York: St. Martin's Press, 1991), 219.
4. Chandler's plan failed at that time because of two dissenting votes in the American League. The National League owners, including Walter O'Malley of the Brooklyn Dodgers and Horace Stoneham of the New York Giants, voted their unanimous approval.
5. "Chandler Avoids Coast League Bolt," *New York Times*, 4 April 1950, 47.
6. "Higher Rank Seen for Coast League," *New York Times*, 2 November 1950, 40.
7. "Coast Loop in Revolt Over Baseball Draft," *New York Times*, 30 August 1951, 27.
8. The best recent discussion of the House Subcommittee's hearings and the antitrust exemption is in "The Irrelevance of Baseball's Antitrust

Exemption: A Historical Review," by Mitchell Nathanson, *Rutgers Law Review* 58, no. 1 (2005).

9. "Major League Plan Would Assist PCL," *Los Angeles Times*, 15 November 1951, C1.
10. "Coast League Nabobs Laud Recommendations," *Los Angeles Times*, 15 November 1951, C33.
11. "New Proposal Dims PCL's Major Hopes," *Los Angeles Times*, 29 November 1951, C1.
12. Quoted in *The Minors*, by Neil J. Sullivan, 224.
13. Ibid. Typical of many writers who covered baseball in San Francisco, *Examiner* sports editor Curley Grieve wrote in one of his columns: "It could be that, in the long run, San Francisco would be better off to let the Seals and the Coast League collapse in order to hasten the arrival of the major-league clubs here and Los Angeles. The Coast League and a couple of ball parks are the only barriers to major-league entry right now. And it's a cinch that neither city will be completely satisfied until it gets under the big tent where it belongs" ("League Pulls a Blunder," *San Francisco Examiner*, 5 December 1953, 20).
14. "Fagan Offers to Sell Seals," *San Francisco Call-Bulletin*, 15 May 1953, 3G; "Details of Fagan Proposal," *San Francisco Examiner*, 16 May 1953, 20.
15. "Fagan Offers to Sell Seals," *San Francisco Call-Bulletin*, 15 May 1953, 3G.
16. "Seals Franchise for sale," *San Francisco Chronicle*, 15 May 1953, 1H.
17. Lloyd Johnson and Miles Wolff, eds., *The Encyclopedia of Minor League Baseball* (Durham, N.C.: Baseball America, 1993), 224, 270.
18. "Fagan Sells Seals to Coast League," *San Francisco Examiner*, 25 September 1953, 39; "PCL Awards Seal Franchise to Miller," *San Francisco Examiner*, 25 September 1953, 3930 October 1953, 37.
19. "Fagan Sells Seals to Coast League," *San Francisco Examiner*, 25 September 1953, 39.
20. Ibid.; "PCL Buys Seals—Miller, Heath in Charge," *San Francisco Chronicle*, 25 September 1953, 7.
21. "Miller moves ahead," Ibid., 26 September 1953, 1H; "The New Man in Charge," *San Francisco Examiner*, 26 September 1953, 19.
22. "PCL Awards Seal Franchise to Miller," *San Francisco Examiner*, 30 October 1953, 37.
23. "Veeck in S.F. to Bid for Seals," *San Francisco Examiner*, 3 December 1953, 44.
24. Ibid.
25. Ibid.
26. Ibid.; "Bill Veeck Confers with Gov.," *San Francisco Chronicle*, 4 December 1953, 1H; "'Raise $100,000,' Brick Laws Advises," *San Francisco Examiner*, 4 December 1953, 42.
27. "League Pulls a Blunder," *San Francisco Examiner*, 5 December 1953, 20.
28. "Seals Open Survival Fight," *San Francisco Chronicle*, 4 December 1953, 1H.
29. Ibid.
30. "90 Men with Grand Might Save a Tiny Band," *San Francisco Chronicle*, 5 December, 1953, 4H.
31. "'Little People' Seek $100,000 at $10 a Share," *San Francisco Chronicle*, 8 December, 1953, 1H.
32. "Seal Sale Near 25G," *San Francisco Examiner*, 10 December 1953, 37.
33. "'Little People' Seek $100,000 at $10 a Share," *San Francisco Chronicle*, 8 December 1953, 1H.
34. "Checks Still Flow to Seals," *San Francisco Chronicle*, 10 December 1953, 3H; "The Wonderful Fairy Tale of PCL Meeting," *San Francisco Chronicle*, 13 December 1953, 3H.
35. "Miller Wins Fight to Keep the Seals," *San Francisco Chronicle*, 12 December 1953, 1; while Fagan was willing to give on the "recapture clause," he was adamant in retaining his right to take back the franchise in the event the major leagues put a team in San Francisco.
36. "Damon Miller Thanks Public," *San Francisco Chronicle*, 13 December 1953, 2H.
37. "Seals to Play Only Two Nights," *San Francisco Chronicle*, 21 April 1954, 1H.
38. "'Little Corpers' Gave Up Pay," *San Francisco Chronicle*, 10 September 1955, 3H.
39. "A Financial Flop This Year, PCL Decides to Junk Playoffs," *San Francisco Chronicle*, 21 September 1954, 1H.
40. "'Little Corpers' Gave up Pay," *San Francisco Chronicle*, 10 September 1955, 3H.
41. Johnson and Wolff, *The Encyclopedia of Minor League Baseball*, 281; " 'Little Corp' Is Now 'Little Corpse,' " *San Francisco Chronicle*, 11 September 1955, 2H.
42. "Big Cash Outlay May Kill Option," *San Francisco Chronicle*, 3 September 1955, 1H.
43. "Seals Face Hour of Decision," *San Francisco Chronicle*, 12 September 1955, 1.
44. "Pattersons Agree to Purchase Seals," *San Francisco Chronicle*, 4 September 1955, 1H.
45. Ibid.; "Overheard," *San Francisco Examiner*, 8 September 1955, 24; "Poll Those 466 and Learn Why," *San Francisco Chronicle*, 9 September 1955, 1H; "Seals Face Hour of Decision," *San Francisco Chronicle*, 12 September 1955, 1.
46. "Pattersons Out, Seals Win Stay," *San Francisco Chronicle*, 13 September 1955, 1.
47. Ibid.
48. "Seals Sell Bradford, Baxes and Melton," *San Francisco Chronicle*, 22 September 1955, 3H.
49. "The Seals Will Be Saved, S.F. Promised," *San Francisco Chronicle*, 25 September 1955, 1.
50. "Perini to Explore Toledo–S.F. Tieup," *San Francisco Chronicle*, 7 October 1955, 1H; "Here's Some Good Baseball News," *San Francisco Chronicle*, 8 October 1955, 3H; "Cleveland Manager Meets with Fagan on Sale of Seals," *San Francisco Chronicle*, 19 October 1955, 1H; "Sale of Seals to Greenberg Stalled," *San Francisco Chronicle*, 20 October 1955, 1H; "Cleveland Would Stock Seals' Club," *San Francisco Chronicle*, 21 October 1955, 1H; "Braves Will Make Bid for S.F. Franchise," *San Francisco Chronicle*, 22 October 1955, 1H; "Greenberg Cancels S.F. Deal," *San Francisco Chronicle*, 23 October 1955, 1H; "Milwaukee Prexy, PCL Boss Confer," *San Francisco Chronicle*, 8 November 1955, 1H; "Milwaukee Rejects $200,000 Sale Tag," *San Francisco Chronicle*, 11 November 1955, 1H.
51. "Heath Planning to Quit Seals," *San Francisco Chronicle*, 27 October 1955, 1H; "Sacs Fire Freitas, Open Door to Tom," *San Francisco Chronicle*, 28 October 1955, 1H.
52. "Milwaukee Rejects $200,000 Sale Tag," *San Francisco Chronicle*, 11 November 1955, 1H.
53. "Classified Ad from Mr. Miller," *San Francisco Chronicle*, 13 November 1955, 2H.
54. "One PCL Club Fought Sale," *San Francisco Call-Bulletin*, 29 November 1955, 22.
55. "Red Sox Purchase Seal Franchise," *San Francisco Chronicle*, 29 November 1955, 1H.
56. "Sale of Seals to Greenberg Stalled," *San Francisco Chronicle*, 20 October 1955, 1H.
57. "Greenberg Cancels S.F. Deal," *San Francisco Chronicle*, 23 October 1955, 1H; "Chronicle Poll of Baseball Opinion," *San Francisco Chronicle*, 11 September 1955, 5H.

Robinson, Race, and Brooklyn

Leverett T. Smith

BARACK OBAMA'S election last fall to the presidency of the United States is generally regarded as a culmination of the civil-rights movement in this country. Looking backward toward the beginnings of that movement, the eye falls on events in New York City just after the end of World War II and particularly on the career of Jackie Robinson. A whole lot has been written about Robinson; a recent look at SABR's Baseball Index shows 1,296 books and articles containing significant material about Robinson.[1]

It's an intimidating number, and I haven't even begun to read all of those books and articles. In fact, it would be silly to say I've even tried. What I will do here is explore the various writings about Robinson that have passed through my library over the sixty years since a copy of his *My Own Story* turned up.[2] My treatment will be biased; I'm a lifelong New York Giants fan, for whom Robinson and the Brooklyn Dodgers were always "the enemy."

Jackie Robinson was undoubtedly a more complex human being than the mythic figure he has become. Even such serious academic historians as Eliot Gorn and Warren Goldstein seem to oversimplify his case in the following statement from *A Brief History of American Sports*.

> For if the Jackie Robinson saga was a sports-world version of the early stage of the Civil Rights movement—restrained, self-sacrificing, aiming for justice and reconciliation, idealizing integration—the story of Muhammad Ali is just as powerfully rooted in the Black Power and black separatist movements of the late 1960s and early 1970s.[3]

Jackie never seemed restrained, particularly on the basepaths, to this Giants fan: He was a menace. I suspect that Gerald Early's characterization of Robinson as "a complicated and admittedly often disturbing and unappealing man" is the truer one. Early's essay "Jackie Robinson, Amiri Baraka, Paul Robeson, and a Note on Politics, Sports, and the Black Intellectual" from *Tuxedo Junction: Essays on American Culture* is well worth reading for its portrait of Robinson, for its summary of Baraka's views (for Baraka, Robinson was "the Frankenstein's monster of American racial pathology"),[4] and for his mention that Martin Duberman's "exhaustive" biography of Paul Robeson[5] contains material on Robinson. Another essay on Robinson appears in Early's *The Culture of Bruising*, in which he compares Robinson and Willie Mays.[6]

Jackie Robinson in his autobiographies tended more and more to acknowledge his own complexity. I used to own a paperback copy of the 1948 *My Own Story* (as told to Wendell Smith), undoubtedly given to me then by some rabid Dodger fan. I never would have bought it myself. Now I'm glad I have read it, even though it minimizes (but does not erase) the difficulties Robinson encountered through his first year in the majors. The mood of Robinson's *Baseball Has Done It* (edited by Charles Dexter), interviews with African American major leaguers, is both combative and celebratory, as the title suggests.[7] The title of Robinson's 1972 autobiography, *I Never Had It Made*, suggests an emphasis on conflict.[8] There's an edition from Ecco Press currently available in bookstores.

It's no coincidence that some of the best books ever written on the subject of baseball have Jackie Robinson as their subject. Roger Kahn's solemn and operatic *The Boys of Summer* seems as vivid and substantial now as it did when published in 1971.[9] The boys of summer are the Jackie Robinson Dodgers, and "the dominant truth of the Jackie Robinson Dodgers was integration."[10] Robinson himself "bore the burden of a pioneer and the weight made him more strong."[11] Robinson's own ruin involved both the death of his first son and his own physical disintegration. Kahn finds himself shocked "to realize I was slowing my own pace so as not to walk too quickly for Jackie Robinson."[12] Quite probably the best academic study of any aspect of baseball is Jules Tygiel's *Baseball's Great Experiment: Jackie Robinson and His Legacy*, available in a Vintage paperback.[13] Tygiel sets Robinson's career in the contexts of the Negro Leagues, Major League Baseball, and American culture at large. Several essays on Robinson, ancillary to *Baseball's Great Experiment*, are gathered in Tygiel's *Extra Bases*.[14] Kahn's *Memories of Summer* contains more material on Robinson.[15]

Over the years Robinson's life has been the subject of several biographies. Arnold Rampersad's *Jackie Robinson: A Biography* is thorough, exhaustive, comprehensive, and well written.[16] It will prove one of the essential works on Robinson. Rampersad was well prepared to write Robinson's life, having produced fulsome biographies of black intellectual and literary figures W. E. B. DuBois and Langston Hughes, the latter in two volumes. In addition, Rampersad helped Arthur Ashe with his autobiography *Days of Grace*, so he was already familiar with the intersection of sport and race.[17] Finally, the Robinson family was enthusiastic about his writing the biography, and family papers and family members were available to him. Jackie's family is a particularly strong presence in the book, as they were in his life.

NATIONAL BASEBALL HALL OF FAME LIBRARY, COOPERSTOWN, N.Y.

Jackie Robinson with the Montreal Royals, 1946. "Jackie never seemed restrained," writes Terry Smith, "particularly on the basepaths, to this Giants fan: He was a menace."

Of the book's seventeen chapters, two deal with his college career and the sports he participated in there and seven deal with his baseball career—one on the Negro Leagues, one on his year with Montreal, and five on his seasons with the Dodgers. The five other chapters probably constitute the largest amount of space devoted to a baseball player's life subsequent to his playing days. The reason for this is the way Rampersad chooses to present Robinson, not simply as a baseball player but, as the author puts it, "someone chosen for a great task."[18] Late in the book Rampersad gets it all into a single sentence. "In 1947, black and handsome, athletically gifted but also cool and astute in his play, stoically enduring insult and injury, Robinson had revolutionized the image of the black man in America."[19] Rampersad's Robinson is Martin Luther King's Robinson. King calls Robinson "a pilgrim walking the lonesome byways toward the high road of Freedom. He was a sit-inner before sit-ins, a freedom rider before freedom rides."[20] Like few other ballplayers—perhaps only Babe Ruth—Jackie Robinson has significance far beyond his ball playing, and Rampersad keeps his focus on this.

Robinson's daughter Sharon has published *Stealing Home* (HarperCollins, 1996), a memoir of the Robinson family, focusing on their lives beyond his ball playing.[21] She subordinates Robinson the ballplayer to his life's mission, "which began with integrating Major League baseball [and] continued in other areas after he retired."[22] Sharon Robinson speaks of her father as being more interested in public service and the civil- rights movement than in his various business enterprises.

She spends very little time on Robinson's baseball career. *Stealing Home* is a family story, about being black and growing up with a celebrity father in the 1950s and 1960s. There is, however, a memorable passage in which Sharon Robinson reveals her sense of the importance of her father's pioneering in baseball. On their property in Stamford, Connecticut was a lake on which the children and their friends would skate during the winter. It was Jackie's job to "test the ice." Armed with a shovel and broomstick, he would slowly make his way to the deepest part of the pond. Watching him, his daughter senses his bravery. "He was as brave then as when he entered baseball, a feat it took me years to appreciate. It dawned on me only gradually what it meant for him to break the baseball color line, the courage it took for him to enter uncharted, and dangerous, waters. . . . He had to feel his way along an uncleared path like a blind man tapping for clues. That was Jackie Robinson. And that was my dad—big, heavy, out there alone on the lake, tapping his way along so the ice would be safe for us."[23]

Though these two books are clearly the place to begin, there are several other biographies of Robinson that reward reading. Arthur Mann's *The Jackie Robinson Story*[24] is particularly interesting, because it was written so close to the events themselves, by a participant in at least some of them. The book's thesis is that

Robinson's triumph is "not a triumph of Negro or white. It was a triumph of baseball."[25] Baseball itself is the hero of Mann's story. Mann writes of Reese and Robinson that "this was the Branch Rickey dream come true, and the only thing he ever tried to prove: that real baseball playing transcends all theories of class, race, religion, color, and politics. The play is indeed the thing, and success on the sporting field has to spring from skill alone and the amalgamation of all skills for the good of the team."[26]

Carl Rowan's 1960 biography of Robinson, *Wait Till Next Year: The Life Story of Jackie Robinson*, takes another tack entirely, its title surely ironic. The book's authors are listed as "Carl T. Rowan with Jackie Robinson," and many passages in the book are in Jackie and Rachel's own words. Writing at the start of the civil-rights movement, Rowan concludes that "future generations will remember [Robinson] not as the baserunner who worried pitchers to their doom, but as the proud crusader against pompous bigots and timid sentinels of the status quo—another symbol of a new Negro American."[27]

Race continues to be prominent in two biographies published in the 1980s, Harvey Frommer's *Rickey and Robinson: The Men Who Broke Baseball's Color Barrier*[28] and Maury Allen's *Jackie Robinson: A Life Remembered*.[29] Though largely superseded by Rampersad and, in Frommer's case, by Lee Lowenfish's *Branch Rickey: Baseball's Ferocious Gentleman*,[30] both books are still valuable because they make extensive use of interviews. Allen's book, particularly, is full of quoted material from interviews. A third biography, David Falkner's *Great Time Coming*, focuses on the public Robinson, as Falkner was denied access to the family and archival material, and has the distinction of being the first biography to look extensively at Robinson's life after his retirement from baseball.[31]

Scott Simon's *Jackie Robinson and the Integration of Baseball* addresses Robinson's first season with the Dodgers.[32] The focus is on the tribulations Robinson experienced leading up to and during that first year. Simon puts Robinson's difficulty quite simply: for him, the baseball diamond was "not simply a playing field" but a kind of war zone where the fight for racial equality occurred.[33] Robinson's story as Simon presents it is "a heroic American legend," Robinson himself, blind and dying at age 53, "a martyr for the cause of racial integration."[34] Distinguished by its brevity, Simon's book is the second volume of *Turning Points*, a series featuring "preeminent writers offering fresh, personal perspectives on the defining events of our time."[35] Simon acknowledges predecessors in his enterprise "with much more complete volumes," mainly Rampersad and Tygiel.[36] He confesses in his epilogue that "there is no need for a new chronicle about Jackie Robinson's arrival in major league baseball. But it has been my privilege to try to tell one."[37] Nevertheless, his version is as readable as it is brief.

Something of an anomaly among these books is Joseph Dorinson and Joram Warmund's *Jackie Robinson: Race, Sports, and the American Dream*.[38] Dorinson and Warmund have edited a selection of papers from a 1997 academic conference on the Brooklyn campus of Long Island University commemorating Robinson's major-league debut fifty years earlier, but their interest goes beyond the strictly academic. They describe the collection as a "heady mix of journalism, scholarship, and memory," its authors as "scholars, sportswriters, journalists, ballplayers, and baseball fans."[39] These many voices "describe conditions prior to Robinson's arrival, offer new perspectives on the events surrounding the integration of baseball, present reminiscences of the era, explore the impact of his breakthrough, and assess how far African-Americans have traveled in Robinson's wake."[40] It's a nice complement to Rampersad's monumental biography, its many authors sometimes happily disagreeing.

Perhaps the most interesting section for SABRites is "Measuring the Impact on Baseball." This section begins with an essay by David Shiner arguing that Robinson's appearance "challenged the dominant conception of offensive strategy in white baseball at the time."[41] He brought over from the Negro Leagues a style of play that combined speed and power. Samuel Regalado's essay shows how the player pool expanded enormously after Robinson's appearance, including not only African Americans, but players from Central and South America.[42] Finally, Lee Lowenfish's essay details the machinations among the Dodgers' owners that enabled baseball's expansion to proceed.[43]

Robinson's life, though, is inextricably tied to the history of the city of Brooklyn, and it's not just that his body is buried there. Frederic Roberts's essay "A Myth Grows in Brooklyn: Urban Death, Resurrection, and the Brooklyn Dodgers" engagingly considers the meanings of the connectedness of the team and the city.[44] Several novels do this as well. Every Dodger fan should have a copy of Philip Goldberg's *This Is Next Year*, a chronicle of Brooklyn in 1955, on his or her bookshelf. Ballantine Books published a paperback edition in 1991.[45] Jay Neugeboren's *Sam's Legacy* is, among other things, a portrait of Brooklyn in the early 1970s with its "changing neighborhoods."[46] The Dodgers are a faint but unmistakable presence in the book, and the nature of "race" a major theme. The protagonist in the course of the novel has to emotionally adjust to the fact that his father has left Brooklyn to retire in—take a wild guess!—Los Angeles. So far as I know, the only edition of this book is the 1974 hardcover from Holt, Rinehart and Winston. For a scary look at Brooklyn in the 1980s, try Thomas Boyle's crime novel *Only the Dead Know Brooklyn*.[47] The Dodgers are still a presence, in fact more of a presence than in *Sam's Legacy*. In *Only the Dead Know Brooklyn*, the subjects of race, gentrification, and the Dodgers are embodied in the figure of a psychotic killer, an albino African American who wears a Brooklyn Dodgers warm-up jacket and tells people he is the illegitimate son of Jackie Robinson. Penguin published a paperback of this book in 1986. Frederic Roberts gives it considerable attention in his essay mentioned above.

The borough and the ballclub both evoke plenty of memories. Perhaps the most fervent collection of these ballclub reflections is Peter Golenbock's *Bums: An Oral History of the Brooklyn Dodgers*.[48] Golenbock's book contains plenty of talk from Dodger players, other employees, journalists, and fans. A complement to Golenbock's book is Myrna Katz Frommer and Harvey Frommer's *It Happened in Brooklyn: An Oral History of Growing up in the Borough in the 1940s, 1950s, and 1960s*.[49] Coffee table–sized, this book offers both memories and photographs of the borough and its inhabitants (dozens were interviewed) during those years. Though Robinson and the Dodgers are a comparatively small part of this experience, Robinson made Brooklyn "a special kind of place."[50] It evokes much nostalgia, but the notion that Brooklyn is a changing place is also present.

Two more recent books depict what it was like to be a Dodger fan and a Dodger. Thomas Oliphant in *Praying for Gil Hodges: A Memoir of the 1955 World Series and One Family's Love of the Brooklyn Dodgers* describes what it was like to root for the Dodgers while growing up in a family devoted to liberal causes, particularly integration.[51] Oliphant combines his own and others' memories of Jackie Robinson's arrival in Brooklyn and the team's subsequent addition of other African American players. "It helped," he says, "that Brooklyn itself was for that time the most tolerant and diverse place in America."[52] Carl Erskine calls his memoir of his time pitching in Brooklyn *What I Learned from Jackie Robinson*.[53] Erskine is concerned to acknowledge that Robinson's quest for racial equality extended to equality for all people, including Erskine's Down-syndrome son Jimmy. Erskine concludes that "we all benefited from Jackie, and he helped us all understand ourselves and each other

NATIONAL BASEBALL HALL OF FAME LIBRARY, COOPERSTOWN, N.Y.

Robinson and Branch Rickey. "This was the Branch Rickey dream come true," writes Arthur Mann in The Jackie Robinson Story, *"and the only thing he ever tried to prove: that real baseball playing transcends . . . class, race, religion, color, and politics."*

better. . . . He had helped his race, but he helped mine more."[54] Here is Erskine on living in Brooklyn in the 1950s: "It was like living in a small town. . . . Brooklyn had been that ephemeral middle ground. It was rural in aspects—beach-filled with crisp, clean, ocean breezes—and also had a strong cultural base."[55]

Brooklyn, through these eyes, seems a little too good to be true, and in fact the borough was changing rapidly during these years, as both Oliphant and others interviewed by the Frommers notice. Relying on human memory is not always a good way to discover what happened. Henry Fetter, for instance, looks at National League attendance figures during Robinson's rookie season and finds that Robinson's presence had no discernible effect, despite the memories of many. This makes Fetter wonder about the idea "that Brooklyn provided a fortuitously welcome setting for this tale of racial tolerance."[56] Eschewing individual memory is also a focus for Jonathan Eig in his *Opening Day: The Story of Jackie Robinson's First Season*.[57] "I have tried in these pages *not* to imagine what Jackie Robinson went through in 1947," he writes. "I have tried at every turn to present verifiable facts. . . . The facts speak for themselves, and I think they speak much more powerfully than the myths that have come to cloud Robinson's story."[58]

Three books on Robinson and the Dodgers published in the late 1990s deserve special mention. *Jackie Robinson: An Intimate Portrait* is an extraordinary picture book with an accompanying text by Robinson's wife Rachel.[59] The text itself seems rather thin, but there are many useful details. For instance, after they moved to Stamford, Connecticut, the Robinsons named their dog after supposed mentor Branch Rickey. This would suggest a relatively complicated relationship with the Mahatma. The pictures, though, are the more interesting part of the book. There's one of Robinson leaving the Brooklyn clubhouse, looking very old. In the background a cat looks up at him. There are wonderful pictures with political implications: Robinson shaking hands with President Eisenhower at a formal dinner in 1953; later, Robinson sitting at a lunch counter with Malcolm X.

Carl E. Prince's *Brooklyn's Dodgers* is also a useful academic book, published in 1996 by Oxford University Press.[60] Subtitled *The Bums, the Borough, and the Best of Baseball*, it attempts to show how the team embodied many of the social and political concerns of the day. It's an intriguing effort to see a major-league team in its cultural context. Then there's Jules Tygiel's *The Jackie Robinson Reader*, published in 1997 by Dutton.[61] Though much of the material will initially seem familiar to the SABRite, Tygiel's stated concern is to make of the anthology "an alternative biography of Robinson."[62] While there are excerpts from the usual books—Kahn's and Tygiel's, for instance—there's also a good deal of material collected from newspapers and magazines, and this makes the book especially valuable.

Tygiel's anthology also reminds me again of all the books about Robinson and the Dodgers I haven't read, but a Giants fan needs to keep a certain distance. I'm always comforted by the fact that when the Dodgers no longer wanted Robinson's services they traded him to the Giants. To my mind, this is evidence that Giants owner Horace Stoneham was no dummy. As he said in a letter to Robinson, "I can't help thinking it would have been fun to have had you on our side for a year or two."[63] And to this Giants fan it seems no more heretical than Leo Durocher's sudden transfer from the Dodgers to the Giants during the 1948 season, or hated Giant Sal Maglie's appearance as a Dodger pitching mainstay in 1956.

A few books covering the 1972 baseball season commemorate Jackie Robinson in the year of his death. Roger Angell's *Five Seasons: A Baseball Companion* contains just a page on Robinson, but most of it needs to be quoted here. Angell remembers a scene from some twenty years before, one that convinced him that "we had asked [Robinson] to do too much for us."

> It was something that had happened during an insignificant weekday game between the Giants and the Dodgers back in the nineteen-fifties. Robinson, by then an established star, was playing third base that afternoon, and during the game something happened that drove him suddenly and totally mad. I was sitting close to him, just behind third, but I had no idea what brought on the outburst. It might have been a remark from the stands or from one of the dugouts; it was nothing that happened on the field. Without warning, Robinson began shouting imprecations, obscenities, curses. His voice was piercing, his face distorted with passion. The players on both teams looked at each other, uncomprehending. The Giants third-base coach walked over to murmur a question, and Robinson directed his screams at him. The umpire at third did the same thing, and then turned away with a puzzled, embarrassed shrug. In time, the outburst stopped, and the game went on.[64]

Clearly, Jackie Robinson's psyche suffered as much, if not more, than his body did from the stress.

Joel Oppenheimer's book on rooting for the 1972 New York Mets, *The Wrong Season*,[65] concludes with a eulogy of Robinson. At its end, Oppenheimer remembers Robinson the baseball player: "We will talk about the stance, the bat held high, the head looming, and the ball bouncing off the wall in deep left center, and the crazy garbage truck run, the pigeon toes . . . and in a world where he was clean, and where, yes, Dixie Walker was clean too, with his long-bred hatred, and the point for both was to score the runs and make the flashing play."[66] The point for Oppenheimer? "For sure . . . Jackie deserved better than us." In an extraordinary time, an extraordinary man, Jackie Robinson. ■

Notes

Parts of this article appeared originally in SABR's Bibliography Committee Newsletter, July 1997.

1. The Baseball Index, Society for American Baseball Research, www.baseballindex.org/.
2. Jackie Robinson and Wendell Smith, *My Own Story* (New York: Greenberg, 1948).
3. Eliot Gorn and Warren Goldstein, *A Brief History of American Sports* (New York: Hill and Wang, 1993), 218.
4. Gerald Early, "Jackie Robinson, Amiri Baraka, Paul Robeson, and a Note on Politics, Sports, and the Black Intellectual," in *Tuxedo Junction: Essays on American Culture* (New York: Ecco Press, 1989), 208–14.

5. Martin Duberman, *Paul Robeson* (New York: Knopf, 1988).
6. Early, *The Culture of Bruising: Essays on Prizefighting, Literature, and Modern American Culture* (New York: Ecco Press, 1994), 146–54.
7. Robinson, *Baseball Has Done It*, ed. Charles Dexter (Philadelphia: Lippincott, 1964).
8. Robinson, *I Never Had It Made* (1972; New York: Ecco Press, 1995).
9. Roger Kahn, *The Boys of Summer* (New York: Harper and Row, 1972.
10. Ibid., xvi.
11. Ibid., xix.
12. Ibid., 402.
13. Jules Tygiel, *Baseball's Great Experiment: Jackie Robinson and His Legacy* (New York: Vintage, 1984).
14. Tygiel, *Extra Bases: Reflections on Jackie Robinson, Race, and Baseball History* (Lincoln: University of Nebraska Press, 2002).
15. Kahn, *Memories of Summer: When Baseball Was an Art and Writing about It a Game* (New York: Hyperion, 1997).
16. Arnold Rampersad, *Jackie Robinson: A Biography* (New York: Knopf, 1997).
17. Arthur Ashe and Rampersad, *Days of Grace: A Memoir* (New York: Knopf, 1993).
18. Rampersad, *Jackie Robinson: A Biography* (New York: Knopf, 1997), 155.
19. Ibid., 391.
20. Ibid., 7.
21. Sharon Robinson, *Stealing Home: An Intimate Family Portrait by the Daughter of Jackie Robinson* (New York: HarperCollins, 1996).
22. Ibid., 23.
23. Ibid., 45.
24. Arthur Mann, *The Jackie Robinson Story* (New York: Grosset and Dunlap, 1956).
25. Ibid., 154.
26. Ibid., 218.
27. Carl T. Rowan, with Jackie Robinson, *Wait Till Next Year: The Life Story of Jackie Robinson* (New York: Random House, 1960), 339.
28. Harvey Frommer, *Rickey and Robinson: The Men Who Broke Baseball's Color Barrier* (New York: Macmillan, 1982).
29. Maury Allen, *Jackie Robinson: A Life Remembered* (New York: Franklin Watts, 1987).
30.Lee Lowenfish, *Branch Rickey: Baseball's Ferocious Gentleman* (Lincoln: University of Nebraska Press, 2007).
31. David Falkner, *Great Time Coming: The Life of Jackie Robinson, from Baseball to Birmingham* (New York: Simon and Schuster, 1995).
32. Scott Simon, *Jackie Robinson and the Integration of Baseball* (New York: John Wiley and Sons, 2002), 53.
33. Ibid., 3.
34. Ibid., 4.
35. Ibid., 9.
36. Ibid., 164.
37. Ibid., 151.
38. Joseph Dorinson and Joram Warmund, eds., *Jackie Robinson: Race, Sports, and the American Dream* (Armonk, N.Y.: M. E. Sharpe, 1998).
39. Ibid., xii, xi.
40. Ibid., xxi.
41. David Shiner, "Jackie Robinson and the Third Age of Modern Baseball," in *Jackie Robinson: Race, Sports, and the American Dream*, 149.
42. Samuel O, Regalado, "Jackie Robinson and the Emancipation of Latin American Baseball Players," in *Jackie Robinson: Race, Sports, and the American Dream*, 157.
43. Lee Lowenfish, "The Two Titans and the Mystery Man: Branch Rickey, Walter O'Malley, and John L. Smith as Brooklyn Dodgers Partners, 1944–1950," in *Jackie Robinson: Race, Sports, and the American Dream*, 165.
44. Frederic Roberts, "A Myth Grows in Brooklyn: Urban Death, Resurrection, and the Brooklyn Dodgers," in *Baseball History* (summer 1987): 4–26.
45. Philip Goldberg, *This Is Next Year* (New York: Ballantine Books, 1992.
46. Jay Neugeboren, *Sam's Legacy: A Novel* (New York: Holt, Rinehart, and Winston, 1974).
47. Thomas Boyle, *Only the Dead Know Brooklyn* (New York: Penguin, 1986).
48. Peter Golenbock, *Bums: An Oral History of the Brooklyn Dodgers* (New York: Putnam, 1984).
49. Myrna Katz Frommer and Harvey Frommer, *It Happened in Brooklyn: An Oral History of Growing up in the Borough in the 1940s, 1950s, and 1960s* (New York: Harcourt, Brace, 1993).
50. Ibid., 15.
51. Thomas Oliphant, *Praying for Gil Hodges: A Memoir of the 1955 World Series and One Family's Love of the Brooklyn Dodgers* (New York: St. Martin's Press, 2005).
52. Ibid., 55.
53. Carl Erskine, *What I Learned from Jackie Robinson: A Teammate's Reflections On and Off the Field* (New York: McGraw-Hill, 2005).
54. Ibid., 147.
55. Ibid., 126.
56. Dorinson and Warmund, *Jackie Robinson: Race, Sports, and the American Dream*, 188.
57. Jonathan Eig, *Opening Day: The Story of Jackie Robinson's First Season* (New York: Simon and Schuster, 2007).
58. Ibid., 281.
59. Rachel Robinson and Lee Daniels, *Jackie Robinson: An Intimate Portrait* (New York: Harry N. Abrams, 1996).
60. Carl E. Prince, *Brooklyn's Dodgers: The Bums, the Borough, and the Best of Baseball, 1947–1957* (New York: Oxford University Press, 1996).
61. Jules Tygiel, ed., *The Jackie Robinson Reader: Perspectives on an American Hero* (New York: Dutton, 1997).
62. Ibid., vii.
63. Rampersad, *Jackie Robinson: A Biography*, 308.
64. Roger Angell, *Five Seasons: A Baseball Companion* (New York: Simon and Schuster, 1977), 51.
65. Joel Oppenheimer, *The Wrong Season* (Indianapolis: Bobbs-Merrill, 1973).
66. Ibid., 157.

The Commissionor versus His Employer

Selig and His Predecessors

Ron Kaplan

In the Best Interests of Baseball? The Revolutionary Reign of Bud Selig
by Andrew Zimbalist
John Wiley and Sons (2007)
$14.95, paperback. 250 pages. Photos, notes

ALLAN H. "BUD" SELIG has nominally been in charge of the national pastime longer than any commissioner since Judge Kenesaw Mountain Landis. Needless to say, the game has expanded beyond what the sixteen original owners could ever have imagined. Such success has been a blessing and a curse, and the complexities for those in the game's highest office have grown exponentially.

Andrew Zimbalist—his previous sports titles include *Baseball and Billions: A Probing Look Inside the Big Business of Our National Pastime*; *May the Best Team Win: Baseball Economics and Public Policy*; and *National Pastime: How Americans Play Baseball and the Rest of the World Plays Soccer*—presents a generally withering look at the nine men who have held the august office. He titles two chapters "The Undistinguished Middle I" and "II," which might strike some readers as overly harsh. Only half the book actually deals with Selig's background and administration; the rest is a brief history of those who came before him.

Landis, who held the office from 1921 until his death in 1944, was appointed by baseball owners desperate for leadership following the Black Sox scandal. He certainly had his faults: vain, despotic, racist, and generally ruling the game with an iron, if sometimes uneven, hand. After Landis "cleaned up" the game to the owners' initial satisfaction, his successors were faced with the challenges that progress and history wrought.

Albert B. "Happy" Chandler (1945–51), who took office following Landis's death, witnessed the most significant event in the game—the breaking of the color line—against the popular consensus of the owners. He continued to battle with them over various issues, including television contracts and the continued association by some baseball personnel with gamblers and similar unsavory characters. The postwar years brought other problems, including the incursion by different forms of entertainment as well as "white flight" to the suburbs. Chandler, tired of the constant conflicts with the owners, resigned in the middle of the 1951 season.

NATIONAL BASEBALL HALL OF FAME LIBRARY, COOPERSTOWN, N.Y.

Allan H. "Bud" Selig, commissioner of baseball on an interim basis beginning in 1992 and officially elected in 1998. His term has been marked by the steroid scandals but also by increased attendance and the resurgence of the minor leagues.

Ford Frick (1951–65) was "a lowly sports journalist" before becoming the National League's public-relations representative and then its president. Zimbalist characterizes him as "a man who was singularly unprepared to take the office to a new level." Yet he was forced by circumstances to sit in office during tumultuous times. As a difficult economy continued into the mid-1950s, the Philadelphia Athletics, St. Louis Browns, and Boston Braves relocated to Kansas City, Baltimore, and Milwaukee, respectively. The threat of a new major league led to expansion in the early 1960s, which led to Frick's claim to infamy when he dictated that Roger Maris's home-run record would bear the burden of a special notation in the record book. (In light of the recent revelations about performance-enhancing drugs, many sports pundits are taking another look at such a designation.)

General William Eckert (1965–68), snidely referred to by an owner as "the unknown soldier," followed Frick during a relatively calm period. Not that he had much of a chance to make a mark, even if he had had a basic knowledge of the game (which he did not); he was dismissed less than halfway into his term.

Bowie Kuhn (1969–84) seemed to be the baseball man the owners had hoped for, but he battled Charles O. Finley over the sale of three of his top players for top dollar. Kuhn voided the transaction, invoking the "best interest" clause. He oversaw another round of expansion and the passage of free agency from theory to reality. Kuhn also took time to ban two of the game's all-time icons—Willie Mays and Mickey Mantle—because of their employment by casinos. He was not extended a new contract when his second term expired.

Although he brought a freshness to the office that was heretofore unknown, Peter Ueberroth (1984–89) couldn't seem to apply the magic from his accomplishments in the 1984 Olympics to baseball. It was on his watch that owners engaged in collusive actions to keep free-agent signings on the cheap.

Bart Giamatti (1989) might have been the ideal candidate for the office because of his brilliance, love for, and knowledge of the game. But he died of a broken heart, forced to banish Pete Rose for his gambling sins. Giamatti had been commissioner for less than six months.

Fay Vincent (1989–92), Giamatti's right-hand man and close friend, did a commendable job as his successor, particularly during the 1989 "Earthquake" Series between the Oakland A's and San Francisco Giants. But he stood up to the owners one time too many.

In fact, Zimbalist offers, that was the case with almost every commissioner: butting heads against the group that was essentially his employer. Evidently they wanted a firm and wise leader, but not if he constantly ruled against their interests.

Selig came with his own set of limitations, although Zimbalist does give him credit for his passion and knowledge. He was instrumental in securing a franchise for Milwaukee—welcoming a bankrupt Pilots team following their sole season in Seattle—after his beloved Braves had relocated to Atlanta. Selig eventually became an owner of the Brewers, a major conflict-of-interest issue, when he assumed the post first of acting commissioner and then commissioner proper.

A particular issue relating to his conflict of interest was contraction. While head of the Brewers, Selig had accepted a loan from Minnesota Twins' owner Carl Pohlad, which was in itself a violation of the rules. When it came time to select teams that would be considered for contraction, the Twins were named as a possible candidate, which would have made an aging Pohlad quite happy.

Selig has "guided" baseball through the most turmoil in the long history of the game, including a devastating work stoppage and, most recently, the shadow of performance-enhancing drugs and its impact on the perception of ethics and the national pastime. (This last item is not addressed in the book, which was originally published in 2006. No doubt the assertion that Selig turned a blind eye while some of baseball's highest-profile players "juiced" will be addressed in future books.)

NATIONAL BASEBALL HALL OF FAME LIBRARY, COOPERSTOWN, N.Y.

Ford Frick, commissioner, 1951–65. Described by Andrew Zimbalist as "singularly unprepared to take the office to a new level," Frick oversaw multiple franchise relocations in the 1950s and expansion in the 1960s.

Has Selig's "reign" been revolutionary? To be sure, there have been many changes: escalating salaries, increased attendance, and the resurgence of the minor leagues, among other things. Were they Selig's doings, or would they have happened regardless of who sat in the commissioner's chair? If the reader believes the latter, then Zimbalist's premise doesn't fit.

In the Best Interests is full of the inner workings of the game, aspects the average fan has little knowledge of or interest in. But for those interested in the history of baseball's smoke-filled rooms, Zimbalist offers a concise, if unflattering, rendering of the office and the men who held it. ■

Who Has the Major-League Record for the Longest Consecutive-Games Run-Produced (CGRP) Streak?

Herm Krabbenhoft

IN ORDER for a baseball team to achieve its ultimate objective (winning the World Series), it must first, during the regular season, win the most games in its division (or, since 1994, have the best winning percentage among the second-place teams) and thereby proceed to postseason play. Moreover, the absolutely essential component for winning the number of games necessary to qualify for MLB's Octoberfest is scoring runs—i.e., more runs than the opposing team scores. Accordingly, the run can be considered the most important statistic for a baseball team—and, thus, for each of the players on the team. Therefore, contributing to the scoring of runs is, without question, the supreme offensive objective for each of the individual players on the team.

During the past 25 to 30 years, several high-powered (and relatively complex) methodologies and formulas to evaluate the offensive contributions a player makes to his team have been introduced by estimating the number of runs for which the player is responsible—such as, for example, batting runs (BR, Pete Palmer) and runs created (RC, Bill James).[1, 2]

However, in this article I'm going to employ the two fundamental statistics that for decades have been used to ascertain a player's proficiency in contributing to the scoring of runs by his team—(1) runs scored (which has been officially recorded since the very beginning of Major League Baseball in 1876) and (2) runs batted in (which, although unofficially tabulated since 1907, became an official statistic in 1920). Specifically, my focus is on the readily calculable metric for evaluating a player's ability to generate runs—runs produced. Runs produced (RP) is defined as "runs scored plus runs batted in minus home runs"; see equation 1.[3] The runs-produced statistic was created more than sixty years ago and was first charted for major-league players in 1956—see the companion article, "Who Invented Runs Produced?"[4]

Equation 1. RP = R + RBI – HR

Switching gears for a moment, let's consider performances in consecutive games. From the perspective of consistency, performance streaks are an important aspect of the game. For example, baseball's record books identify the players who hold the top marks for most consecutive games hitting safely (Joe DiMaggio), getting a walk (Roy Cullenbine), reaching base safely, i.e., getting on base via a hit, a walk, or being hit by a pitch (Ted Williams), scoring a run (Billy Hamilton), batting in a run (Ray Grimes), hitting a home run (Dale Long, Don Mattingly, and Ken Griffey Jr), and so on.

What about the record for the most consecutive games producing a run—that is, either scoring a run or batting in a run?

Resorting to the various baseball record books and encyclopedias to find out the answer to this important question is fruitless.

So, a few years ago, I initiated a research program to ascertain the players who for each league and for each season achieved the longest consecutive-games streaks for scoring at least one run, batting in at least one run, and producing at least one run. In a previous article I presented my findings for the players who achieved the longest consecutive-games run-scored (CGRUNS) streaks annually in each circuit during the period 1945–2008.[5] Subsequently, I determined the players who achieved the longest CGRUNS streaks for the period 1920–44.[6] Similarly, I carried out analogous research to find out the AL and NL league leaders for the longest consecutive-games run-batted-in (CGRUNBI) streaks for each season during the period 1920–2008.[7]

In this article, I present the results of my research to provide the answer to the query given in the title of this article.[8]

It is appropriate to mention at the outset that over the years there has been a considerable amount of debate on the (mathematical) reasonableness of the "minus home runs" term in the runs-produced formula.[9] Fortunately, that issue has absolutely no relevance in the determination of CGRP streaks—because the focus of the CGRP streaks is on the number of consecutive games for producing at least one run rather than on the number of runs produced (or how the runs were produced).

HISTORICAL BACKGROUND

The longest known streak for most consecutive games scoring a run in the major leagues is 24—by Billy Hamilton Philadelphia (NL), 1894.[10-12] The record for the longest CGRUNS streak in the American League is 18—by Red Rolfe of the 1939 New York Yankees and by Kenny Lofton of the 2000 Cleveland Indians.[10-12] The modern (i.e., post-1900) National League record for the longest CGRUNS streak is 17—by Rogers Hornsby of the 1921 St. Louis Cardinals and by Ted Kluszewski of the 1954 Cincinnati Redlegs.[10, 12]

With regard to the longest CGRUNBI streaks, the major-league record (since 1920, when RBI became an official statistic) is 17—by Ray Grimes of the 1922 Chicago Cubs.[13-15] The longest CGRUNBI streak in American League history is 14—by Tris Speaker of the 1928 Philadelphia Athletics.[13, 14]

The AL and NL records for the longest CGRP streaks, unknown prior to my research efforts, are presented in this article.

RESEARCH PROCEDURES

To unequivocally ascertain the record for the longest CGRP streak, one needs to examine accurate runs-scored records and accurate runs-batted-in records for every major-league player—from a game-by-game perspective—for every season from 1920 forward. There are two primary sources of game-by-game runs-scored and runs-batted-in information for the period 1920–2008.

The official baseball records, also known as the official Day-By-Day (DBD) records, are available on microfilm at the National Baseball Hall of Fame Library in Cooperstown. All seasons from 1920 forward are available.

The Retrosheet daily records. These are available online at the Retrosheet website. Currently, the Retrosheet database includes the following seasons—AL: 1921–26, 1954–2008; NL: 1921–26, 1929, 1953–2008. The daily data from 1953 to the present come from the Retrosheet files; the daily data before 1953 (e.g., from the 1920s) come from the official baseball records.[16]

I used the Retrosheet daily records for each of the seasons in the Retrosheet database. Dave Smith (Retrosheet) graciously wrote a computer program to extract the longest CGRP streak for each player for each season in the Retrosheet database. While the information contained in the Retrosheet database is not official, it is generally regarded as being highly reliable—virtually all of the entries in the player daily records are corroborated by verified play-by-play data.

For the seasons not yet in the Retrosheet database (AL: 1920, 1927–53; NL: 1920, 1927, 1928, 1930–52), I used the official DBD records. Regrettably, the official DBD records—particularly those before 1970—contain some errors in the entries for runs scored and runs batted in. For example, as reported previously, I discovered—and corrected—26 runs-scored errors which impacted 19 players (including four Hall of Famers) from the 1945–69 Detroit Tigers. Each of the corrections I proposed has been sanctioned by the Elias Sports Bureau (the official statisticians of Major League Baseball).[17] Similarly, I discovered—and corrected—45 RBI errors involving 33 players (including three Cooperstown enshrinees) from the 1945–69 Detroit Tigers.[18] Based on these findings, it is not unreasonable to suspect that there probably are analogous numbers of runs-scored errors and runs-batted-in errors in the official DBD records for the players of the other major-league teams. Moreover, as reported in the newsletter for the Baseball Records Committee, Trent McCotter discovered—and corrected—68 RBI errors impacting 59 players (including 15 Hall of Famers) in the official DBD records for the period 1920–39.[19] Fortunately, there appear to be no runs-scored errors or runs-batted-in errors in the official DBD records for the players on the Detroit Tigers from 1970 to the present (and, hopefully, on the other major-league teams).[20]

In order to manage the game-by-game runs-scored and runs-batted-in information in the error-plagued official DBD records, I followed this two-step procedure for all of the seasons—including those in the Retrosheet database—from 1920 through 1952 (NL) and 1920–53 (AL):

First, I ascertained the longest (unverified) CGRP streak for each player for each team for each season. Thus, I determined the unverified annual leader for the longest CGRP streak for each league.

Then, I examined the pertinent box scores (provided in the *New York Times* and/or *Sporting News*) to corroborate or refute the relevant runs-scored and runs-batted-in information in the official DBD records. For the 1920–27 seasons, for which the newspaper box scores do not provide RBI information, I again benefited enormously from the depository of play-by-play information in the Retrosheet vault. As it developed, during the period 1920–27, there were 70 player-games in which the unverified CGRP-streak leader extended his streak by only getting at least one RBI (i.e., he did not score a run in those games). Dave Smith again came through by providing me with the batting lines (including RBIs) for 40 of those 70 player-games. Note that these batting lines have not yet been proofed by Retrosheet. Nonetheless, I deem their RBI information to be just as reliable as the RBI information presented in the unproofed newspaper box scores. For the remaining 30 player-games, I relied on the text accounts in the newspapers from the cities of the teams involved in the games. That task was facilitated by the generous cooperation of several SABR members who provided photocopies of the pertinent player-game accounts presented in newspapers to which they had access.[21]

The importance of conducting these corroborations is clearly demonstrated by the CGRP streaks achieved by Paul Waner, Chuck Klein, Billy Rogell, Lonny Frey, and Del Ennis.[22-26] Thus, the lengths of the CGRP streaks achieved by the league leaders presented in table 1 are accurate. However, it must also be pointed out that I corroborated only the lengths of the CGRP streaks of the players listed as league leaders. Thus, it is possible that another player could have fashioned a longer CGRP streak than the indicated league leader but, because of an unrecognized error (either in runs scored or in runs batted in) in his official DBD record, he did not emerge as the *unverified* league leader.

Before proceeding to the results of my CGRP streak research, I should explain the criteria I used to ascertain what events extend a CGRP streak (or, in other words, what events terminate a CGRP streak). The official Major League Baseball rules do not specifically cover CGRP (or CGRUNS or CGRUNBI) streaks.[27] Therefore, I used the following guidelines to define the extension or termination of a CGRP streak:

- If a player scores at least one run or bats in at least one run in a game, that game extends the CGRP streak.
- If a player completes at least one plate appearance in a game but does not score at least one run or bat in at least one run, that game terminates the CGRP streak.
- If a player is used only as a pinch runner in a game and does not score at least one run, that game terminates the CGRP streak.
- If a player is used only as a defensive player in a game (and thus does not have a completed plate appearance or a pinch-running appearance), that game does not terminate the CGRP streak.
- If a player is announced as a pinch-hitter and is then replaced by another pinch-hitter (and thus does not have a completed plate appearance), that game does not terminate the CGRP streak. Likewise, if a player enters the game as a pinch-hitter, but, before he can complete his plate appearance, the inning ends via a caught-stealing or a pickoff, that game does not terminate the CGRP streak.

The critical aspect to these guidelines is that, if a player had at least one opportunity to either score a run or bat in a run in a game, he must have scored at least one run or batted in at least one run in order to extend his CGRP streak; if he had at least one opportunity to either score a run or bat in a run and did not either score at least one run or bat in at least one run, his CGRP streak is terminated.

RESULTS

Table 1 presents the players who achieved the longest CGRP streak within each league for each season from 1920 through 2008.

Table 1. The American and National League Players with the Longest CGRP Streaks, 1920–2008

Year	AL Player (team)	CGRP Streak	NL Player (team)	CGRP Streak
1920	George Sisler (STL)	18	Ross Youngs (NY)	13
1921	Babe Ruth (NY)	23	Zack Wheat (BRK)	18
1922	Ken Williams (STL)	23	Ray Grimes (CHI)	19
1923	Harry Heilmann (DET)	21	Heinie Groh (NY)	14
			Irish Meusel (NY)	14
1924	Harry Hooper (CHI)	14	Ray Grimes (CHI)	19
	Bill Lamar (PHI)	14		
	Gene Robertson (STL)	14		
1925	Al Simmons (PHI)	30	Rogers Hornsby (STL)	22
1926	Babe Ruth (NY)	14	Taylor Douthit (STL)	22
1927	Lou Gehrig (NY)	19	Paul Waner (PIT)	32
	Ty Cobb (PHI)	19		
1928	Heinie Manush (STL)	18	Pie Traynor (PIT)	19
1929	Mule Haas (PHI)	17	Dick Bartell (PIT)	16
	Harry Heilmann (DET)	17	Pie Traynor (PIT)	16
	Jack Rothrock (BOS)	17		
1930	Lou Gehrig (NY)	24	Travis Jackson (NY)	19
1931	Babe Ruth (NY)	19	Mel Ott (NY)	20
1932	Jimmie Foxx (PHI)	19	Billy Herman (CHI)	17
1933	Joe Cronin (WAS)	33	Chuck Klein (PHI)	12
			Danny Taylor (BKN)	12
1934	Billy Rogell (DET)	22	Chick Hafey (CIN)	15
1935	Bob Johnson (PHI)	16	Lonny Frey (BKN)	17
1936	Hal Trosky (CLE)	17	Ken O'Dea (CHI)	16
1937	John Stone (WAS)	17	Paul Waner (PIT)	22
1938	Earl Averill (CLE)	21	Frank McCormick (CIN)	15
1939	Red Rolfe (NY)	18	Morrie Arnovich (PHI)	17
1940	Joe DiMaggio (NY)	19	Debs Garms (PIT)	16
1941	Lou Boudreau (CLE)	18	Terry Moore (STL)	16
1942	Tommy Henrich (NY)	24	Mel Ott (NY)	14
			Joe Medwick (BKN)	14
1943	Gene Moore (WAS)	17	Bill Nicholson (CHI)	16
1944	Doc Cramer (DET)	16	Whitey Kurowski (STL)	15
1945	Gene Moore (STL)	16	Phil Cavarretta (CHI)	24
1946	Joe DiMaggio (NY)	16	Whitey Kurowski (STL)	12
			Stan Musial (STL)	12
1947	Pat Mullin (DET)	15	Johnny Mize (NY)	16
1948	Joe DiMaggio (NY)	14	Wally Westlake (PIT)	13
	Tommy Henrich (NY)	14	Stan Musial (STL)	13

Year	AL Player (team)	CGRP Streak	NL Player (team)	CGRP Streak
1949	Ted Williams (BOS)	21	Stan Musial (STL)	12
			Enos Slaughter (STL)	12
1950	Billy Goodman (BOS)	17	Roy Hartsfield (BOS)	18
	Sam Chapman (PHI)	17		
1951	Nellie Fox (CHI)	18	Stan Musial (STL)	16
1952	Ferris Fain (PHI)	17	Del Ennis (PHI)	11
1953	Gil McDougald (NY)	16	Duke Snider (BKN)	16
1954	Larry Doby (CLE)	15	Ted Kluszewski (CIN)	24
1955	Mickey Mantle (NY)	16	Gus Bell (CIN)	12
			Willie Mays (NY)	12
1956	Jim Rivera (CHI)	15	Lee Walls (PIT)	14
1957	Minnie Minoso (CHI)	12	Don Blasingame (STL)	14
	Mickey Mantle (NY)	12		
1958	Pete Runnels (BOS)	14	Ed Bouchee (PHI)	12
1959	Minnie Minoso (CLE)	11	Willie Mays (SF)	15
	Bill Tuttle (KC)	11		
1960	Rocky Colavito (DET)	11	Billy Bruton (MIL)	14
1961	Harmon Killebrew (MIN)	16	Billy Williams (CHI)	12
1962	Lee Thomas (LA)	16	Frank Robinson (CIN)	12
			Ed Bailey (SF)	12
1963	Rocky Colavito (DET)	12	Bill White (STL)	12
	Al Kaline (DET)	12	Willie Mays (SF)	12
1964	Norm Siebern (BAL)	14	Tommy Davis (LA)	15
1965	Tony Conigliaro (BOS)	13	Bill Mazeroski (PIT)	15
1966	Floyd Robinson (CHI)	13	Pete Rose (CIN)	13
	Jimmie Hall (MIN)	13	Gene Alley (PIT)	13
			Jose Pagan (PIT)	13
1967	Al Kaline (DET)	13	Hank Aaron (ATL)	14
	Tony Conigliaro (BOS)	13		
1968	Reggie Jackson (OAK)	11	Roberto Pena (PHI)	12
	Ed Stroud (WAS)	11		
1969	Don Buford (BAL)	13	Matty Alou (PIT)	14
	Tony Oliva (MIN)	13		
1970	Reggie Smith (BOS)	15	Jose Cardenal (STL)	13
			Tony Perez (CIN)	13
			Bobby Tolan (CIN)	13
1971	Roy White (NY)	12	Willie Stargell (PIT)	17
	Reggie Jackson (OAK)	12		
1972	Bill Freehan (DET)	14	Johnny Bench (CIN)	19
1973	John Mayberry (KC)	12	Rusty Staub (NY)	16
1974	Al Kaline (DET)	10	Cesar Cedeno (HOU)	14
	Bernie Carbo (BOS)	10		
	Graig Nettles (NY)	10		
	Jeff Burroughs (TEX)	10		
1975	John Mayberry (KC)	14	Rusty Staub (NY)	15
1976	Reggie Jackson (BAL)	14	Jay Johnstone (PHI)	12
	Larry Hisle (MIN)	14	Mike Schmidt (PHI)	12
			Dusty Baker (LA)	12
1977	Ralph Garr (CHI)	15	Ron Cey (LA)	20
1978	Lyman Bostock (CAL)	16	Gene Richards (SD)	14
1979	Eddie Murray (BAL)	17	Omar Moreno (PIT)	14
1980	Mickey Rivers (TEX)	14	Mike Schmidt (PHI)	14
1981	Amos Otis (KC)	13	Mike Schmidt (PHI)	13
1982	Lou Whitaker (DET)	14	Bob Horner (ATL)	15
	Kent Hrbek (MIN)	14		
1983	Frank White (KC)	15	Jose Cruz (HOU)	12
1984	Larry Parrish (TEX)	14	Carmelo Martinez (SD)	12
1985	Don Mattingly (NY)	15	Hubie Brooks (MON)	12
1986	Tony Bernazard (CLE)	17	Tim Raines (MON)	15
1987	Paul Molitor (MIL)	23	Jack Clark (STL)	14
1988	Wade Boggs (BOS)	20	Tim Raines (MON)	14
			Keith Hernandez (NY)	14
1989	Jim Rice (BOS)	14	Von Hayes (PHI)	14
1990	Alan Trammell (DET)	13	Gregg Jefferies (NY)	13
	Frank Thomas (CHI)	13		
1991	Willie Randolph (MIL)	18	Fred McGriff (SD)	13
1992	Robin Ventura (CHI)	15	Delino DeShields (MON)	12
			Barry Bonds (PIT)	12
1993	Alan Trammell (DET)	15	Matt Williams (SF)	17
1994	Jose Canseco (TEX)	15	Larry Walker (MON)	14
1995	Edgar Martinez (SEA)	18	Dante Bichette (COL)	14
			Matt Williams (SF)	14
1996	Chuck Knoblauch (MIN)	27	Eric Young (COL)	18
			Steve Finley (SD)	18
1997	Tony Phillips (ANA)	17	Andres Galarraga (COL)	24
1998	Paul O'Neill (NY)	21	Jeff Kent (SF)	13
1999	Roberto Alomar (CLE)	18	Edgardo Alfonzo (NY)	16
			Reggie Sanders (SD)	16
2000	Kenny Lofton (CLE)	18	Jeff Bagwell (HOU)	17
2001	Mike Cameron (SEA)	17	Albert Pujols (STL)	22
2002	Jim Thome (CLE)	15	Austin Kearns (CIN)	13
			Rich Aurilia (SF)	13
2003	Carlos Lee (CHI)	16	Todd Helton (COL)	15
2004	Ichiro Suzuki (SEA)	15	Jeff Bagwell (HOU)	16
2005	Torii Hunter (MIN)	14	Todd Helton (COL)	16
	Gary Sheffield (NY)	14		
2006	Jim Thome (CHI)	20	Jose Reyes (NY)	18
2007	Kevin Youkilis (BOS)	16	Russell Martin (LA)	15
2008	Ian Kinsler (TEX)	18	Lance Berkman (HOU)	21

DISCUSSION

Inspection of table 1 reveals that, since the RBI statistic was officially recognized in 1920, Joe Cronin of the 1933 Washington Senators compiled the longest CGRP streak in the major leagues—a 33-gamer. Cronin began his streak on May 25 at home against the Browns. The streak came to a close on June 30 in Detroit, as Tommy Bridges kept the all-star shortstop from producing a run, although the Tigers' right-hander lost the game, 2–1. Curiously, it was Bridges who previously had shut down Cronin in the run-production department—on May 24, the Tigers hurler tossed a one-hitter, defeating the Senators 3–1. During his 33-CGRP streak, Cronin scored a total of 34 runs and batted in 45 runs; he hit two homers. Thus, according to the RP formula, he produced a total of 77 runs. During his 33-CGRP streak his longest CGRUNS streak was a seven-gamer and his longest CGRUNBI streak was a ten-gamer.

Prior to Cronin's 33-CGRP streak in 1933, the longest CGRP streak in the American League was the

NATIONAL BASEBALL HALL OF FAME LIBRARY, COOPERSTOWN, N.Y.

Paul Waner, Pirates outfielder, in 1927 scored or batted in a run in 32 consecutive games—the National League record.

30-gamer by Al Simmons of the 1925 Philadelphia Athletics. Preceding Simmons for the AL record were Babe Ruth and Ken Williams, who each assembled a 23-gamer—the Yankees outfielder achieved his in 1921; the Browns flyhawk, in 1922. George Sisler of the 1920 Browns was the junior circuit's first leader for the longest CGRP streak; he put together an 18-gamer. On the flip side, the longest CGRP streak in the AL since Cronin's 33-gamer is the 27-CGRP streak produced by Chuck Knoblauch of the 1996 Minnesota Twins.

In the National League, the longest CGRP streak is 32 games, a feat achieved by Paul Waner for the 1927 Pittsburgh Pirates.[22] Big Poison was able to produce at least one run in each of the games he played from May 18 through June 21. Prior to Paul Waner's record 32-CGRP streak, the chronology of the National League record for the longest CGRP streak is Ross Youngs (13 in 1920), Zack Wheat (18 in 1921), Ray Grimes (19 in 1922 and 1924), Rogers Hornsby (22 in 1925), and Taylor Douthit (22 in 1926). With respect to the longest CGRP streak in the senior circuit since Waner's 32-gamer, three players fashioned 24-game skeins—Phil Cavarretta (1945 Cubs), Ted Kluszewski (1954 Redlegs), and Andres Galarraga (1997 Rockies). With respect to the longest CGRP streaks in the twenty-first century, two senior-circuiteers have put together strings of at least 20 games—Albert Pujols of the 2001 Cardinals had a 22-gamer, and Lance Berkman of the 2008 Astros had a 21-gamer.[28]

Table 2. Players with the Longest CGRP Streak for Each AL and NL Team, 1920–2008

AL Team	Player (Year)	CGRP Streak	NL Team	Player (Year)	CGRP Streak
Red Sox	Ted Williams (1949)	21	Braves	Roy Hartsfield (1950)	18
White Sox	Jim Thome (2006)	20	Dodgers	Ron Cey (1977)	20
Indians	Earl Averill (1938)	21	Cubs	Phil Cavarretta (1945)	24
Tigers	Billy Rogell (1934)	22	Reds	Ted Kluszewski (1954)	24
Yankees	Earle Combs (1925)	26	Giants	Mel Ott (1931)	20
Athletics	Al Simmons (1925)	30	Phillies	Lenny Dykstra (1993)	16
Orioles	Ken Williams (1922)	23	Pirates	Paul Waner (1927)	32
Twins	Joe Cronin (1933)	33	Cardinals	Rogers Hornsby (1925)	22
				Taylor Douthit (1926)	22
				Albert Pujols (2001)	22
Angels	Tony Phillips (1997)	17	Astros	Lance Berkman (2008)	21
Rangers	Will Clark (1998)	18	Mets	Jose Reyes (2006)	18
	Ian Kinsler (2008)	18			
Royals	Frank White (1983)	15	Nationals	Tim Raines (1986)	15
	Mike Sweeney (1999)	15		Vladimir Guerrero (2000)	15
Brewers	Paul Molitor (1987)	23	Padres	Steve Finley (1996)	18
Mariners	Edgar Martinez (1995)	18	Rockies	Andres Galarraga (1997)	24
Jays	Lloyd Moseby (1987)	15	Marlins	Cliff Floyd (2001)	13
Rays	Fred McGriff (1999)	16	Diamondbacks	Travis Lee (1999)	12
				Tony Womack (2001)	12
			Brewers	J. J. Hardy (2008)	15

NATIONAL BASEBALL HALL OF FAME LIBRARY, COOPERSTOWN, N.Y.

Joe Cronin, holder of the longest consecutive-game run-produced streak in MLB history—33, which he achieved in 1933.

In terms of having assembled (or tying) the longest CGRP streak the most times between 1920 and 2008, the American League features four three-time champions, each a Hall of Famer—Babe Ruth (23 in 1921, 14 in 1926, and 19 in 1931); Joe DiMaggio (19 in 1940, 16 in 1946, and 14 in 1948); Al Kaline (12 in 1963, 13 in 1967, and 10 in 1974), and Reggie Jackson (11 in 1968, 12 in 1971, and 14 in 1976). Nine junior-circuiteers picked up a pair of trophies for the longest CGRP streak—Harry Heilmann (1921 and 1929), Lou Gehrig (1927 and 1930), Gene Moore (1943 and 1945), Mickey Mantle (1955 and 1957), Minnie Minoso (1957 and 1959), Rocky Colavito (1960 and 1963), Tony Conigliaro (1965 and 1967), Alan Trammell (1990 and 1993), and Jim Thome (2002 and 2006).

In the National League, Stan Musial captured the throne four times (12 in 1946, 13 in 1948, 12 in 1949, and 16 in 1951). Two senior-circuiteers each copped three CGRP gold medals—Willie Mays (1955, 1959, and 1963) and Mike Schmidt (1976, 1980, and 1981). And, nine players picked up a pair of blue ribbons—Ray Grimes (1922 and 1924), Pie Traynor (1928 and 1929), Paul Waner (1927 and 1937), Mel Ott (1931 and 1942), Rusty Staub (1973 and 1975), Tim Raines (1986 and 1988), Matt Williams (1993 and 1995), Jeff Bagwell (2000 and 2004), and Todd Helton (2003 and 2005).

The players who make up table 1 are an interesting mix. Perhaps it's not surprising that many of them were subsequently enshrined in the Hall of Fame—24 players from the junior circuit and 23 players from the senior loop were CGRP league leaders at least once. But, there were also a number of players whom one would probably not have expected to have emerged with the longest CGRP streak in his league—such as Bill Lamar of the 1924 Athletics, Danny Taylor of the 1933 Dodgers, Ken O'Dea of the 1936 Cubs, Roy Hartsfield of the 1950 Braves, Jim Rivera of the 1956 White Sox, Roberto Pena of the 1968 Phillies, Carmelo Martinez of the 1984 Padres, and Tony Bernazard of the 1986 Indians.

In addition to the league record holders (Joe Cronin in the AL and Paul Waner in the NL), it is also useful to list those players who compiled the longest CGRP streak for each franchise during the period 1920–2008. Table 2 provides the players from each AL team and each NL team who compiled the longest CGRP streak from 1920 through 2008. [Note: Table 2 includes franchise-shifted clubs such as the St. Louis Browns (1920–53) to the Baltimore Orioles (1954–2008).]

It may also be of interest to note that the American League team with the most league leaders (and co-leaders) for the longest CGRP streak is the New York Yankees—their players claimed the gold medal in 18 seasons. Next in line with 13 blue ribbons are the Detroit Tigers. Among the expansion teams, the Texas Rangers (and their predecessor, the Washington Senators) have had their players claim the most (6) first-prize trophies. In the National League, the Giants (New York and San Francisco combined) led the way—their players occupied the throne 14 times. Next in line with 13 first-place finishes each are the Pirates and the Cardinals. Among the expansion teams, New York Mets players won the most (6) first-place medals.

Finally, table 3 presents a list of the longest known CGRP streaks (that is, those of at least 20 games) from 1920 onward.

Examination of table 3 reveals that, since 1920, there have been 31 CGRP streaks of at least 20 games—20 from the junior loop and 11 from the senior circuit. Each of the 16 original teams (including those that have relocated) is represented by at least one player with a CGRP streak of at least 20 games—except the Braves and Phillies. In contrast, only three of the 14 "expansion" teams (including those that have relocated) have had a player with a CGRP streak of at least 20 games—the AL Milwaukee Brewers, the Colorado Rockies, and the Houston Astros.[28] It is also noted that three players assembled a pair of CGRP streaks of at least 20 games—Babe Ruth (23 in 1921 and 20 in 1930), Paul Waner (32 in 1927 and 22 in 1937), and Ted Williams (21 and 20, both in 1949).

CONCLUSIONS

The answer to the question posed in the title of this article has been determined. The longest CGRP streak in the major leagues (1920–2008) is the 33-gamer by

Table 3. Players Who Have Achieved CGRP Streaks of at Least 20 games

Player	Team	Year	Runs	RBI	Runs + RBI	CGRP Streak
Babe Ruth	Yankees	1930	150	153	303	20
Mel Ott	Giants	1931	104	115	219	20
Joe Vosmik	Red Sox	1938	121	86	207	20
Ted Williams	Red Sox	1949	150	159	309	20
Ron Cey	Dodgers	1977	77	110	187	20
Wade Boggs	Red Sox	1988	128	58	186	20
Jim Thome	White Sox	2006	108	109	217	20
Jack Tobin	Browns	1921	132	59	191	21
Harry Heilmann	Tigers	1923	121	115	236	21
Earl Averill	Indians	1938	101	93	194	21
Ted Williams	Red Sox	1949	150	159	309	21
Paul O'Neill	Yankees	1998	95	116	211	21
Lance Berkman	Astros	2008	114	106	220	21
Rogers Hornsby	Cardinals	1925	133	143	276	22
Taylor Douthit	Cardinals	1926	96	52	148	22
Billy Rogell	Tigers	1934	114	101	215	22
Paul Waner	Pirates	1937	94	74	168	22
Albert Pujols	Cardinals	2001	112	130	242	22
Babe Ruth	Yankees	1921	177	171	348	23
Ken Williams	Browns	1922	128	155	283	23
Paul Molitor	Brewers	1987	114	75	189	23
Lou Gehrig	Yankees	1930	143	174	317	24
Tommy Henrich	Yankees	1942	77	67	144	24
Phil Cavarretta	Cubs	1945	94	97	191	24
Ted Kluszewski	Redlegs	1954	104	141	245	24
Andres Galarraga	Rockies	1997	120	140	260	24
Earle Combs	Yankees	1925	117	61	178	26
Chuck Knoblauch	Twins	1996	140	72	212	27
Al Simmons	Athletics	1925	122	129	251	30
Paul Waner	Pirates	1927	114	132	245	32
Joe Cronin	Senators	1933	89	118	207	33

NATIONAL BASEBALL HALL OF FAME LIBRARY, COOPERSTOWN, N.Y.

In 1997, Andres Galarraga of the Rockies scored or batted in a run in 24 consecutive games—a team record and tied (with Phil Cavarretta of the Cubs and Ted Kluszewski of the Reds) for second-best in the National League.

Joe Cronin of the 1933 American League Washington Senators. The longest CGRP streak in the National League (1920-2008) is 32, by Paul Waner of the 1927 Pittsburgh Pirates. In addition, the players who hold the record for the longest CGRP streak for each major league team are listed in table 2.

With regard to future research, my plan is to extend the CGRP-streak study back to 1901, the year that the American League became a major league. However, it is noted that this will be an arduous task—since there are no known day-by-day compilations of RBI records (official or unofficial), it will be necessary to generate them by going through the pertinent newspaper accounts for every major-league game. To facilitate this process, the focus will be on individual franchises, the first franchise to be undertaken by me being the 1901–19 Detroit Tigers. Hopefully, other researchers will want to carry out analogous studies for their favorite teams.

Permissions

The longest-CGRP-streak information for the seasons included in the present Retroshseet database and provided here in tables 1–3 was obtained free of charge from and is copyrighted by Retrosheet. Interested parties may contact Retrosheet at www.retrosheet.org.

Acknowledgments

It is a pleasure to thank the following people for their wonderful help and cooperation in the CGRP- streak research I have carried out—Dave Smith (Retrosheet), utilizing the computer program he wrote to extract the longest CGRP streak for each player in each season of the Retrosheet database, provided me with this critical information. Dave also shared the Retrosheet batting lines of those players from the period 1920–27 so I could corroborate or refute the pertinent RBI information in the official DBD records. Thanks are also extended to all of the Retrosheet volunteers who over the years have provided and/or inputted play-by-play information to create the invaluable Retrosheet database. Each of these Retrosheeters is truly a baseball-research enabler—many thanks to each of you! Tim Wiles and Freddy Berowski (National Baseball Hall of Fame Library) were superbly helpful to me in my efforts to review (and photocopy) the official DBD records for most of the seasons in the period 1920–53. Trent McCotter gave me copies of the official DBD records for many seasons in the period 1920–33. Seymour Siwoff, Steve Hirdt, and John McCarthy (Elias Sports Bureau) have been very supportive of my efforts to employ accurate runs-scored and runs-batted-in information in my research, by officially sanctioning the corrections of the errors I've discovered. The following SABR members have been tremendously helpful by providing photocopies of newspaper game accounts and box scores so as to corroborate or refute runs-scored and/or runs-batted-in information in the official DBD records: Ron Antonucci, David Ball, Cliff Blau, Steve Boren, Bob Buege, Keith Carlson, John Delahanty, Chris Eckes, Mike Lynch, Austin Macdonald, Bob McConnell, Bill Nowlin, Rick Riccardi, and Dixie Tourangeau. In addition, SABR members Clem Comly, Bill Deane, and Jim

Smith have provided valuable information for my "Longest CGRP Streaks" project. And, I gratefully express my appreciation to my friend Gary Stone for his invaluable help with photocopying the official DBD records of hundreds of players and especially for the insightful discussions I had with him. ■

Notes

1. Paul Dickson, *The Dickson Baseball Dictionary*, 3d ed. (New York: Norton, 2009), 92. Batting runs (BR) is the linear-weights measure of a player's offensive performance, representing the number of runs for which a batter is personally responsible through batting; devised by Pete Palmer and originally described by John Thorn and Pete Palmer (with David Reuther) in their book *The Hidden Game of Baseball: A Revolutionary Approach to Baseball and Its Statistics* (Garden City, N.Y.: Doubleday 1984).
2. Dickson, *Dickson Baseball Dictionary*, 728. Runs created (RC) is an estimate of the number of runs that would result from a player's offensive contributions, as derived from one of several formulas; created by Bill James and first described in his self-published *Baseball Abstract* (1978); see also James's commercially published *The Bill James Baseball Abstract* (New York: Ballantine, 1982).
3. John Thorn and Pete Palmer, eds., *Total Baseball* (New York: Warner Books, 1989), 2292.
4. Herm Krabbenhoft, "Who Invented Runs Produced (RP)?" *The Baseball Research Journal* 38, no. 1 (summer 2009), 135–138.
5. Herm Krabbenhoft, "The Longest Streaks of Consecutive Games in Which a Detroit Tiger Scored a Run, 1945–2008," *The Baseball Research Journal* 37 (2008): 123.
6. Herm Krabbenhoft, "The Longest Streaks of Consecutive Games in Which a Detroit Tiger Scored a Run, 1920–1944," manuscript in preparation.
7. Herm Krabbenhoft, "The Longest Streaks of Consecutive Games in Which a Detroit Tiger Batted in a Run, 1945–2008, manuscript in preparation.
8. Some of the results presented here were described in my presentation "Corrections and Consecutive Games Streaks: Detroit Tigers (1945–2006)," given at the Society for American Baseball Research convention (SABR 37), St. Louis, July 26–29, 2007.
9. For example, see the following: Archie Motley, Phil Tortora, "19th Hole: The Readers Take Over," *Sports Illustrated* (29 November 1976), 117; J. R. Booth, "Fake Formula Unmasked," *The Sporting News* (24 October 1983), 7; Bill James, "Logic and Methods in Baseball Analysis," *The Bill James Baseball Abstract* (1984), 17–19; John Thorn and Peter Palmer, *The Hidden Game of Baseball* (Garden City, N.Y.: Doubleday, 1984), 64; Bill James, "Beyond the Basics—Runs Produced," *The Bill James Baseball Abstract* (1987), 25; Tom M. Tango, "Runs Produced—Should We Subtract the Home Run or Not?" www.tangotiger.net/runsproduced.html.
10. Seymour Siwoff, *The Elias Book of Baseball Records* (New York: Elias Sports Bureau, 2009), 12.
11. Steve Gietschier, *Complete Baseball Record and Fact Book* (St. Louis: The Sporting News, 2008), 18.
12. Lyle Spatz, ed. *The SABR Baseball List and Record Book: Baseball's Most Fascinating Records and Unusual Statistics* (New York: Scribner, 2007), 144.
13. Siwoff, *Elias Book of Baseball Records* (2009), 26.
14. Gietschier, *Complete Baseball Record and Fact Book* (2008), 30.
15. Spatz, ed., *SABR Baseball List and Record Book*, 145.
16. Personal communication (7 March 2009) from Dave Smith of Retrosheet—in an email message to me, Dave wrote: "The season totals for players on our site come from Pete Palmer's data base of 15 years ago. The newer seasons come from our data. The daily data back to 1953 come from our files. All the earlier ones (1920s) come from the official totals."
17. Herm Krabbenhoft, "The Authorized Corrections of Runs-Scored Errors in the Official Baseball Records (1945–2007) for Detroit Tigers Players," *The Baseball Research Journal* 37 (2008): 115.
18. Herm Krabbenhoft, "The Authorized Corrections of Runs-Batted-In Errors in the Official Baseball Records for Detroit Tigers Players, 1945–2007," manuscript in preparation. It is also mentioned that, following my Completely Closed Circuit Principle, I unearthed an additional 54 RBI errors involving a total of 31 players (including six more Hall of Famers).
19. Trent McCotter, "Hitting a Home Run and Not Being Credited with an RBI," newsletter of the SABR Baseball Records Committee (August 2008, 2; and October 2008, 2). See also Trent McCotter, "Record RBI Streak Discovered: Hall of Famer Tris Speaker Put Together a String of 14 Consecutive Games with an RBI in 1928 That Was Unrecognized for 79 Years," *Baseball Digest*, May 2008, 62.
20. Personal communication (14 November 2006) from Dave Smith of Retrosheet)—in an email message to me, Dave wrote: "At this point, I do not know of any errors on runs or RBI for any Tiger after 1970. If any arise, I will let you know immediately, since this will undoubtedly impact your streak studies."
21. It is appreciated that the process of corroborating the runs-scored and runs-batted-in information in the official DBD records by resorting to the runs-scored and runs-batted-in information in newspaper box scores is not a priori, guaranteed fool-proof verification of the official DBD records—because it is conceivable that the box-score information and the official DBD information are both erroneous. Nonetheless, using newspaper box scores to corroborate the official DBD records certainly represents a good-faith effort—which was very beneficial in the present research effort, as described in references 22–26.
22. According to the uncorroborated 1927 official DBD records for Paul Waner, his longest CGRP streak was a 23-gamer—from May 28 through June 21; he did not score a run or bat in a run in the games on May 27 and June 22. The runs-scored information provided in the box scores presented in the *New York Times* corroborated the runs-scored information in the official DBD records. However, comparing the runs-batted-in information in his official DBD information with that provided in Waner's batting lines obtained from the Retrosheet event files revealed a discrepancy—for the game on May 27, the official DBD records show Waner with no runs batted in; the (unproofed) Retrosheet batting line shows that Waner was credited with one RBI, indicating that his CGRP streak actually began before May 28 and is longer than the 23 games indicated by his official DBD records. That the Retrosheet batting line for Paul Waner is indeed correct was conclusively demonstrated by examining the text accounts and batter-by-batter, play-by-play accounts provided in three newspapers—the *Pittsburgh Post*, the *St. Louis Post-Dispatch*, and the *St. Louis Star*. In each of these newspapers it was clearly stated that Paul Waner batted in a run in the first inning. For example, here's the play-by-play account provided in the *St. Louis Star* for the Pirates batting in the first inning. "L. Waner singled to center. L. Waner stole second as Cuyler was called out on strikes. P. Waner singled to center, scoring L. Waner. Wright hit into a double play, Thevenow to Frisch to Bottomley. One run." So, Paul Waner did have one RBI in the game on May 27. And, according to his official DBD records, Waner produced at least one run in each of the eight games he played in from May 18 through May 26; he did not produce a run in the game he played on May 17. Fortunately, the Retrosheet event files also have the daily batting lines for each of Waner's games from May 17 through May 26. Significantly, the Retrosheet daily lines also show that Waner did not produce a run in the game on May 17 and that he did produce at least one run in each of the eight games from May 18 through May 26. Thus, Waner actually compiled a 32-CGRP streak from May 18 through June 21.
23. According to the uncorroborated 1933 official DBD records for Chuck Klein, he had a 12-CGRP streak—from May 2 through May 17. However, comparison of the runs-scored and runs-batted-in information in his official DBD records with that provided in the box scores presented in the *New York Times* revealed a discrepancy in the first game of the doubleheader on May 13. The official DBD records for this game credit Klein with no runs scored and one run batted in; the box score presented in the *New York Times* shows no runs scored and no runs batted in for Klein. Resorting to the game account presented in the *Chicago Tribune*, which

described in detail how the Phillies scored in the third inning, we learn that Klein did indeed bat in a run—"Fullis got the second of his three singles with one out in this inning and stopped at second on Bartell's single to left. The runners moved up on Tinning's first wild pitch and when Klein grounded out Fullis scored and Bartell took third." Thus, the official DBD is correct with regard to Klein having an RBI in that game—and, therefore, his 12-CGRP streak is accurate.

24. According to the unchecked 1934 official DBD records for Billy Rogell, he had an 18-CGRP streak—from July 22 (second game) through August 9; he did not produce a run in the games on July 22 (first game) and August 10. However, comparison of the runs-scored and runs-batted-in information in his official DBD records with that provided in the box scores presented in the *New York Times* revealed a discrepancy for the game on August 10. The *New York Times* box score for this game shows Rogell credited with one RBI, indicating his 18-CGRP streak was not terminated in that game. The game accounts presented in three newspapers (the *Cleveland Plain Dealer*, the *Cleveland Press*, and the *Detroit News*), provide batter-by-batter details for each of Detroit's six runs and incontrovertibly show that Rogell batted in the Tigers' run in the seventh inning—"Cochrane flied out. Gehringer singled to right. Goslin made his fourth consecutive hit, a drive to left center. Gehringer took third on the hit. Hildebrand was taken out and Mel Harder substituted. Rogell flied to Holland and Gehringer scored after the catch." Thus, Rogell did have an RBI in the game on August 10, thereby extending his CGRP streak to 19 games. Furthermore, according to the corroborated runs and RBI information in his official DBD record, Rogell produced at least one run in each of his next three games before being shut down in the run-production department in the second game on August 14. Therefore, Rogell's CGRP streak was 22 games.
25. According to the unverified 1935 official DBD records for Lonny Frey, he had a 17 CGRP streak—from May 8 through May 26. However, comparison of the runs-scored and runs-batted-in information in his official DBD records with that provided in the box scores presented in the *New York Times* revealed a discrepancy in the game on May 18. The official DBD records show Frey with no runs scored and one run batted in; the newspaper box score shows Frey with no runs scored and no runs batted in. The game account presented in the *New York Times* describes each of the two runs the Dodgers scored: "Al Lopez opened with a single off Thevenow's glove, Mungo fanned and Jimmy Jordan dropped a bunt that left both men safe when Vaughan took Blanton's throw and failed to get his foot on second. Frenchy Bordagaray rapped a clean single to center, scoring Al, and when Frey hit to Floyd Young the substitute second sacker made a low throw to Vaughan that allowed Jordan to tally and sent Frenchy to third." Thus, it appears that, initially, the official scorer did not give credit to Frey for an RBI. However, after the game story and box score went to press, the official scorer decided that, since there was only one out when Frey batted, Jordan would have scored even if Young had not committed his throwing error. Consistent with this explanation is the official DBD record for the Pirates pitcher, Blanton—both of the runs charged to him were earned runs. Thus, the official DBD records show Frey with one RBI—and, therefore, his 17-CGRP streak is correct.
26. According to the unchecked 1952 official DBD records for Del Ennis, he had a 13-CGRP streak—from July 23 through August 7. However, comparison of the runs-scored and runs-batted-in information in his official DBD records with that provided in the box scores presented in *The Sporting News* and the *New York Times* revealed a discrepancy in the second game of the doubleheader on July 29. The official DBD records for this game credit Ennis with no runs scored and one run batted in; the newspaper box scores for this game show no runs scored and no runs batted in for Ennis. Moreover, according to newspaper accounts, the details for each of the four runs the Phillies scored in that game reveal that Ennis did not score or bat in any runs—Granny Hamner scored the first run in the fourth inning when he was trapped off third base, but he came home on a throwing error by Bobby Adams. Richie Ashburn's inside-the-park homer accounted for the second run. Eddie Watikus drove home Willie Jones with a single in the ninth and then later scored the winning run on a hit by Johnny Wyrostek. Therefore, Ennis did not actually achieve a 13-CGRP streak; his longest CGRP streak that season—according to his corroborated official DBD record—was actually an 11-gamer (from May 10 [one] through May 22—i.e., a couple of months before his refuted 13-CGRP streak), which still turned out to be the longest CGRP streak in the NL in 1952.
27. The Official Baseball Rules (2008) are available online at mlb.com. "Rule 10.23 Guidelines for Cumulative Performance Record" deals with consecutive streaks: (A) Consecutive Hitting Streaks, (B) Consecutive-Game Hitting Streaks, and (C) Consecutive-Game Playing Streaks. There is no reference to Consecutive-Game Run-Scoring Streaks, Consecutive-Game Run-Batting-In Streaks, or Consecutive-Game Run-Producing Streaks. With regard to Consecutive-Game Hitting Streaks, the rule states, "A consecutive-game hitting streak shall not be terminated if all of a batter's plate appearances (one or more) in a game result in a base on balls, hit batsman, defensive indifference or obstruction or a sacrifice bunt. The streak shall terminate if the player has a sacrifice fly and no hit." With regard to Consecutive-Game Playing Streak, the rule states, "A consecutive-game playing streak shall be extended if a player plays one half-inning on defense or if the player completes a time at bat by reaching base or being put out. A pinch running appearance only shall not extend the streak."
28. Herm Krabbenhoft, "Lance Berkman Joined Select Group of Run Producers in 2008," *Baseball Digest*, May 2009, 40.

Who Invented Runs Produced?

Herm Krabbenhoft

REFERRAL to the glossary of statistical terms in the first edition (1989) of *Total Baseball* by John Thorn and Pete Palmer allows one to easily find not only the meaning and utility of numerous baseball statistics but also the persons credited with inventing them.[1] For example:

> **Assist average.** Assists divided by games played. Stat created by Philadelphia baseball writer Al Wright in 1875.
>
> **Average bases allowed.** A pitcher's total bases allowed, divided by his innings pitched—what might be termed opponents' slugging average. Created by Alfred P. Berry in 1951.
>
> **Linear weights.** A system created by Pete Palmer to measure all the events on a ball field in terms of runs.
>
> **On-base percentage.** Created by Allan Roth and Branch Rickey in its current form [hits plus walks plus hit by pitch, divided by at-bats plus walks plus hit by pitch] in the early 1950s. . . . When OBP was adopted as an official stat in 1984, the denominator was expanded to include sacrifice flies.
>
> **Runs created.** Bill James's formulation for run contribution from a variety of batting and baserunning events. In its basic expression, the formula is [(hits + walks) x (total bases)] divided by (at-bats + walks).
>
> **Total average.** Tom Boswell's formulation for offensive contribution from a variety of batting and baserunning events. The concept of the numerator is bases gained; that of the denominator is outs made [total bases + steals + walks + hit by pitches] divided by [at-bats − hits + caught stealing + grounded into double plays].
>
> **Runs produced.** Runs batted in plus runs scored minus home runs.

Curiously, the inventor of the runs-produced (RP) statistic is not mentioned. Similarly, other sources of such information have provided only the definition or formula for runs produced—nothing at all about its creator. For example, the third edition (2009) of *The Dickson Baseball Dictionary* gives the following for runs produced: "An informal statistical measurement that equals runs scored plus runs batted in, minus home runs. Of unknown origin, the measure was evaluated by Bill James (*Baseball Abstract*, 1987)."[2]

Because of my interest in determining who has the major-league record for the longest consecutive- games run-produced (CGRP) streak,[3,4] I deemed it appropriate to find out who created the runs-produced statistic.[5]

So, who did invent runs produced?[6]

Here's the fascinating chronology of my discovery.

In a phone conversation with fellow SABR member Seymour Siwoff (Elias Sports Bureau), I mentioned my CGRP-streak research (and the need for accurate data for runs and RBIs alike on a game-by-game basis). Seymour told me that he recalled runs-produced stats first being presented in *Sports Illustrated*—a couple of years after its first year of publication, which was 1954. Similarly, in an email exchange with Pete Palmer, Pete thought that runs produced "was introduced by *Sports Illustrated*, maybe in the '50s or '60s."

With that lead, I went through every "baseball season" issue of *Sports Illustrated* from 1955 through 1964, looking for anything on runs produced. Here's what I came up with:

> **1955.** Nothing at all on runs produced. In each weekly issue, *SI* included an information box (titled "Major League Baseball") that gave the scores of the previous week's games and the individual leaders in BA, RBI, HR, and pitching W–L.
>
> **1956.** Each weekly issue of *SI* included "The X-Ray Box," which (in addition to the usual stats) presented a chart for the top five "runs produced" leaders for each league.

In the first baseball-season issue (May 14, page 52), the column headings in the runs-produced chart were

> **Player's name (team and batting average)**
> **Runs Scored**
> **RBI**
> **Total Runs Produced**

In the next issue (May 21, page 46), the column headings in the RP chart were

Player's name (team and batting average)
Runs Scored
Teammates Batted In
Total Runs Produced

Note the difference for the third column heading in the first two issues—"RBI" (i.e., *Runs* Batted In) in the May 14 issue and "*Teammates* Batted In" in the May 21 issue.

It is pointed out that *SI* provided no explanation whatsoever of the change from "RBI" to "Teammates Batted In."

For the remainder of the 1956 baseball season, the column heading "Teammates Batted In" was used.

In the end-of-the-season "X-Ray" (October 7, page 55), the distinction between "RBI" and "Teammates Batted In" is crystal clear (though not expressed by *SI*). For example, Mantle (the AL RBI leader) is listed in a chart of "month-by-month leaders" with a total of 130 RBI; in the Runs Produced chart, he is listed with 78 teammates batted in. Thus, "Teammates Batted In" is equal to RBI minus HR (Mantle having hit 52 home runs in his 1956 triple-crown season).

It is emphasized that in none of the baseball articles accompanying "The X-Ray Box" was any mention made or discussion given of runs produced (or of "teammates batted in").

1957. Each weekly issue of SI was organized essentially just like those in 1956—"The X-Ray Box" included a runs-produced chart with the same column headings:

Player's name (team and batting average)
Runs Scored
Teammates Batted In
Total Runs Produced

1958. Exactly the same as in 1957 (and 1956).

1959. The "X-Ray Box" was replaced by "Baseball's Week," which included text by Les Woodcock as well as some performance charts, including "Runs Produced," which was exactly the same as those employed in 1958 (and 1957 and 1956)—with one significant midseason addition. Beginning with the July 13 issue (page 10), and continuing for the rest of the baseball season, the column heading "Teammates Batted In" was asterisked, the asterisk directing the reader to the explanation "Derived by subtracting HRs from RBIs."

1960. Same as in 1959—"Baseball's Week," which included text by different authors as well as some performance charts, including "Runs Produced," which for the column heading "Teammates Batted In" had an asterisk indicating the explanation "Derived by subtracting HRs from RBIs."

1961. Same as in 1960.

1962. Identical to 1961.

1963. Similar to 1962. However, the performance charts provided only runs-produced information—no columns for "Runs Scored" and "Teammates Batted In."

1964. No performance charts; text only—no mention of runs produced.

In none of the baseball articles published in *Sports Illustrated* from 1955 through 1964 was any mention made of the creator of runs produced; likewise for the period 1965–2008.[7, 8]

So, I wrote the following summary and emailed it to Seymour Siwoff, Pete Palmer, and John Thorn:

> The batting performance statistic, "Runs Produced" (which is defined as Runs Scored plus Runs Batted In minus Home Runs) first appeared in *Sports Illustrated* in 1956 (May 14 issue, page 52). A "Runs Produced" chart was included in nearly every issue of SI during the baseball season from 1956 through 1963. The specific person(s) deserving credit for creating the "Runs Produced" statistic has/have not yet been identified.

Thorn wrote back the following: "This sticks in my memory—that the inventor of the *SI* Runs Produced formula was none other than Bob Creamer."

That Bob Creamer could have been the creator of the runs-produced statistic seemed unlikely to me for the following reason. In the *Sports Illustrated* issue with the very first presentation of the runs-produced statistic (May 14, 1956), "The X-Ray Box" accompanied the article "End of Round One" with the by-line "Baseball by Robert Creamer." ("Round One" referred to the fact that each club was supposed to have played every other team in its league at least once.)

While Creamer provided his assessments on the round-one performance of each team in each league, he gave only brief mention to individual performances (through May 6), and then only of a few players—Mickey Mantle (who was ahead of Ruth's 1927-season homer pace), Whitey Ford (who won his first four decisions), Bill Wight (who lost his first four starts), and Cardinals pitchers Tom Poholsky, Jackie Collum, and Ellis Kinder (who combined to pitch a "rare three-man shutout"). Creamer made absolutely no mention of runs produced.

So, I asked Thorn for contact information for Bob Creamer. Thorn responded that, while he didn't have contact info for Creamer, another SABR member might—Marty Appel. (Appel had been public-relations director for the New York Yankees during the middle 1970s and is the author of the book, *Now Pitching for the Yankees: Spinning the News for Mickey, Reggie, and George* [Kingston, N.Y.: Total / Sports Illustrated, 2001].)

I sent an email summarizing the situation to Appel, asking for Creamer's contact information. Appel replied: "Happy to provide it; very interesting story. I'll be surprised if Bob was the creator, in that I don't see him as a 'stat guy,' but you never know!"

Next, I sent an email to Creamer, including some of the salient points from above. I concluded my missive with the following:

> So, I wanted to contact you to find out if you are the creator of the Runs Produced stat. I would greatly appreciate it if you would please let me know if you did indeed originate Runs Produced and your recollections of *SI* including RP in their weekly coverage of baseball during the 1956–1963 period.

I was hoping that, even if Creamer was not the inventor of runs produced, he would recall who was.

Pay dirt! Two days later, Bob Creamer sent the following email to me:

> My computer has been down—it's still not working right—or I'd have answered your email before this.
>
> I'll be honest and admit that I was delighted to get your message.
>
> Yes, in 1956 in working up a weekly stat report for *Sports Illustrated* I suggested the Runs Produced idea. Les Woodcock, another original member of the *SI* staff, worked closely with me and helped refine it. At first I thought adding runs scored and runs batted in was enough, but that gave an over-preponderance to home-run hitters, who got two RPs for a home run, the one they batted in and the one they scored. To level the playing field, so to speak, and to give more weight to less powerful hitters who nonetheless seemed to get around the bases and score a lot, we arbitrarily decided to deduct home run totals. The Runs Produced stat was sometimes dismissed by mathematical purists and I confess I was surprised and pleased when Total Baseball included it among its many measures of batting performance. I'd always felt that despite its mathematical flaw it was a good honest way of evaluating an offensive player's worth. I had that belief reinforced in the 1950s by my great friend Seymour Siwoff of Elias, who said something to the effect that while it may not be mathematically valid, "It works!" (Seymour, who was a tremendous help to us at Sports Illustrated in those early days of the magazine, often spoke with exclamation marks in his voice.)
>
> The Runs Produced stat had its origins a decade earlier, in 1946, just after World War II, when a bunch of us returning from military service to southern Westchester County formed a softball team and joined a Sunday league (Sunday because lots of people still had to work Saturdays in those days and evening games were difficult for guys who commuted to jobs in New York City). I was the manager for some reason and because I was smart enough to keep myself on the bench most of the time (I wasn't much of a player) I was able to keep a meticulous scorebook of all our games. Because of my fondness for stats (I love Marty Appel but he pegged me wrong on that one) I kept working up lists of team leaders in various categories.
>
> I had an On Base Percentage that included not just hits and bases on balls but getting on base because of errors. We had a little right-fielder who batted about .220 but could bunt beautifully and was fast as a rabbit going down the line to first, with the result that pitchers, catchers and infielders hurrying to throw him out made error after error. Jay had a very high OBP and a remarkably high number of runs scored. We also had a rotund third-baseman who could hit and drive in runs but who didn't get around the bases to home plate that often. Jay would be high on the list of runs scored, and Fred would be among the leaders in RBIs. I got the idea of adding runs scored and runs batted in to see who overall were the best run producers on the team.
>
> That Runs Produced figure worked well in softball because we didn't play on a fenced field and home runs were hard to come by. But when Les Woodcock and I applied the Runs Produced idea

to major league baseball it became distorted by the great number of homers, which led us to the idea of deducting them from the overall total. And there we were.

How I do run on. Sorry for the length, but it was a pleasure.

So: Mission accomplished!

Bob Creamer (with refinement input from Les Woodcock) is the inventor of runs produced. ■

Notes

It is a pleasure to thank all the persons who contributed to this chronology—Seymour Siwoff, Pete Palmer, Gary Stone (who helped me search some of the issues of *Sports Illustrated*), John Thorn, Marty Appel, and, especially, Bob Creamer.

1. John Thorn and Pete Palmer, eds., *Total Baseball*, 1st ed. (New York: Warner Books, 1989), 2286–93.
2. Paul Dickson, *The Dickson Baseball Dictionary*," 3d ed. (New York: Norton, 2009), 729.
3. Herm Krabbenhoft, "Lance Berkman Joined Select Group of Run Producers in 2008," *Baseball Digest*, May 2009, 40–43.
4. Herm Krabbenhoft, "Who Has the Major-League Record for the Longest Consecutive-Games Run-Produced (CGRP) Streak?" *The Baseball Research Journal* 38, no. 1 (Summer 2009): 125–134.
5. The runs-produced (RP) statistic should not be confused with the statistic estimated runs produced (ERP) devised by Paul Johnson. As reported on pages in *The Bill James Baseball Abstract* (1985), Johnson's ERP "is a method for estimating run production which is more accurate than even Bill James' runs created formula" (276–81). The ERP formula is: ERP = 0.16 x {2 x [TB + BB + HB] + H + SB – [0.605 x (AB + CS + GIDP – H)]}.
6. The Baseball Almanac (www.baseball-almanac.com) states the following in its section "Career Leaders for Runs Produced": "Runs produced is a SABERmetric statistic that describes a hitter's overall effectiveness by measuring his ability to produce runs for (his) team either by scoring them himself or driving them in at the plate. Runs produced was created by baseball great Bill James during the 1970's and the way it is calculated is adding runs to runs batted in [and] then subtracting home runs." Likewise, in *The Hidden Game of Baseball: A Revolutionary Approach to Baseball and Its Statistics* (Garden City, N.Y.: Doubleday, 1984), John Thorn and Pete Palmer (with David Reuther) wrote the following: "Bill James, at about the same time [i.e., that Steve Mann introduced his run-productivity average in an unpublished 1977 manuscript] came up with a similar formula, since shunned, with values based on runs plus RBIs minus home runs" (64). However, in *The Bill James Baseball Abstract* (1984), James wrote that "there is another road toward the same truth [ascertaining a player's contributions to offense, i.e., his runs created] that I would like to say something about. That is the statistic 'Runs Produced'" (17–19). James concluded his discussion with the following statement: "Ah, well, I didn't build the road" (i.e., invent runs produced). Then, three years later, James in *The Bill James Baseball Abstract* (1987) wrote: "Runs produced were invented by Spiro Agnew, an attempt to measure the same thing [as total average—i.e., to sum up the total effectiveness of an offensive player]. The 'formula,' of course, is runs + RBI – home runs (Spiro never was too complex)" (25).
7. In a subsequent (13 November 2008) search of the SI Vault on the *Sports Illustrated* website (www.Vault.sportsillustrated.cnn.com) for the term "runs produced" for the period 1954–present, I found that runs-produced charts were included in some post-1964 issues: 1965, once each month [(April 19 [the 1964 season RP rankings], May 3, June 7, July 12, August 16, September 13, and October 11); 1966, once every other month (April 25, June 20, and August 15); 1968 (August 19); 1976 (June 21, October 25, and November 29); 1982 (July 5); and 1999 (June 21). In none of the articles in which runs-produced statistics were presented (with or without RP charts) was any mention made of the creator of the RP statistic. In the "Scoreboard" (a collection of snippets on a variety of current topics, edited by Robert W. Creamer [e.g., Philadelphia Flyers Bobby Clarke's thoughts on the NHL's decision to crack down on fighting and related violence by introducing more stringent penalties]) in *Sports Illustrated* (21 June 1976) was the following statement about runs produced: "A baseball statistic called Runs Produced, which first appeared in *Sports Illustrated* 20 years ago, is based on the premise that runs are what count most in baseball. The figure is arrived at by adding the runs a player scores to the runs he bats in and then subtracting from that amount the number of home runs he hits. Players at or near the top in Runs Produced invariably are the ones who win ball games, those who get on base and score, those who drive other base runners in. For example, last year's Runs Produced leaders were Joe Morgan of Cincinnati in the National League and Fred Lynn of Boston in the American. Not by coincidence, each was voted Most Valuable Player in his league, even though neither finished first in any of the so-called Triple Crown categories—batting average, home runs, runs batted in. If you're wondering why the Reds are moving away from the pack, or why Texas and Kansas City are running one–two, here are this season's top Run Producers in each league through games of last Friday." The accompanying chart provided the following information (Player, Team, Runs Produced): National League—Griffey (CIN, 85), Morgan (CIN, 79), Perez (CIN, 75), Rose (CIN, 72), Schmidt (PHI, 72); American League—Mayberry (KC, 65), Otis (KC, 65), Burroughs (TEX, 63), Chambliss (NY, 62), Hargrove (TEX, 62), Hisle (MIN, 62). Later in the "Scoreboard" in *SI* (25 October 1976), Creamer reiterated the position that "while hitters who win batting titles and home-run championships get the publicity, the most valuable players tend to be the ones who are at or near the top in runs produced." An accompanying chart provided the top ten in each league in runs produced—in the American League, Thurman Munson of the Yankees finished second in runs produced with 167 (Rod Carew of the Twins finished first with 178); in the National League, Joe Morgan of the Reds was first with 197 (with teammate Pete Rose second with 183). Creamer's prognostication turned out to be on the money, as Munson and Morgan each later claimed the Most Valuable Player Award in his league. These two commentaries are apparently the only editorial texts on runs produced provided in *Sports Illustrated*. However, in a later issue of *SI* (29 November 1976), in the "19th Hole" (where readers expressed their thoughts about *SI*'s treatment of a given topic), two people wrote to criticize runs produced. Archie Motley (Chicago) claimed that, in order to have a meaningful statistic, home runs should not be subtracted. And, Phil Tortora (Milford, Connecticut) opined that the "runs-produced theory does not take into consideration the player's team"—i.e., a player on a good-hitting club will likely produce more runs than if he were on a poor-hitting team.
8. Similarly, an analogous online search of *The Sporting News* at www.paperofrecord.com for the period 1954–2003 showed that, while runs-produced statistics have appeared numerous times over the years since 1962 (particularly in the columns of Edgar Munzel, Peter Gammons, and Moss Klein), no indication of the inventor of runs produced was ever provided.

Remembering the Golden Age of Baseball

Preserving the Past

Vi Owen

FOR AS LONG as I can remember I have had an unquenchable passion for baseball. Beginning in the 1920s, when I was about five years old, I'd watch my big brother, Marv, playing sandlot games, then high-school and college games. The biggest thrill of all was witnessing his sparkling professional play in a major-league career that took him all the way to the World Series.

Now, as a senior citizen, I enjoy traveling back in time to *my* golden age of baseball—the 1930s and 1940s. Those were the glory days of Babe Ruth, Charlie Gehringer, Lefty Grove, Hank Greenberg, Bob Feller, and scores of other great ballplayers.

At some time in the 1920s, Babe Ruth came to San Jose, California, to play in the exhibition game at old Sodality Park on San Carlos Street in San Jose.

My parents took me to the game. I was about seven years old and knew little about the great career of Babe Ruth. In fact, I spent most of the time at the old wooden ballpark running up and down the wooden planks (not stairs). I seldom even looked at the playing field or at Babe Ruth.

In the 1980s Marv, then a retired major-leaguer, gave me all the memorabilia he had carefully preserved from those exciting decades—contracts, baseball cards, newspaper articles and box scores, fan letters, pictures, game programs, correspondence, and more. Reviewing this wealth of material and reliving the memories that went with it, I knew I had to write a book about my brother's career. He agreed to be the consultant.

As a "rookie" writer, I faced a huge challenge. Would a female senior citizen writing about baseball be taken seriously? Added to this were the physical and financial limitations imposed by age and the great investment of time that would be needed to complete the project. Balanced against those confines were several tremendous assets, the most valuable being Marv himself, coupled with the wealth of material he had preserved from that wonderful era. When added to my own burning desire to see the job through, these plusses far outweighed the drawbacks.

If a slow, low-key approach was all I could manage, so be it. Still, how could I go about finding the inner circle of baseball? With whom could I network? In pursuit of answers to these questions I set out on a fantastic, never-to-be-forgotten journey.

COURTESY OF VIOLA OWEN

Left to right: *Hank Greenberg (first base), Charlie Gehringer (second base), Billy Rogell (shortstop), and Marv Owen (third base), the Tigers infield, 1930s.*

My first step into digging for background information to establish the setting of the book was to visit the places where it had all begun. Starting with California's Santa Clara Valley, where we had grown up, I enlarged my search to other areas of the Pacific Coast. Finally, I moved on to Detroit, where Marv's greatest professional triumphs had taken place. Whenever possible, I collected pictures along the way.

At the same time I joined groups such as the Society for American Baseball Research and the Pacific Coast League Historical Society and participated in their activities. Attending national and regional baseball conferences, I met fans, sportswriters, editors, publishers, and retired players. Many of these people who shared my passion for baseball had great stories to tell. All were helpful and friendly. They renewed my vigor and expanded my thinking. Nevertheless, it was easy to get sidetracked. Hunting through old photos and finding a picture of a tall, shy, awkward thirteen-year-old girl (me), I remembered what it was like to stay for the first time in a large city hotel. The excitement of being in a hotel elevator filled with famous baseball players. The incredible thrill of watching my brother play third base for a major-league club.

How different it was from our small hometown.

Another photo triggered recollections of a true incident that took place in 1939. Marv, then with the Chicago White Sox, and Hank Greenberg of the Detroit

COURTESY OF VIOLA OWEN

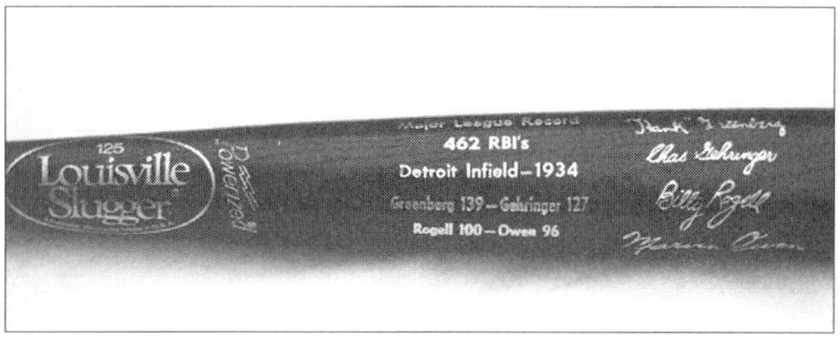

Top: *Louisville Slugger model 125, commemorating the 462 RBIs compiled by the 1934 Tigers infield.* Bottom: *Ball autographed by Hall of Famers for Marv Owen at the baseball centennial celebration in Cooperstown in 1939.*

Tigers had the honor of playing in the baseball centennial celebration at Cooperstown, New York. They were greatly impressed by seeing lined up at home plate the five Hall of Fame charter members—Walter Johnson, Babe Ruth, Ty Cobb, Tris Speaker, and Honus Wagner—in addition to Hall of Famers George Sisler, E. T. Collins, Nap "Larry" Lajoie, Cy Young, C. C. "Pete" Alexander, and Connie Mack. (Lou Gehrig was ill and unable to attend the celebration.)

Hank, who had brought along two official baseballs, muttered to Marv that, much as he would like to have them autographed, he was too bashful to approach these heroes of the game with the request. Marv swallowed his own shyness. "Let me do it," he offered. At his request, each Hall of Famer signed both baseballs. Hank kept one of them and presented the second to Marv, who for decades kept it in a fur-lined box in a safety deposit box.

Anecdotes and photographs such as these played an important part in the finished book. To start with, however, I outlined the material in projected sequence. Once I had a fairly complete book proposal, I sent it off to editors at publishing houses that I hoped would be interested in publishing the manuscript.

While this audacious move failed to result in the offer of a contract for publication, each editor I had contacted answered my letters personally. Many offered suggestions. One even gave the proposal a lengthy, constructive critique by phone.

But even though I followed their suggestions in the book's many rewrites, in the end the editors still regretfully expressed the opinion that the market for the book was too limited. With no contract for publication forthcoming, I had a hard decision to make. Ten years' work had gone into the book. It was the best I could make it, but was it worth publishing?

With all my heart, I believed that it was. Accordingly, I decided to see it through as a self-publishing venture.

In 1996, soon after I celebrated my seventy-seventh birthday, *Adventures of a Quiet Soul: A Scrapbook of Memories* made its debut in print. While I haven't made a fortune, following through on my dream has proven to be well worth the effort in every way.

All of the many reviews were positive. Some, indeed, were extremely flattering. Dave Anderson of the *New York Times* wrote, "Your book is dazzling. It's a priceless labor of love."

It *was* a labor of love—for baseball and my brother.

Traveling back in time to my golden age of baseball proved to be quite a journey! ■

Corrections

The National Pastime, volume 25, 2005

"Sisler Confronts the Evil Empire," by Roger Godin, 123–26. Page 123: The American League pennant winner in 1924 is misidentified, and the number of games that the St. Louis Browns finished out of first place is wrong. The Washington Senators won the pennant, and the Browns finished 17 games in back of them.

The National Pastime, volume 28, 2008

"Ten Days in August: A Last Chance for Brooklyn," by Henry D. Fetter, 63–67. Page 66: "If Walter O'Malley actually pulled a world-championship team out of its hometown right after such a triumph, he would have been the first team owner in a major sport to make such a move—and to date the only one." In an endnote to this sentence, the author acknowledges the near-precedent of the NFL's Boston Redskins moving to Washington after the 1936 season. A stronger precedent was that of the Cleveland Rams, who won the NFL championship in 1945 and were relocated to Los Angeles the next year.

The Baseball Research Journal, volume 37, 2008

"History versus Harry Frazee: Re-revising the Story," by Daniel R. Levitt, Mark L. Armour, and Matthew Levitt, 26–41. Page 28: In the caption to the photo, the second player from the left is misidentified as Harry Hooper. The player's identity is unknown. The player to the far right is identified as Ralph Comstock; the possibility that this player is also misidentified has been raised but not confirmed.

"Beating the Klan: Baseball Coverage in Wichita Before Integration, 1920–1930," by Brian Carroll, 51–61. Page 52: Segregation of the public schools in Wichita in 1906 is said to be "a move that the Klan aggressively fought for." After being suppressed in the 1870s, the Ku Klux Klan was reconstituted but not until 1915, and it did not organize in Kansas until the early 1920s. For clarification—also on page 52: The sentence beginning "In the context of what quickly became an economically depressed decade for most Americans" refers to the 1930s, not the 1920s.

"The OBP Triple Crown," by Bill Nowlin, 105–6. Page 106: In the table, Ty Cobb is correctly listed as leading the league in BA and OBA in 1909, but he is erroneously omitted from the list in the paragraph below the table.

"Where Have You Gone, Carl Yastrzemski: A Statistical Analysis of the Triple Crown," by John E. Daniels, 107–14. Page 107: The Triple Crown is said to have been won 14 times, but the accompanying table lists 13. The table is correct. (Bill Nowlin in "The OBP Triple Crown" in the same issue counts 10, but he counts players, not the times won [Rogers Hornsby and Ted Williams each won twice], and he starts at 1903 thereby excluding Nap Lajoie in 1901).

Contributors, page 131: In the entry for Bill Nowlin, the year of publication for *When Boston Still Had the Babe: The 1918 World Champion Red Sox* should read 2008.

Contributors

PHIL BIRNBAUM is the editor of *By the Numbers*, the newsletter of the SABR Statistical Analysis Committee. A native of Toronto, he now lives in Ottawa where he works as a software developer.

CLIFFORD BLAU is a retired CPA living in White Plains, N.Y. This is his second article for *The Baseball Research Journal*.

RICHARD CREPEAU, professor of history at the University of Central Florida, is author of *Baseball: America's Diamond Mind, 1919–1941* (Nebraska, 2000).

STEVEN M. DAY, an epidemiologist and medical researcher with the Life Expectancy Project in San Francisco, publishes extensively in peer-reviewed medical journals. He is a fellow of the American Academy of Cerebral Palsy and Developmental Medicine and of the Royal Society of Medicine and a member of the Gerson Lehrman Group's Council of Healthcare Advisors.

MARK FIMOFF, an electronic engineer, is author of the "Mystery Photo" column in the SABR Pictorial History Committee Newsletter.

VINCE GENNARO, author of *Diamond Dollars: The Economics of Winning in Baseball* (Maple Street, 2007), is a consultant to MLB teams. His analytical work on the business of baseball has been featured in the *Wall Street Journal*, *CNNMoney*, and the *New York Times*. He has written for the *Hardball Times* and *Yahoo! Sports* and teaches sports-business management in graduate programs at Columbia University and Manhattanville College. He is executive director of Manhattanville's Sports Analytic Institute.

TOM HANRAHAN works for the U.S. military trying to figure out how to put unmanned aircraft into the air while promising not to hit any passenger jets, Cessnas, or hot-air balloons. After hours he comes home to his wife, does volunteer work, preaches some Sundays, and enjoys being the luckiest man alive since Lou Gehrig.

CHARLES D. JOHNSON, a court administrator, lives in San Francisco with his daughters, Adelaide and Clementine. They can often be found in View Box 315 at AT&T Park, cheering on the Giants.

RON KAPLAN is the sports and features editor for the *New Jersey Jewish News*. His freelance work has appeared in publications including *Mental Floss*, *Baseball America*, *Irish America*, *ForeWord Magazine*, and the *Cleveland Plain Dealer*. He hosts Ron Kaplan's Baseball Bookshelf (http://rksbaseballbookshelf.wordpress.com), a blog about baseball literature and other media.

JOHN A. KNOX is assistant professor of geography at the University of Georgia, where he teaches atmospheric science and physical geography. A native of Birmingham, Alabama, where he watched Hank Aaron, Reggie Jackson, and Bo Jackson play at historic Rickwood Field, he has coauthored one college textbook and more than two hundred columns and articles in science publications and the popular press.

HERM KRABBENHOFT has been a Detroit Tigers fan since 1945, his year of birth. One of his favorite memories: On May 3, 1959, he sat in the bleachers at Briggs Stadium and watched Charlie Maxwell launch his "Sunday Slugger" career by blasting four consecutive homers as the Tigers swept a doubleheader from the Yankees. Krabbenhoft still has his scorebooks for those games.

LEE LOWENFISH is author of *Rickey: Baseball's Ferocious Gentleman* (Nebraska, 2007), winner of the 2008 Seymour Medal. The biography has been issued in paperback with a new introduction by the author.

NORMAN L. MACHT, having recovered from the birth of *Connie Mack and the Early Years of Baseball*, is now conceiving volume 2.

BOB MCCONNELL is a founding member of SABR and author of *Going for the Fences: The Minor League Home Run Record Book*, second edition (SABR, 2009).

ALAN M. NATHAN, professor of physics at the University of Illinois since 1977 and a fellow of the American Physical Society, is the author of more than 80 publications in scientific journals. His research specialty is experimental nuclear/particle physics. He has written numerous papers on the physics of baseball, primarily on the physics of ball–bat collision and on baseball aerodynamics. His website devoted to the physics of baseball is www.npl.uiuc.edu/~a-nathan/pob.

VI OWEN, author of *Adventures of a Quiet Soul: A Scrapbook of Memories* (1996), writes from Aptos, California.

ROBERT J. REYNOLDS is an epidemiologist in the department of symptom research at M. D. Anderson Cancer Center in Houston. His baseball-research interests include new methods of performance measurement and aggregate processes. In spite of recent trends he remains a steadfast fan of the San Francisco Giants.

JIM REISLER, a SABR member for more than twenty years, is the author of *A Great Day in Cooperstown: The Improbable Birth of Baseball's Hall of Fame* (Carroll and Graf, 2006) and *Babe Ruth: Launching the Legend* (Macmillan, 2004).

CHUCK ROSCIAM is a retired navy captain with 43 years of active service, a SABR member since 1992, an amateur catcher for more than forty years, and the creator of www.baseballcatchers.com. He has published articles in *The Baseball Research Journal* and *The National Pastime*.

SCOTT SCHLEIFSTEIN, a lifelong Yankees fan, is as surprised as anyone by his continued interest in the championship Oakland A's teams of the early 1970s. This is his second article about them. When he's not musing about Charlie Finley's Mustache Gang, Scott practices promotion marketing law in New York.

ERIC SEIDMAN, a Phillies fan, writes for *Baseball Prospectus* and *Fangraphs*. He works as an accountant for a movie studio in Philadelphia and is pursuing an MBA.

LEVERETT T. SMITH, a member of SABR since 1973, is author of *The American Dream and the National Game* (Bowling Green University Popular Press, 1975). Since the mid-1990s he has reviewed books for the Bibliography Committee Newsletter.

CHRISTOPHER J. YOUNG is assistant professor at Indiana University Northwest where he teaches early American history. The idea for the article presented here came from his childhood memory of seeing broken records strewn among the seats at Comiskey Park the day after Disco Demolition Night.